Southern West Virginia
and the Struggle
for Modernity

CONTRIBUTIONS TO SOUTHERN APPALACHIAN STUDIES

1. *Memoirs of Grassy Creek: Growing Up in the Mountains on the Virginia–North Carolina Line.* Zetta Barker Hamby. 1998

2. *The Pond Mountain Chronicle: Self-Portrait of a Southern Appalachian Community.* Edited by Leland R. Cooper and Mary Lee Cooper. 1998

3. *Traditional Musicians of the Central Blue Ridge: Old Time, Early Country, Folk and Bluegrass Label Recording Artists, with Discographies.* Marty McGee. 2000

4. *W.R. Trivett, Appalachian Pictureman: Photographs of a Bygone Time.* Ralph E. Lentz II. 2001

5. *The People of the New River: Oral Histories from the Ashe, Alleghany and Watauga Counties of North Carolina.* Edited by Leland R. Cooper and Mary Lee Cooper. 2001

6. *John Fox, Jr., Appalachian Author.* Bill York. 2003

7. *The Thistle and the Brier: Historical Links and Cultural Parallels Between Scotland and Appalachia.* Richard Blaustein. 2003

8. *Tales from Sacred Wind: Coming of Age in Appalachia. The Cratis Williams Chronicles.* Cratis D. Williams. Edited by David Cratis Williams and Patricia D. Beaver. 2003

9. *Willard Gayheart, Appalachian Artist.* Willard Gayheart and Donia S. Eley. 2003

10. *The Forest City Lynching of 1900: Populism, Racism, and White Supremacy in Rutherford County, North Carolina.* J. Timothy Cole. 2003

11. *The Brevard Rosenwald School: Black Education and Community Building in a Southern Appalachian Town, 1920–1966.* Betty J. Reed. 2004

12. *The Bristol Sessions: Writings About the Big Bang of Country Music.* Edited by Charles K. Wolfe and Ted Olson. 2005

13. *Community and Change in the North Carolina Mountains: Oral Histories and Profiles of People from Western Watauga County.* Compiled by Nannie Greene and Catherine Stokes Sheppard. 2006

14. *Ashe County: A History; A New Edition.* Arthur Lloyd Fletcher. 2009 [2006]

15. *The New River Controversy; A New Edition.* Thomas J. Schoenbaum. Epilogue by R. Seth Woodard. 2007

16. *The Blue Ridge Parkway by Foot: A Park Ranger's Memoir.* Tim Pegram. 2007

17. *James Still: Critical Essays on the Dean of Appalachian Literature.* Edited by Ted Olson and Kathy H. Olson. 2008

18. *Owsley County, Kentucky, and the Perpetuation of Poverty.* John R. Burch, Jr. 2008

19. *Asheville: A History.* Nan K. Chase. 2007

20. *Southern Appalachian Poetry: An Anthology of Works by 37 Poets.* Edited by Marita Garin. 2008

21. *Ball, Bat and Bitumen: A History of Coalfield Baseball in the Appalachian South.* L.M. Sutter. 2009

22. *The Frontier Nursing Service: America's First Rural Nurse-Midwife Service and School.* Marie Bartlett. 2009

23. *James Still in Interviews, Oral Histories and Memoirs.* Edited by Ted Olson. 2009

24. *The Millstone Quarries of Powell County, Kentucky.* Charles D. Hockensmith. 2009

25. *The Bibliography of Appalachia: More Than 4,700 Books, Articles, Monographs and Dissertations, Topically Arranged and Indexed.* Compiled by John R. Burch, Jr. 2009

26. *Appalachian Children's Literature: An Annotated Bibliography.* Compiled by Roberta Teague Herrin and Sheila Quinn Oliver. 2010

27. *Southern Appalachian Storytellers: Interviews with Sixteen Keepers of the Oral Tradition.* Edited by Saundra Gerrell Kelley. 2010

28. *Southern West Virginia and the Struggle for Modernity.* Christopher Dorsey. 2011

29. *George Scarbrough, Appalachian Poet: A Biographical and Literary Study with Unpublished Writings.* Randy Mackin. 2011

30. *The Water-Powered Mills of Floyd County, Virginia: Illustrated Histories, 1770–2010.* Franklin F. Webb and Ricky L. Cox. 2011

31. *School Segregation in Western North Carolina: A History, 1860s–1970s.* Betty Jamerson Reed. 2011

Southern West Virginia and the Struggle for Modernity

Christopher Dorsey

Contributions to Southern Appalachian Studies, 28

McFarland & Company, Inc., Publishers
Jefferson, North Carolina, and London

To Lowell O'Dell.
You will be missed.

LIBRARY OF CONGRESS CATALOGUING-IN-PUBLICATION DATA

Dorsey, Christopher, 1972–
 Southern West Virginia and the struggle for modernity / Christopher Dorsey.
     p.   cm. — (Contributions to Southern Appalachian studies ; 28)
 Includes bibliographical references and index.

 ISBN 978-0-7864-6049-6
 softcover : 50# alkaline paper ∞

 1. West Virginia — History. 2. Economic development — West Virginia. 3. West Virginia — Civilization. 4. West Virginia — Politics and government. I. Title.
 F241.D67   2011
 975.4 — dc23   2011021776

BRITISH LIBRARY CATALOGUING DATA ARE AVAILABLE

© 2011 Christopher Dorsey. All rights reserved

No part of this book may be reproduced or transmitted in any form or by any means, electronic or mechanical, including photocopying or recording, or by any information storage and retrieval system, without permission in writing from the publisher.

On the cover: *inset* massive explosion and mountaintop removal site (Giles Ashford); *foreground* Tamarack Economic and Cultural Center in Beckley, West Virginia (Roger Spencer Photography)

Manufactured in the United States of America

McFarland & Company, Inc., Publishers
 Box 611, Jefferson, North Carolina 28640
 www.mcfarlandpub.com

Table of Contents

Acknowledgments   ix
Introduction   1

ONE. The Rediscovery of Appalachia and the Coming of Industrialization   13

TWO. Life and Death in the Early Company Towns   31

THREE. The Coming of the Unions and the Paint Creek–Cabin Creek Strike   47

FOUR. Profiles in Corruption and Failed Government: The Matewan Massacre and the Battle for Blair Mountain   62

FIVE. FDR's Legacy: The Great Depression and Continuing Problems with Public Welfare, Agriculture, and Unemployment   73

SIX. Health and the Mountaineer: Perspectives on Public and Occupational Health   105

SEVEN. Democracy Lost: Political Corruption and the Impact on Political Involvement   120

EIGHT. Culture, Identity, and Modernization   136

NINE. Mountaintop Removal and the Battle for Hearts and Minds   158

Conclusion   183
Chapter Notes   189
Bibliography   205
Index   215

Acknowledgments

Several organizations and individuals were instrumental in the development of this book. First, the U.S. Navy's Graduate Education Voucher Program allowed me the funding and time necessary to pursue graduate studies at Syracuse University. The faculty and staff of the Master of Social Science program at the Maxwell School were first rate, and the interdisciplinary nature of the program created a perfect environment for this type of project. Although the entire faculty was supportive and extremely helpful, I would like to convey special thanks to Dr. Norman Kutcher, Dr. Mehrzad Boroujerdi, and Dr. Stephen S. Webb. To Dr. David H. Bennett, I extend an especially heartfelt thanks. Without his understanding, flexibility, and direction, this book would not have been possible.

I would also like to thank those who were helpful during the research process. Of particular note are Robert Fletcher, D.D.S., Nicholas County Prosecuting Attorney James "P.K." Milam, Principal Bill Dobbins, and the staff at Summersville Public Library who, through their assistance with access, support, and personal interviews, provided a wealth of information. Finally, I would like to thank the families, friends, and citizens of southern West Virginia. Despite the negative stereotypes and the educational and economic roadblocks that remain even today, the true mountaineer spirit strives to persevere and overcome.

For the purpose of this study, "southern West Virginia" refers to Mason, Jackson, Roane, Calhoun, Gilmer, Lewis, Upshur, Randolph, Pocahontas, Webster, Braxton, Clay, Nicholas, Kanawha, Putnam, Mason, Cabell, Wayne, Lincoln, Boone, Fayette, Greenbrier, Monroe, Summers, Mercer, McDowell, Wyoming, Raleigh, Mingo, and Logan Counties. The reason for this is a combination of geography, economics, and socio-economic drivers. According to 2008 U.S. Census data, of the 30 counties listed, 24 were above the state's 2008 average percentage of people living below the poverty level (17.1 percent). Only one county (Putnam) was below the national average of 13.2 percent. Although other West Virginia counties also have high percentages of people living below the poverty level, the more northern and panhandle counties do not experience the problem on the same scale. On average, counties within the boundaries of this study have 20.9 percent of the population living below the poverty level while 15.3 percent of those outside the boundaries live in poverty. Additionally, the panhandle and adjoining counties are more closely aligned with the economies and societies of Ohio, Pennsylvania, Maryland, and Northern Virginia; therefore, when one thinks about Central Appalachia, these counties, along with bordering counties in eastern Kentucky and southwestern Virginia, tend to come to mind.

Introduction

John Denver's folk-country song "Take Me Home, Country Roads" carries emotional and inherently powerful connotations for many West Virginians. I did not personally realize this power until several years after I left the mountains of southern West Virginia for a career in the military. This realization occurred during one of my short visits to my ancestral home while calling on one of my neighbors and kin, Lowell O'Dell. On this day, our conversation opened my eyes to the intrinsic power of place for many West Virginians, past and present.

Lowell exemplified the type of role model I had as a youth. Hardworking, humorous, friendly, and a lover of the outdoors, Lowell spent the majority of his life working in a decaying lumber industry. Unfortunately, Lowell was taken from this world much too early by cancer, but his love of life and family and his contagious laughter will live on in the hearts and minds of friends and relatives. Lowell lived in a remote mountain community in Nicholas County, about a 45-minute drive from the town of Summerville. Bounded by Anglins Creek and dotted with small family farms cut out of the thick hardwood forest, the Hill was my home for the majority of my youth. Lowell had grown up there as well, and most of his brothers lived only a few miles away. In fact, the entire mountain was (and is) mostly inhabited by O'Dells, Dorseys, Nutters and other members of a kinship band that had called this "their" mountain home for generations. I always enjoyed stopping by to see Lowell while home on leave and our conversations often included a discussion of the benefits and hardships of military life, as Lowell had also left the hills of southern West Virginia for service decades earlier, but returned at the end of his term.

While Lowell and I discussed military service and my plans regarding a career in the Navy, he explained his reasoning for not making a career of the military. "I just needed to get back home," he said. He spoke of family, friends, and particularly the power of place which continues to tie West Virginians to the land of their ancestors. Lowell knew exactly where the boundaries of this place-self bond lay; it was not at the borders of the state or even the county, although these are important aspects of identity. His "West Virginia" was even more defined. According to Lowell, the boundaries of home began "as soon as I turned off the paved road [a small one-lane road] onto that little dirt road headed down the holler. When I hit that road, I knew I was home."

By defining his bounds of "home" as well as its compelling pull on the individual and therefore identity, Lowell had summed up a truth that resonates throughout Denver's "Country Roads." For most West Virginians, those little country roads, almost dark even at mid-day under the cover of tall oak, hickory, and maple trees, are just where they belong. Even after twenty years of military service and travel across the country and around the world, every time I turn off that same paved road down the holler, I feel it too.

Only I did not return. And may not, save short visits to see family and friends. I have become yet another expatriate West Virginian that obtained an education and moved on to areas with more opportunities. Yet it is difficult to break the bonds woven by generations (since the 18th century) of kinfolk, the occasional nostalgic draw of a simpler life, and a sense of place and identity that many find inescapable. It is with this visceral interest that I undertake the challenge of addressing the recent history of a unique portion of my home state (which I will always call it) and its long struggle to escape the unfortunate historical baggage of corruption,

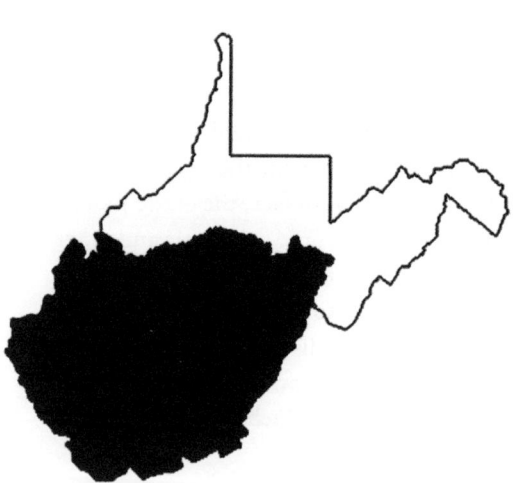

Fig. 1. Southern West Virginia.

violence, and social and cultural upheaval, as well as a crisis of identity that each generation of West Virginians has faced in one way or another.

A significant and vigorous discussion has taken place over the years regarding the underlying causes of over a century of disparity between southern West Virginia (as part of a greater Appalachian construct) and mainstream America. This disparity has been discussed in terms of economic, education, public health, and some would argue culture. Many lay this blame on the host of capitalists who rushed into the state to take advantage of West Virginia's virgin resources following the Civil War. This argument, however, fails to show the dynamic nature of the interaction between American economic, political, and social movements and the residents of southern West Virginia. An analysis of this complex connection does not support laying all of the blame for the region's woes at the feet of the Gilded Age industrialists alone.

Southern West Virginia's story is not a straightforward one of exploitation and coercion, although both occurred quite frequently. As Northeastern and European capitalists descended, or more accurately ascended, upon the mountain region, many were welcomed with open arms by state officials as well as many local elites. In several cases, southern West Virginians from all walks of life — officials, merchants, professions, and farmers — welcomed the opportunities of industrialization and modernization. In *Coal Towns: Life, Work, and Culture in Company Towns of Southern Appalachia*, Crandall Shifflett argues that West Virginia officials promised to "be a doormat for all with capital to invest."[1]

Greedy and power-hungry officials were not the only people to welcome outside investment. Contrary to most contemporary beliefs, sections of southern Western Virginia (formerly Virginia) had a long history of industrial and entrepreneurial practices, particularly in the Kanawha Valley region. This history included significant involvement in furs, ginseng, and salt works. John Edmund Steally III discussed in great detail the national significance, and complexity, of the early salt works of the Kanawha region in his article "Kanawha Prelude to Nineteenth-Century Monopoly in the United States: The Virginia Salt Combination." Dissertations such as John Sherwood Lewis's "Becoming Appalachia: The Emergence of an American Subculture, 1840–1860" and Rebecca Bailey's "Matewan Before the Massacre: Politics, Coal, and the Roots of the Conflict in Mingo County, 1793–1920" also provide evidence demonstrating the importance of both the fur and ginseng trade to the greater American economic picture during the early 19th century.[2]

Something happened along the way, however. After the initial rush of Gilded Age investment and development, many southern West Virginians began to question the price they had paid for their modicum of modernization. Large scale introduction of railroads, coal mines, and an expanding lumber industry brought about significant, unexpected, and, to some, devastating changes. The exodus of young men from subsistence farming and ancestral lands to company towns disrupted generations-old family and social power structures. New elites were formed that challenged agricultural and (to some degree) small-scale industrial elites already established in the region. These new elites were the local advocates of the absentee land and company owners, local officials on company payrolls, and savvy local entrepreneurs who capitalized on land grabs in the wake of railroad, mining, and timber expansion.

The company towns that sprung up throughout the region further accelerated the breakdown of subsistence-based norms as a "white, mountain-born and mountain-reared agricultural society reorganized around the opportunities and horrors of industrial capitalism."[3] Filling the needs of the explosion of industry, the population of formerly remote counties swelled with foreign immigrants looking to make their mark in America and African Americans fleeing an oppressive post–Reconstruction South and its Jim Crow laws. This massive population growth and a lack of legitimate legal authority and familial control resulted in conditions in many communities where gambling, drinking, womanizing, and violence became commonplace. The only true power was that of the quasi-police force employed by the parent companies to maintain some semblance of order and provide a coercive mechanism when required.[4]

The rise of the Progressive Age coincided with, and obviously influenced, this realization of the negative aspects of rapid and unchecked industrialization. The greater Progressive movement was embraced in the hills and hollers of southern West Virginia, but with little success. Following decades of violent labor disputes, legal battles, and government corruption on a massive scale, the absentee industrialists and their local surrogates still held a firm grip on the control of labor, and arguably the society of southern West Virginia itself. According to Shifflett, by the first decade of the 20th century, "the region was reduced to the status of a colony of corporate America."[5] It would remain this way until at least the Great

Depression; some argue the condition still remains to some degree. In fact, some economists believe the current "anti-capitalist mentality [held by many in the region] is mostly rooted in stories from our state's historical experience with industry, specifically in coal mining."[6]

Although the internal colony theory of Appalachian history has its merits, it sheds little light on the resistance movements that took place not only during the Progressive Era but during the initial stages of the post–Civil War industrialization of southern West Virginia. This history of resistance had many facets and included economic, social, and personal motivators, and to some degree dispels the myth that Appalachian residents were easily fooled bumpkins who gave up their lands, minerals, and culture with no understanding what they were doing. In fact, to many local businessmen and farmers, the industrialists were seen as rivals for economic gain and openly challenged as such. Many saw the influx of industry as threat to an agrarian, more Jeffersonian way of life, while others felt the flood of outsiders posed a direct challenge to cultural, ethnic, and moral norms fostered over generations of subsistence farming (aside from the few early industrial areas) by an ethnically homogeneous group of descendants of Scots-Irish immigrants who came to the area in the Colonial period.[7]

While acknowledging the resistance movements throughout the period, southern West Virginians for the most part did not become benefactors of the wealth that was extracted from their mountains and valleys. The cycle of coal and lumber company dominance, fostered by assistance from corrupt government officials, resulted in an immense exodus of resource wealth from the state with little benefits to the residents who were providing the very labor by which it was (and is) extracted. According to Jack Weller (whose study of Appalachia based on missionary work in southern West Virginia in the 1960s provides an insightful but incomplete picture of the region's society, culture, and psychology), these 19th century inhabitants and their descendants were "people whose ancestry goes back to the very early settlers of our nation, who have yet to experience what it means to be living in a land of opportunity and abundance."[8]

The mountaineers' experience has not occurred in a vacuum, either. Throughout its history, West Virginia has played a role in and been affected by major economic, political, and social movements of the greater mainstream American experience. What has occurred, however, is that in most cases southern West Virginia's role in these movements has been one of a supplier of resources instead of recipient. Even in cases where resources were provided directly to the region and its inhabitants, such as the New Deal programs and Lyndon Johnson's War on Poverty, the region still to arguably managed more resources (more intangible than material) than it gained.

Although many of the lost resources discussed are tangible, such as land and mineral rights, lumber, and natural beauty, southern West Virginia has also faced a loss of several vital intangible resources that have (and continue to) proven detrimental to modernization and development in the region. These intangible losses include a political marginalization and apathy that has gripped the area for generations, the loss of a self-generated identity in the face of nationwide stereotyping, and perhaps the most dangerous to current success of the state, the outmigration of southern West Virginia's most educated and motivated young adults. The loss of these resources has occurred as a result of a failure of the region to escape the yoke of its complex, volatile, and often misunderstood history.

As the themes of this work are presented, I hope to demonstrate the historical burdens that have amalgamated themselves into the identity, culture, and psyche of southern West Virginians in a manner which, even to this day, plays a role in many of the state's ongoing problems, such as outmigration, poverty, educational gaps, and lack of adequate industrial growth. These problems, rooted in a century of historical encumbrances, can only be tackled by first coming to grips with the ghosts of the region's past and facing the next century by looking forward instead of backward. It is with an understanding eye on the past, not an anchor to it, that progress will be made.

The first four chapters are presented in a chronological order and in traditional historical format. These chapters discuss major movements and issues from the end of the Civil War through the Great Depression to establish an historical foundation upon which the remaining chapters will build. Chapters Five through Nine, while still chronological, address issues in a more thematic light, focusing on issues such as poverty, welfare, political corruption, and issues of identity and place.

Chapter One provides a brief historical backdrop of the region necessary for understanding how southern West Virginia society evolved following the Civil War. Secondly, the impact of post–Civil War political, economic, and social movements on the region will be examined. Starting in the last two and a half decades of the 19th century, dramatic changes in almost all aspects of life drastically and irrevocably changed the face of the region's social, cultural, and political experience. During this period industrial corporations moved into formerly remote regions and with them came powerful forces of change. The introduction of new peoples, ideas, and norms, as well as political and social intervention by absentee industrialists, directly challenged an established power structure based on patriarchal land ownership.[9]

Chapter Two examines the further deterioration of old power bases as coal and lumber towns sprung up across southern West Virginia. The role that company towns played in shaping many aspects of the region's past and present cannot be understated. Vehicles of advancement and modernization, while at the same time harbingers of oppression and poverty, company towns forever changed the face of southern West Virginia. Initially known for their lax moral and legal characteristics, the more rowdy towns became legendary. As these towns grew more stable over time, however, they offered a glimpse of the mainstream American dream to some — steady wages, electricity, and community activities such as movie theatres, swimming pools, and bowling alleys. While many people hold happy memories of their life in a company town, the perception of the company town as a universal good or evil was often determined by the company running the town and the individual superintendent. At an even more fundamental level, as the measure of life in these towns was often "in the eye of the beholder," the true story of company towns is more complex than many histories would have us believe.[10]

Chapters Three and Four explore major attempts at organization in the coalfields of southern West Virginia and the backlash of intimidation and violence that exploded into civil war. This unrest grew out of the complexities of the company town structure and the struggle between labor and management fueled by the national labor movements underway. Between 1900 and 1930, many came to consider the towns for which they had happily left their mountain farms, southern sharecropping fields, or European slums as "prisoner-of-work" camps, due to coercive control of labor and in some cases extra-legal confinement and forced labor.[11] The often absentee owners, at least in the eyes of residents and reformers, "became like plantation owners of the South, keeping their workers uneducated, underpaid, and isolated, while at the same time, controlling elections and even the very culture of [the] people."[12]

This perception of inequality and oppression, in many cases real, was promoted and amplified by the United Mine Workers of America (UMWA) as part of the greater labor movement taking place throughout the country. Dissention between owners and workers, supported by the UMWA, erupted into violence and widespread civil disorder along Paint Creek and Cabin Creek in 1912 and 1913 and in Logan and Mingo Counties in 1919 through 1922. Labor disputes reached unprecedented levels, involving thousands of belligerents and resulting in several declarations of martial law in less than ten years. In the end, despite years of large scale and widespread labor uprisings, the industrialists retained firm control of southern coal fields. They would retain this overt domination until the 1930s, although some would argue it still exists in an only slightly less intimidating form.

More important than the temporary victory of the industrialists is the lasting sense of distrust and fear that hangs over the valleys of southern West Virginia. The legacy of trepidation toward outside investment has hamstrung modernization and economic diversity, while the distrust of local government has severely hampered reform throughout the region. In his dissertation regarding corruption in West Virginia politics, Allen Loughry pondered "the opportunities that have been lost by citizens of West Virginia in so many areas of concern such as education, health care, and infrastructure as a result of a long line of corrupt elected officials."[13]

Chapter Five addresses the momentous changes that occurred during the 1930s as the Great Depression caused a rethinking of government's role in a free society. The resultant programs of the New Deal, while without a doubt saving many families, also acted as a replacement for family support structures and the often dependable (but one-sided) support offered by the structure of the company town. To many, the aid and support of New Deal programs became not short-term measures of recovery, but a long-term, permanent means of maintaining an austere but sustained existence on the fringes of economic viability — an existence that would have been very similar to that of their subsistence-farming ancestors prior to the influx of big industry after the Civil War. Given this tradition of subsistence living, a life on welfare and aid seemed acceptable to many. This "it was good enough for grandpa" mentality has continued to stifle ambition of a portion of the region's residents and limit opportunities for the area's youth.[14]

West Virginia, and particularly southern West Virginia, residents suffer from a myriad of health and medical concerns at a much higher rate than the U.S. average. Just a few of these issues are teenage pregnancy, occupational injury, obesity, smoking, various cancers, and heart and lung diseases.[15] Chapter Six looks at both the historical and contemporary status of public and occupational health in the region, as well as some of the enduring barriers to improved public and occupational health.

Chapter Seven examines the specter of political corruption which continues to haunt southern West Virginia and impact involvement in the democratic process. The chapter will address the legacy of political corruption in southern West Virginia that has grown so pervasive that, according to Allen Loughry, "if political corruption were an Olympic event, West Virginia would be a strong contender for the Gold Medal."[16] Following the April 2010 mine explosion at the Upper Big Branch Mine in Raleigh County, the national spotlight was again fixed on the influence powerful coal operators, such as Massey Energy and its controversial CEO, Don Blankenship, wield in the region. In a political arena tainted by corruption for over a century, many citizens have become cynical or ambivalent in regard to politics or simply removed themselves from the process altogether.

National media attention was also focused on the region as a result of 1960 presidential campaign and President Lyndon Johnson's War on Poverty. Although many in the region received much-needed aid, a "critical magnifying glass" was turned on the mountain communities which "highlighted a poverty that many mountain families felt helpless to control."[17] This portrayal, on a national scale, further stereotyped Appalachian people and helped foster an identity that was incomplete, sensational, and damaging to the psyche of its subjects.

Chapter Eight examines the bonds between culture, stereotypes, and identity. Valid arguments can be made for the existence of an Appalachian culture not wholly alien to, but distinct from, mainstream America. The interaction between the development of this culture, and outside interpretations and perceptions of its existence, have also shaped internal identities of the region's population. Both this distinct culture and internal and external perceptions of it have been influenced by each of the elements discussed in the preceding chapters. Exploring the bonds between Appalachian culture, stereotypes, and the resultant perceptions and paradigms will help to encapsulate how the region's history still plays a pivotal role in contemporary southern West Virginia.

The controversial topic of mountaintop removal provides an excellent example of the ways in which history, culture, stereotypes, economics, and politics still come together to form a complicated and emotional web of identity and existence that is extremely relevant in contemporary southern West Virginia and its foreseeable future. Chapter Nine examines the struggle between environmentalist-activist groups, such as the Coal River Mountain Watch, and multinational energy corporations, such as Massey Energy, for the hearts of minds of southern West Virginia residents.

As the traditionalist- and environmentalist-oriented mountain removal opposition groups and the profit-driven (and at least tacitly employment- and modernization-oriented) coal operators challenge one another in a war of propaganda and legal battles, others are stuck in the middle. State governmental organizations and a weakened United Mine Workers of America currently struggle to walk a fine line between the sustaining jobs and supporting the economy while at the same time defending the real and perceived destruction of the very thing that makes the region unique — the land. At the heart of this modern-day, polarizing struggle between residents and industrialists is the legacy of the collective history of post–Civil War southern West Virginia. This accumulation of historical baggage, in the form of tradition, stereotypes, paradigms, and identity, creates the canvas upon which the state has continued its struggle for development, modernization, and economic viability.

In this struggle over southern West Virginia's future, three groups have developed. The traditionalists reject modernity as an attack on their culture. In defense of a rural, family-oriented mountain life and mountaineer heritage, this group often creates roadblocks to the expansion of industrialization and technological development. Although specific motives may emerge from a need to protect their families, their heritage, or the environment, the enemy at hand is often development and industry. In some cases, their arguments are not only valid but necessary checks to unbridled industrial advancement without regard to the residents' best interests. At other times, however, traditionalist stances can block progressive development as well as help to support those mired in a culture of poverty by creating a mindset that deems a life on the margins as "good old-fashioned living."

In opposition to the traditionalists are the progressives who seek to overcome their past by accepting modernization with open arms, often without regard to the important bond that exists between local history, the land, and contemporary southern West Virginia society. Progressives take several forms, just as do the traditionalists. Some simply wish for a more modern, diversified, and less stereotyped future for the state. Others, however, have pinned further development and financial gain solely on the back of the region's dominant industry — coal. In doing so, this faction of progressives runs the risk of trading jobs and marginal economic stability in the immediate future for any chance of a more diverse and robust economic, (and arguably socially stable) future over the long term.

The third class does not look to the region's history, nor does it look toward a new future. This welfare class has developed over generations out of a metamorphosis of a subsistence farming tradition and public welfare. This metamorphism allows for an existence on the margins of society with the aid of public assistance and kinship bonds. Oddly, this group is at the same time marginalized and supported by traditionalists and progressives alike. Traditionalists, while promoting the concepts of self-sufficiency, moderate living, and hard work, sometimes leave the definition of moderate living and self-sufficiency open enough to include those who subsist on limited work and government support. At the same time, progressives argue the need to advance and diversify while elements of the group, including blue-collar workers, promote the importance of coal. While undoubtedly important, and necessary for at least the next few decades, the promotion of coal above all other industries creates barriers to diversification and likewise supports a coal-centered economy which has played a major role in creating some of the economic conditions that allow the welfare class to exist.

It is imperative that as current and future legislators, educators, and citizens strive for a better tomorrow for southern West Virginia, the past must be remembered, honored, understood, and overcome. This can only occur as traditionalists and progressives find common ground. Both sides must move away from embedded, polarizing positions which by their very nature build roadblocks to constructive discussion and compromise. Only when both sides begin to pull themselves out of stagnant, encumbering, and long-standing ideological and political positions will an environment be created which allows measured modernization. It is this deliberate, nonpartisan approach to modernization that will eventually weaken the economic, social, and cultural foundations that led to the formation of the welfare class.

ONE

The Rediscovery of Appalachia and the Coming of Industrialization

Before the impact of the industrial revolution on southern West Virginia can be discussed, a brief snapshot of the pre-industrial history of the region should be provided. As Billings and Blee accurately argued in *The Road to Poverty*, "Just as scholars have shown that the history of slavery, debt peonage, and the cotton plantation is crucial for understanding the roots of African American poverty and, more generally, social problems in the contemporary South, we contend that the social dynamics of agrarian Appalachia left a lasting imprint on the southern mountains today."[1]

Southern West Virginia's history, while deeply rooted in subsistence farming, also include a small but important history of industrial endeavors, including early businesses centered on the fur and ginseng trade and, most importantly, a salt industry that was intimately involved with national markets in the first half of the 18th century. This history of agrarian predominance punctuated by sparks of entrepreneurial ambition provided the economic and social foundations upon which southern West Virginians attempted to manage the coming of large scale industrialization to the region.

When Will Wallace Havney published *A Strange Land and Peculiar People* in 1873 regarding his travels in Appalachia, a long history of stereotypical perspectives was born of half-truths and sensationalism. Writers often focused on aspects of Appalachian life that enhanced the region's people and their experience as a classical Orientalism-styled "other" in contrast to a greater American culture.[2] Through this clouded view, a region that indeed had its own cultural history was fancied as an example of devolution of civilization. Henry Shapiro argued that by the 1870s, this concept of an Appalachian "other," when compared to "the progress of civilization in America, and Americans' self-consciousness of their progress, was such that the apparent persistence of pioneer conditions among the mountain people created a paradigm in which Appalachia and its inhabitants did seem a strange land inhabited by a peculiar people."[3]

While late 19th century America looked down upon a region that as late as 1850 had been called "uninhabitable,"[4] the area's residents continued to develop their culture and live their lives. In the generations prior to its "rediscovery," southern West Virginia and other mountainous Appalachian areas in Tennessee, Kentucky, and Virginia had developed a strong power structure based on a subsistence farming culture and patriarchal land ownership. This culture was rooted in individualism, hard labor, and strong kinship bonds derived from what Billings and Blee call a patriarchal moral economy. In this model, the difficulty of subsistence farming drove the need for kinship cooperation as a survival mechanism. Over generations, land ownership and patriarchal control of land, and therefore family power, developed throughout Appalachia.[5]

Randall Lawrence echoed this kinship bond born of hard agricultural labor. In his dissertation, "Appalachian Metamorphosis," he argued that these "mountaineers, isolated from the course of national events and preoccupied with earning a living on small mountain farms, organized their lives around work and family life."[6] While mountaineers were not as isolated from national events as Lawrence's statement implies, the kinship-land bond was powerful. The "mountain people's self-sufficiency was predicated on the most highly [commoditized] of goods, land."[7] This relationship between family, land, and power would play a major role when industrialization came to the mountains.

There was more to Appalachia than subsistence farming, however. The standard view of the Appalachian region as an isolated redoubt of Jeffersonian yeoman farmers, while describing a majority of people in the region, does not fully describe the experience of southern West Virginia. Although on a small scale, industry, outside investment and land ownership, as well as non-agricultural labor did in fact exist prior to the 1880s. The existence of these small but vital examples provided Lawrence with valuable ammunition in his argument against the paradigm of pre-industrial Appalachia as "helpless orphan charges" and docile lambs sent to the slaughter at the hands of industrialists.[8]

One. The Rediscovery of Appalachia and the Coming of Industralization 15

Aside from the stock feeding, fur, and ginseng industries which existed in the region dating to the Colonial days, the salt works in the Kanawha region provided small but influential commerce in the area during the first half of the 19th century.[9] Deposits in this area would provide the largest domestic source of salt during the period and act as the catalyst for the first legitimate attempts at the formation of a major industrial-based trust in the United States.[10] Far from being isolated from mainstream American society and industry, the Kanawha salt entrepreneurs "flourished in the environment of economic and political classism, which viewed the best system of political economy as the one that maximized total wealth without regard to distribution."[11] The salt industry in the Kanawha, however, would soon fall victim to another burgeoning industry—the railroad.

The rugged terrain of southwest Virginia (it became West Virginia in 1863) made the construction of major roads and railways difficult in the first half of the 19th century. During this period, the most successful means of transport were the waterways, particularly the Ohio River by way of the Kanawha. This mode of transportation proved to be highly competitive for shipping salt to the meat packing center in Cincinnati. It could not, however, compete with the expansion of railroads in other areas of the nation in the 1840s and 1850s. The salt industry was further hindered by the shift of the national meat packing center to Chicago in the 1850s. The combination of alternate transportation routes and a western shift in meat processing brought about a serious decline in the Kanawha Valley salt industry. By 1890, only one salt work was still in operation in the region.[12]

The expansion of railroads and other industries, however, was significantly disrupted during the Civil War, particularly in border states and areas such as the region of western Virginia that would become West Virginia. Plans such as those undertaken to exploit coal deposits in the Tug Valley in the 1850s[13] were interrupted or delayed by the raiding and occasional battles that took place in the region. Aside from the chaos of Civil War, technology also limited expansion. Early and mid–19th century locomotives had grade restrictions which made laying down track in the steep mountains of southern West Virginia difficult and expensive. It would not be until the late 19th century that geared locomotives allowed for easier access to the more mountainous regions.[14]

Due to warfare, limited technology, and challenging topography, the majority of the minerals and industry of southern West Virginia remained isolated or were bypassed by larger markets through the antebellum and

Civil War periods. This isolation would abruptly end in the 1870s. As the industrial revolution gained momentum, technologies improved, and industrialists gained a firm control of more politicians, many began to eye West Virginia's resources with anticipation. The most important of these resources were the coal and lumber that would fire the furnaces of industrialization and empire.

Following the Civil War, three conditions existed in America that would be important to future social, political, and economic circumstances of southern West Virginia. First, the Republican Party had virtually unopposed dominance of the federal government. Even among Democrats who held office on a national level, there was little to differentiate them from their Republican counterparts. This was due to a political environment in which, perhaps more than any other period in our national history, personal gain, not partisanship, drove policy. During this period, "the ideological contest was not between Republican and Democratic Parties for both were converts to the development faith."[15] According the Richard Hofstadter, "The parties of the period after the post–Civil War were based on patronage, not principle; they divided over spoils, not issues."[16]

Second, the government desperately needed to recoup funds expended during the struggle against the rebellious states. Total direct and indirect cost for the war at the time totaled over ten billion dollars.[17] This amount in 2009 would equate to over 117 billion dollars, by one measure, and to over 14 *trillion* dollars as a relative share of gross domestic product. By comparison, the entire cost of the wars in Afghanistan and Iraq and the "War on Terror" was estimated at 1.7 trillion dollars from September 11, 2001 through 2009.[18]

Finally, the industrial revolution, which had been held back due to the war, returned to the forefront with renewed vigor. Out of these variables rose a formula for rapid expansion of wealth for those ambitious enough to take advantage of the opportunities of the time. The men of economic, and therefore political, prominence in this era "were such as one might expect to arise where great waste is permitted for great accomplishment."[19] Powerful industrialists such as Andrew Carnegie, J.P. Morgan, and John Rockefeller dominated this period, and through whatever means necessary amassed huge fortunes.

The majority of these tycoons were self-made men who had risen from lower- and middle-class beginnings. They held that it was the individual's duty to better themselves and believed the best way for talented men to prosper was through unregulated economies driven by profit and controlled by the most ambitious, if not ruthless, mechanisms at their disposal. As such, most gained or enhanced their power and influence through "exploiting workers and milking farmers, bribing Congressmen, buying legislatures, spying upon competitors, hiring armed guards, dynamiting property, [and] using threats and intrigue and force.[20]

The willingness of these ambitious men to influence politics was only encouraged by the weakness of America's politicians. "Capitalists seeking land grants, tariffs ... freedom from regulatory legislation and economic reform, supplied campaign funds, fees, and bribes and plied politicians with investment opportunities."[21] Under this blanket of legislative protection the robber barons of the Gilded Age looked toward the timber- and coal-rich Appalachian region to fuel their rise to unbelievable wealth and power.

In 1881 a group of ambitious bankers and investors made their way on horseback to the top of Flat Top Mountain in the remote hills on the border of West Virginia and Virginia. At the peak many were shocked to find an outcropping with a twelve-foot-thick seam of coal, and they immediately began making plans to extract it.[22] This group of investors was similar to hordes of others, mostly from Northeastern cities or Britain, that invested heavily in coal speculation in the mountains of southern West Virginia beginning as early as the 1870s. The rapid increase in U.S. coal production (Fig. 2) demonstrates both the speed at which a post–Civil War United States expanded its industrial base and the level to which coal-rich territories, such as southern West Virginia, would be impacted by its growth. As this demand grew, so did West Virginia coal's role in maintaining the expansion of the Industrial Revolution in the U.S.

Coal was not the only significant economic resource for the state; above the vast deposits of coal grew virgin hardwood forests. Former Confederate officer Jed Hotchkiss surveyed the region extensively during and after the war and was a major proponent of coal and lumber speculation. In one article published in *Science* in 1892, Hotchkiss examined a portion of 200,000 acres owned by the Guyandot Coal Land Association in Wayne, Logan, and Lincoln Counties. Hotchkiss reported that of the 655 acres sampled, there was an average of 26 large trees per acre, most of which were hardwoods.[23] Some of these trees were massive. On more than one occasion, the ancient behemoths were so large that holes had to be drilled in them and dynamite used to create splits by which the trees could be broken into manageable sizes and transported.[24]

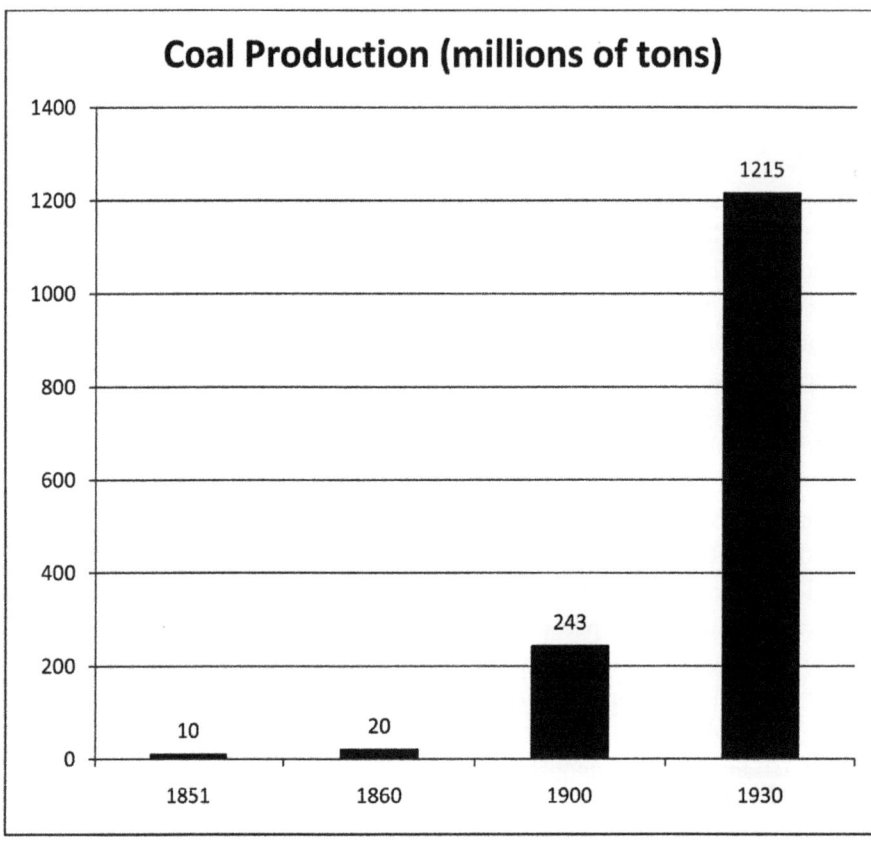

Fig. 2. Coal Production, 1851–1930. Source: Shifflett, pp. 27, 30.

Lumber towns sprang up all across the state. An example of this rapid growth is the town of Richwood in Nicholas County. Initially a small camp on the Cherry River, Richwood in time produced over 3 million board feet of lumber and was home to one of the world's largest tanneries.[25] In one year alone Richwood exported 4,000 carloads of lumber, 1,000 of paper, 300 of leather, and 240 of wooden dishes. In all, close to 6,000 carloads of goods left Richwood for places around the nation and world.[26]

It was known before the Civil War that coal existed in abundance throughout the region. Even with limited transportation routes available, hundreds of boats filled with coal made their way eastward from Appalachia every year between 1830 and the war.[27] After the war, industrialization dramatically increased the need for an energy sources. Before southern

West Virginia's energy wealth could be extracted from the mountains, however, a means of transporting coal and lumber to larger markets was necessary.

Many of the plans for railroads in the region that had been placed on hold for decades were quickly dusted off and put into motion on a grand scale. Between 1870 and 1900, four major railroads extended lines into central Appalachia.[28] Most important to southern West Virginia were the Norfolk and Western (N&W) and the Chesapeake and Ohio (C&O) railroads. The C&O completed its line through the central counties of West Virginia in 1873 but grew slowly for the next decade due to the economic downturn of 1873. The N&W completed its main line along the southern border of the state in 1883.[29] In true Gilded Age fashion, these railroads, particularly the N&W, not only laid the track by which the coal and timber of the region were removed, but promoted investment of its members and others in coal and lumber corporations as well.[30]

Numerous coal and timber operations were established along the railways. Seventy-five mines would eventually operate between Thurmond and Hawk's Nest along the C&O line alone.[31] Hundreds of mines went into operation in Mercer, McDowell, and Mingo Counties along the N&W.[32] Although the majority of investors in mines and timber along the railroads were northerners or British, some West Virginians were heavily involved in the coal and lumber industries as well. The Williamson Mining and Manufacturing was a group of lawyers, politicians, and businessmen from the region. Unfortunately for the group, the N&W failed to complete a branch to the area. Failed ventures such as these often fostered ill feelings between many prominent members of the community and outside industrialists.[33]

Members of the Williamson group were not the only residents hoping to profit from the opportunities offered by the new-found economic interest in the area. In contrast to the stereotypical belief that many Appalachian land owners were waylaid by speculators, some, in fact many, gladly offered up land for cash. A review of the Nicholas *Chronicle* shows not only the willingness of some to part with land, but also the optimism of a modernizing region. In 1881, the *Chronicle* listed thousands of acres for sale, described as excellent farming and mineral lands. On May 20, 1881, over 200,000 acres of land in Nicholas, Clay, and Webster Counties were advertised.[34] Other West Virginians were also willing to buy up the lands their fellow citizens were all too willing to sell.

In this massive transfer of lands, three powerful West Virginian industrialist-politicians amassed huge holdings; these men were Johnson N. Camden, Henry Gassaway Davis, and Stephen B. Elkins. Railroadmen at their core, this trio "would be the first to lay the iron rails of progress into the great interior forests, transforming life in the remoteness of north central West Virginia."[35]

Johnson N. Camden, a U.S. senator from 1881 to 1887, was a major player in all three of the key elements of the industrial revolution in southern West Virginia (timber, railroads, and coal) as well as oil. Camden organized the Camden Consolidated Oil Company and directed the construction of several short rail lines, including the line to Sutton, Camden-on-Gauley, and Richwood. Making use of the new lines, Camden purchased over 200,000 acres of land in Pocahontas, Nicholas, and Webster Counties with Davis and Elkins as partners.[36] Camden also partnered with Davis on the West Virginia Central Railroad and served as president of West Virginia & Pittsburg Railroad Company.[37]

Henry Gassaway Davis served as both a state and U.S. senator. Although a servant of the people, Davis "realized that the vast natural resources of the coal and timber counties might lie untouched by man forever unless transportation to the outside world should be provided."[38]

Apparently Davis saw no conflict of interest in public service and accumulation of personal wealth through programs he would help legislate. According his biographer, Charles M. Pepper: "Public service in the Legislature of West Virginia and the United States Senate had not entirely diverted Senator Davis from his development enterprises. It was during this period that his investments in coal and timber lands were expanded, the railway project for the line to the southwest of Piedmont conceived, matured, and its construction begun."[39]

Davis's son-in-law, Stephen B. Elkins, would also become a senator. He was also extremely wealthy, worth over $15,000,000. When questions over his residency status in West Virginia impacted his political career in Washington, he simply founded the town of Elkins, where he then moved. From this established stronghold, he conducted several business endeavors, including ventures with Camden and Davis such as the West Virginia Central Railroad and the Davis Coal and Coke Company.[40]

These three men, holding massive tracts of land, heavily invested in railroads, and holding powerful political offices, were well positioned take full advantage of the chaotic nature of West Virginia legal structures and

One. The Rediscovery of Appalachia and the Coming of Industralization   21

Southern West Virginia's virgin hardwood forests were filled with massive trees such as this behemoth in Nicholas County (West Virginia and Regional History Collection, West Virginia University Library).

land regulations. It seemed as though the major limit to their control of the area was each other. Even this challenge was mitigated when the three came to a gentlemen's agreement to establish "spheres of influence," not unlike 19th and 20th century imperial nations and superpowers, to avoid conflict among themselves.[41]

Camden, Davis, and Elkins were but a few of the resident industrialists of southern West Virginia. Others, such as John T. McGraw, sold thousands of acres to Northern capitalists like Cornelius Vanderbilt and Seward Webb when local partners did not materialize.[42] This sharing and transition of power was common in late 19th century and highlights two important elements which Ronald Lewis discussed in his study of the timber and railroad industry in West Virginia between 1880 and 1920. Lewis stated that 56 percent of those invested in the lumber industry were residents of West Virginia. While Lewis admits the number does include outside investors who moved into the region to keep watch on their enterprises, this is evidence of a population not caught up in, but fully participating in, the industrialization of the region. At the same time, Lewis conceded that the 46 percent of non-residents most likely operated at a higher volume and therefore saw greater rewards.[43]

To see the depth of absentee and non-resident involvement in investment in the region, one only needs to review any newspaper published between 1870 and the early 20th century, such the Nicholas *Chronicle*. One purchase encompassed 200,000 acres in south-central West Virginia by a British corporation, the West Virginia Land and Lumber Company Limited, in April of 1881.[44] Other lands were obtained by non-residents through government grants. In Clay County 93,000 acres were inherited by the grandson of Secretary of War Simon D. Cameron, to whom Lincoln had granted the land during the Civil War. Joseph Bradley (Cameron's grandson), as a member of the Elk River Coal and Lumber Association, began developing the land, particularly coal at Widen and Dundon and lumber at Swandale.[45]

The *Chronicle* also applauded the "thrifty" work of the Hawks Nest Coal Company, which employed up to 500 workers. The article was optimistic toward the extension of the Hawks Nest and Gauley River Railway Company and stated that the community was "glad to see our country improving so fast."[46] Comments such as these as well as the massive number of land advertisements demonstrate a people that were not "swept up" by modernization but embraced it. Unfortunately for many West Virginians, the positive results of industrial transformation "were limited, superficial, and fleeting."[47]

The expansion of the railroads and explosion of the mining and lumber industries brought about significant and lasting changes to the economy, society, culture, and landscape of southern West Virginia. In the period between 1880 and 1900, fantastic demographic changes swept through the region involving new occupations, exposure to different peoples, and the emergence of the infamous company towns. The way in which these changes were managed and perceived by inhabitants of the region would play a major role in the events that took place during the early 20th century.

One of the major catalysts for social change in southern West Virginia was the population explosion of the late 19th century. The labor demand generated from the rapid growth of mining, lumber, and railroad industries in the region could not be met by the indigenous population alone. Although many farmers did give up the plow for the shovel and ax, farming remained a mainstay for southern West Virginians throughout the period.

More people were needed. To make up for this labor shortfall, companies sought out immigrants from Europe as well as blacks from the Deep South.

Between 1870 and 1900 approximately 11.7 million Europeans came to the United States.[48] Many found their way to the hills of southern West Virginia. Thousands of blacks, Italians, Poles, Hungarians, and others were recruited, enticed, and tricked into coming to the region.[49] This rapid influx of peoples from different racial and ethnic backgrounds changed the demographic makeup of a region that had, ethnically speaking, remained the same for almost two hundred years.[50] The majority of these immigrants worked for either the railroad or mines. Aside from being recruited for those specific purposes, breaking into farming or other business in the area would have been difficult for outsiders, particularly blacks or foreigners due to the kinship-landowning power structure that was still the dominant force away from major mining and railroad operations. The lumber industry, particularly the woodsmen who cut and brought the massive timbers into the camps, seemed to retain more of their local flavor, however. According to Ronald Lewis, the majority of lumbermen between 1866 and 1909 were West Virginia residents.[51]

The subsequent population increase in southern West Virginia was dramatic. McDowell County saw a 137.5 percent increase from 1880 to 1890, 156.8 percent from 1890 to 1900, and 155.3 percent from 1900 to 1910.[52] The population of Central Appalachian Plateau counties in West Virginia can be seen in Fig. 3. An example of the ethnic division of labor can be seen in the census returns of the Falls District of Fayette County in 1880. Of the 38 men who listed the railroad as their occupation, all were Italians born of Italian parents. No other person in the district was listed as Italian.[53] The graphs in Fig. 4 represent the nationality and racial makeup of West Virginia (all counties) miners from 1880 to 1915 and demonstrate the magnitude of the influx of blacks and Europeans to the region.

The new company towns and camps did offer many tempting opportunities to a wide variety of people. Although many farmers resisted the pull of the mines and the company towns, thousands looked toward the opportunities offered by industrialization. Work in the mines provided a means of escaping the patriarchal land ownership practice that over the generations had resulted in increased division of family lands. Many farmers also chose to use the mines as a means of supplementing subsistence farming in order to earn much needed cash.[54] Weary of Jim Crow laws,

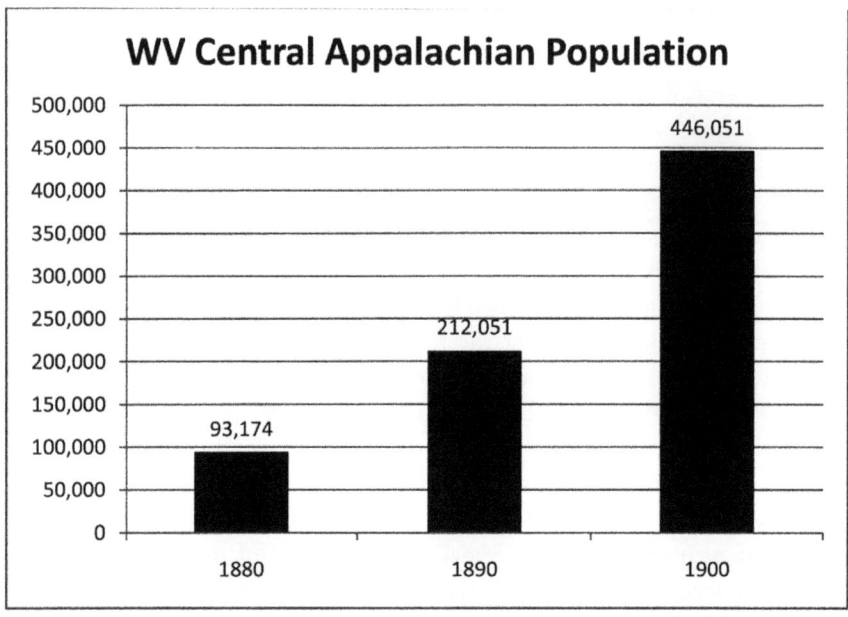

Fig. 3. West Virginia Central Appalachian Population, 1880–1900. Source: Lawrence, p. 51.

blacks also took advantage of a more accepting environment. The town of Keystone, which had a black newspaper and offered access to public office, provided such an environment. The paper, the McDowell *Times*, became "a place of unheard of freedoms" for working and middle class blacks from the Deep South, although wholesale segregation was still the norm.[55]

The growth of company towns also provided women with previously unavailable opportunities. Women left the farm and their families for many reasons. Some did so to escape abusive and domineering husbands. Others simply went to work to help out with family finances and some took teaching positions. The promise of men with money also attracted many, and others simply wanted to experience the freedoms of the socially and morally lax company towns.[56] Songs such as the one below told the story of one type of "company woman."[57]

> Where did you get the pretty little dress?
> That hat you wear so fine?
> Got my dress from a railroadman,
> Hat from a man in the mine.

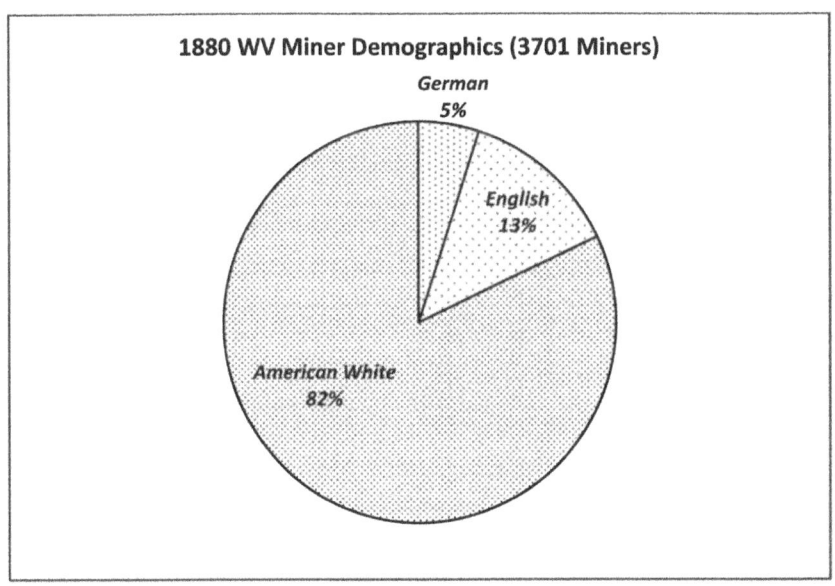

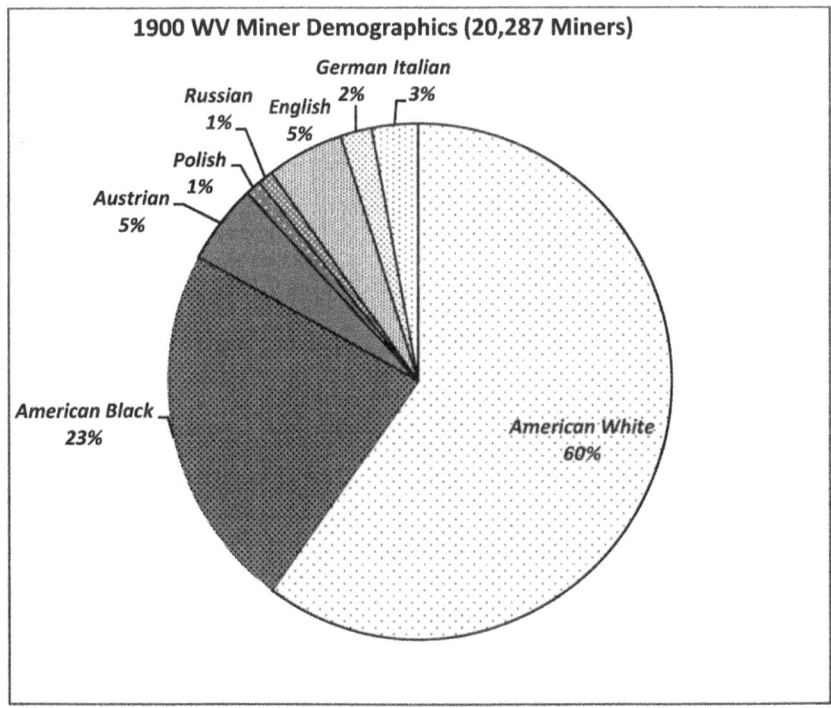

Above and following page: Fig. 4. West Virginia Miner Demographics, 1880–1915. Source: Bailey, Kenneth, p. 119. Groups with less than 1 percent are not included.

1909 WV Miner Demographics (62,189 Miners)
Slav
4%
Lithuanian
1%
English
1%
Hungarian
7%
Russian
2%
Polish
4%
Austrian
1%
American White
56%
American Black
24%

1915 WV Miner Demographics (81,328 Miners)
Italian
11%
Other
8%
Slav
3%
Hungarian
6%
American White
48%
Russian
3%
Polish
3%
Austrian
3%
American Black
15%

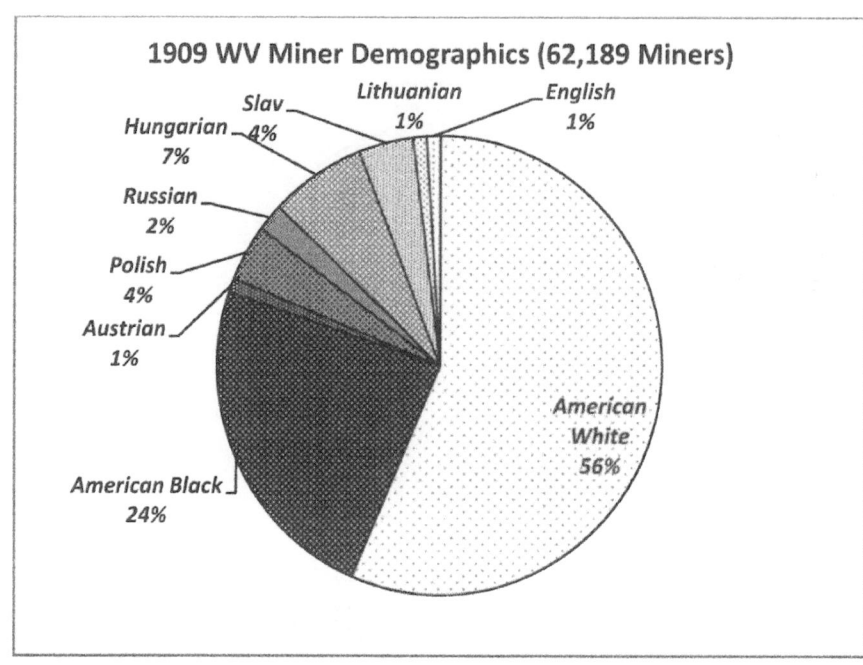

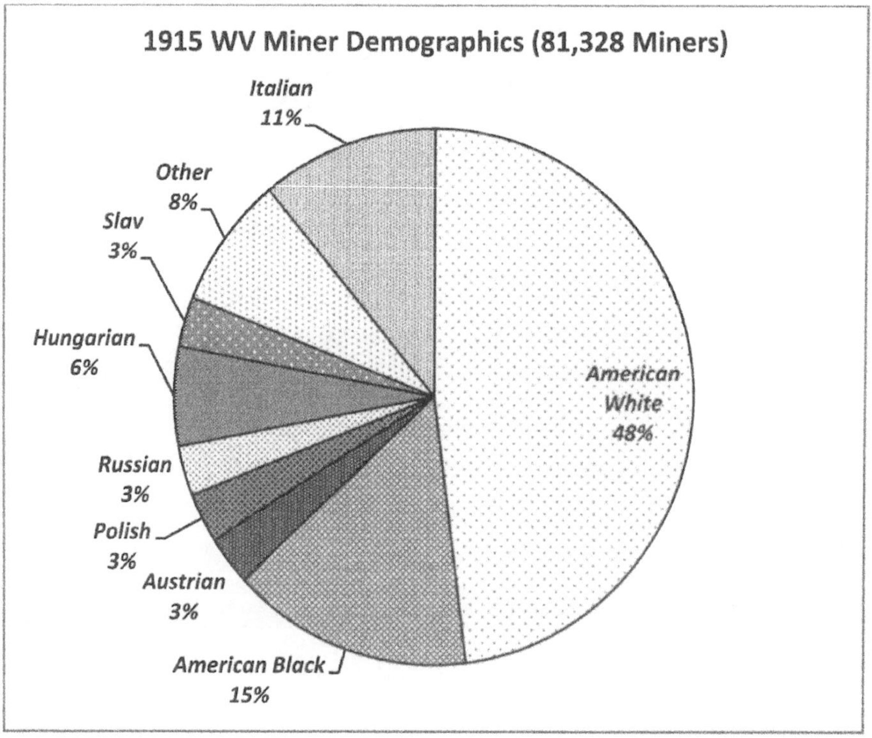

One. The Rediscovery of Appalachia and the Coming of Industralization   27

The company towns provided an avenue to personal and physical freedoms that women throughout the country were beginning to experience as part of the greater women's rights movement sweeping the nation. This limited, but significant, creation of mobility and freedom for women was but one challenge to the old guard of societal norms established through the patriarchal landowning social structure of the mountains.

New forms of labor and business associated with industrialization directly impacted agricultural business in coal counties as well. Between 1880 and 1900 many residents moved away from agriculture as an occupation. The shift in occupations seen from a sample of heads of household in McDowell County in Fig. 6 support this trend.[58] Although the rush of farmers (mostly sons) to the mines would seem to have posed a threat to the farming business in the region, in some cases farming not only survived but prospered due to the growth of industrial operations. As the population burgeoned, so did the demand for food. Aided by a rapidly improving transportation system, many farmers took advantage of the increased local market in agriculture.[59]

For areas not yet fully involved in mining endeavors, farming occupations rose quickly as the demand from nearby counties increased. As seen in Fig. 5, the Summersville District (Township) of Nicholas County saw a threefold increase in farmers between 1870 and 1900. Following a redistribution of occupations between 1900 and 1910, farming was still the predominant occupation in that district by a large margin. In 1870 the next closest occupation to farming was retirement (6), in 1900 it was carpentry (7), and in 1910 teaching held the second spot (12).[60] Even in counties heavily impacted by mining, many saw the number of farms increase between 1880 and 1920.[61]

For generations, the power structure of southern West Virginia was in the hands of a few successful businessmen and the patriarchs of kinship groups that had developed independently as families expanded and solidified their influence up and down isolated valleys. Under this system, "kinship mediated access to land and thus exerted a profound influence" in many cases.[62] As the British and Northeastern companies moved into southern West Virginia, however, the financial decisions of many of these local elites undermined their long-established power base.

In a social construct "where young men's place in the economy was dictated by the life span and inheritance decisions of their fathers,"[63] the sale of large parcels of land to outside investors drove many young men

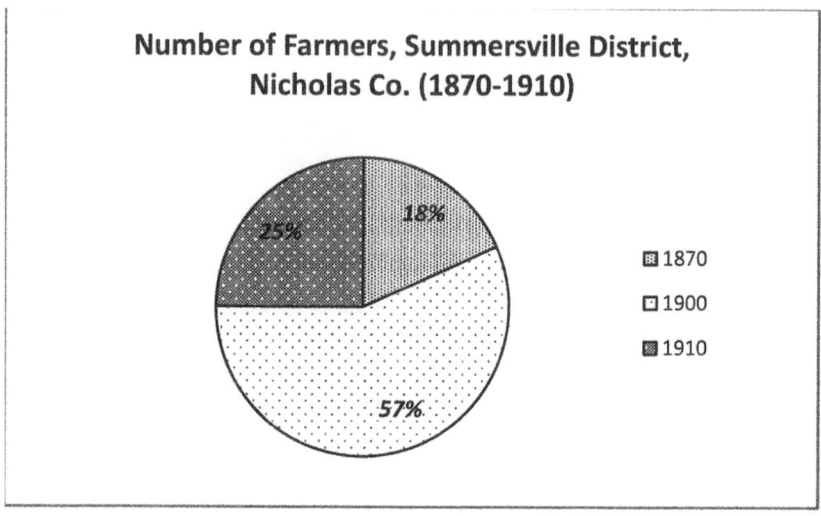

Fig. 5. Number of Farmers, Summersville District, Nicholas Co., 1870–1910. Source: U.S. Census, Summersville District (Township), Nicholas County, 1870, 1900, 1910. All males over 16 years of age who listed an occupation are included.

out of the tight-knit control of the patriarchal power structure and into the hands of the absentee corporations. This transfer of land wealth to outsiders was augmented by the transfer of legal and financial power through the actions of many prominent landowners, small businessmen, and professionals in the established towns. This group provided the base for the growth of a "petty bourgeoisie," as the local elites acted as middlemen for wealthier and more powerful absentee industrialists.[64] Although in many cases these local elites were often able to maintain or increase their financial gains and local prestige through such agreements, they traded their autonomy for new-found wealth.

The fact that their actions resulted in a relegation to pawns of much wealthier absentee industrialists posed a major change in the power structure of the southern West Virginia mountains. Although still powerful in their communities, their prestige and power were often used to persuade, influence, and, when necessary, coerce large populations to fall in line with the will of absentee industrialists.[65] This shift in local power structure, combined with the "growth of a wage labor market in mining and timber at the turn of the century—drawing members away from the family farm," would ultimately prove to be extremely disruptive to social relations in the mountains.[66]

Occupation	1880	1900
Farming	175	44
Keeping House	13	6
Merchant	2	0
Teacher	2	0
Government	1	0
Miller	1	0
Other	4	0
Laborer	0	21
Miner	0	73
Railroad	0	2
Lumber	0	3
Skilled worker	0	12
Professional	0	7
Industrial Management	0	17

Fig. 6. Occupation of Head of Households, 1880–1900. Source: Lawrence, pp. 56–57.

As thousands of people, including large numbers of blacks and European immigrants, went to work in the mining, lumber, and railroad operations, the parent companies often supplied their employees with everything they needed in the form of the company town. The companies "provided goods and services, hired police [which they controlled], and collected garbage" for the residents. Although the company town was "an economic institution that grew naturally out of the market for mine labor," which rose out of "the need to have miners where coal was minable,"[67] the resultant impact on southern West Virginia society was much more subversive and permanent than many predicted.

With the expansion of the coal industry, an "entire society was erected," which in turn "imported populations, established towns, erected an infrastructure, and built a regional economy based on the mining of coal."[68] Within the first years of operation these towns developed into much more than economic necessities, however. Many quickly morphed into centers of not only modernization and economic opportunity but vice, violence, political corruption, and coercive mechanisms of labor and societal domination. These company towns transformed the nature of southern West Virginia politics, society, and culture and would come to symbolize the negative consequences of the great industrial and financial growth of the Gilded Age.

Two

Life and Death in the Early Company Towns

Company towns were not exclusive to southern West Virginia; they occurred in many mining and logging operations throughout the nation from the 1880s until the middle of the 20th century. What made the company town experience unique in southern West Virginia was both its prevalence and long-standing social and political impact. Almost all southern West Virginia miners lived in company towns. Studies have shown that at least 80 percent and perhaps as many as 98 percent of miners lived in company towns.[1] The next closest state was Illinois, with 53 percent of its miners living in company towns.[2] With such direct influence on virtually every miner in southern West Virginia, the impact of the company town was much more pervasive and in many cases longer lasting than it has been in other regions.

Recent scholars, such as Russell Sobel in *Capitalism Unleashed*, have argued that mobility did allow miners to escape the pitfalls of the company town. The basis for this argument was the use of mining company employee turnover rates.[3] Evidence shows that many mining families did exercise this mobility. A study by the Children's Bureau of the U.S. Department of Labor in 1923 determined that one-third of 464 Raleigh County families interviewed had moved at least once in the previous two years. Many had moved so many times they had lost count.[4] Sobel's data, however, may not account for changes in employment due to strikes, part-time employment, the cyclic nature of the coal economy, and health and injury concerns, not to mention the vast surplus of miners available in the state. Even if increased mobility allowed miners to move from one mine to another, the endemic nature of the practice virtually turned the entire region into one large company town. Therefore, many were effectively unable to avoid the pervasive and often coercive influence of the company town.

Crandall Shifflett characterized the company towns of Appalachia into three distinct eras. He defined these periods as frontier, paternalistic, and declining years.[5] During the frontier years, between the founding of the company towns in the 1880s through the first decade of the 20th century, these towns served as the epicenter for the shockwaves of social change that rippled across southern West Virginia. These communities offered new opportunities and problems for thousands of mountaineers that for the most part had lived their lives close to family and separated from outsiders.

Although the historical trend has been to condemn company towns as modern fiefdoms where "from cradle to grave, they [residents] draw breath by the grace of the sometimes absentee coal owner,"[6] these towns were not clear-cut examples of evil or good. They were many things to many people trying to come to grips with the momentous social and political changes that were occurring before their eyes. These changes related to living conditions, community structure, racial and ethnic relations, and perspectives on morality. Aside from the new societal perspectives, the nature of Gilded Age and later Progressive Age ideas worked to reshape the political structure of the region as well. As people in these towns grew accustomed to aspects of modernization such as newspapers, appliances, medical care, transportation, and community organizations such as the YMCA, they also had to deal with political corruption, industrial coercion, and the deadly reality of the dangers of the coal industry.

The social impact of the company towns was multi-faceted. People moving into the new communities from isolated farms were exposed to changes in living conditions, social interactions, and perceptions of societal norms and morals. The availability of company housing provided, to varying levels of adequacy, a new home to former mountain farmers, blacks, and newly arrived immigrants from Europe.[7] In some cases, these houses were often furnished with some of the latest technologies relating to living conditions, all of which could be purchased through the company store. The iconic symbol of the era, the company store, not only provided household necessities and conveniences, but served as a type of town square. It was often where people received their mail and gathered to share news and gossip.[8]

More than any other facet of company town life, company stores symbolized the opportunities and pitfalls of the time. While goods, mail, newspapers, and gossip were now readily available to residents, many company stores took advantage of their position by charging excessive prices and driving miners into debt. This cycle of indebtedness was chronicled in the song "Sixteen Tons" recorded in 1946 by country singer Merle Travis, in which the miner could not die because he owed his very soul to the store.[9] It is the duality of opportunity and oppression that existed in the early company towns, both fostered by the company store, that highlight this complex time in the region's history.

At the heart of the residents' personal lives were the company houses. As with almost every aspect of company town life, the quality of housing varied depending on the town. The following description of company housing for the Elk River Coal and Lumber Company provides an example of good company housing:

> The houses in Widen followed the same floor plan of the typical coalfield settlement housing. The first houses constructed were single story structures with three, four, or five rooms, stone foundations, galvanized steel roofs, and were painted red with white trim. Four room homes had 14 feet square rooms featuring tongue-and-groove floors with closets and fireplaces, a kitchen with a stove, and one unheated room. Widen houses had small front porches and a "good sized back porch," but did not have plumbing or electricity. Early rent ranged from $5 to $7.50 a month.[10]

In many cases, housing was at least on par with that of nearby farms. Some were even of higher quality, such as the brick houses in the town of Borderland (on the Virginia border).[11] Even in the strike- and violence-ridden Paint and Cabin Creek areas, a commission found that general conditions were "very good" in comparison to both union and non-union camps across the nation.[12] The U.S. Department of Labor described one company town as "picturesque" with well-kept roads, lighted streets, sidewalks and with homes, fences, and other structures in "excellent repair."[13] Even in the 'good' towns, however, many residents were "challenged by a combination of crowded living conditions, inadequate water supply, and an almost daily installment of dust, soot, and coke oven fumes."[14] Other towns were far from picturesque; the same 1923 Department of Labor report provided a more general description of company towns and the youth who called them home: "The child of a coal miner in the West Virginia mountains lives very often in what is practically a frontier settlement.

It is remote and isolated, shut in by high, wooded hills, a straggling line of low houses in the wilderness."[15] The report also stated that many houses were "insanitary, ill-ventilated, and cold."[16] Such conditions also undoubtedly contributed to widespread public health issues, which will be discussed in Chapter Six.

Within each town, housing quality often depended on several factors, such as race and ethnicity. Almost all housing compounds were segregated. In the Kaymoor towns along the New River, "the two main clusters of houses at Kaymoor Top were reserved for whites" and at Kaymoor Bottom "white families lived in the choice locations near the tracks while black families were placed in homes high along the Craig Branch in the back rows."[17] American-born whites' housing also generally tended to be less crowded and more centrally located than those of blacks or European immigrants.[18] Segregation was not limited to housing; most recreation, churches, and schools were segregated as well.[19]

This photograph of miners at Price Hill shows the presence of blacks and whites and nature of segregation in the company towns (West Virginia and Regional History Collection, West Virginia University Library).

Nativism also played a role. This anti-immigrant ideology was solidified through the propaganda of the influential Know-Nothing party during the 1850s. As immigration increased and "everywhere traditional relationships were being disrupted" by the social upheaval of the industrial revolution, anti-alien groups, such as the American Protection Association, again sprung up across the nation.[20] Similar to the original Nativist movement of the 1850s, in the years prior to the turn of the century, "the same arguments were repeated" and there was a "proliferation of patriotic societies" that worked to protect the United States from alien threats to the idealized Protestant, Anglo-Saxon way of life.[21]

Many citizens exhibited feelings of not only frustration but superiority. The president of the Borderland coal company had the following to say regarding immigrants: "From the earliest beginning and during the trying times of the company, the majority of men in the field were foreigners ... if these foreigners were left to their own inclinations, conditions in the houses would not be anything like the standard of an American workman.[22] The Bluefield *Daily Telegraph* called a flash flood that damaged several immigrant houses in 1906 an "unpremeditated bath."[23] Similar opinions were held by other native workers. One man complained of the need for someone to "look after the women and children" on payday when "all that foreign element gets drunk."[24]

Regardless of their differences, the residents of company towns enjoyed a new access to modernity. This included more than necessities such as food, clothing, and tools. Former farmers, European peasants, and southern sharecroppers often had access to refrigerators, radios (later in the period), washing machines, medicines, and many other modern niceties.[25] These items made life easier and more enjoyable, and provided comforts that many would never have dreamed of in their previous conditions. These "new necessities" were provided almost exclusively through the company stores.

These stores evolved into "centralized places of communal life and affiliation."[26] As many of the residents' daily needs and wants were met by the company store, it naturally grew into the center of the community. Shifflett describes a typical day at the company store in *Coal Towns*:

> Women appeared early in the morning to pick up quick items for breakfast or in the afternoon for something for supper; children came after school for a soda or ice-cream cone.... Women met and talked about their children, who was sick or well, what they were sewing or what they were fixing for supper

... problems with the neighbor.... Men might brag about the fish they had caught, plan a hunting trip, or talk about the number of tons of coal loaded that day, about a close call in the mines ... or the pain in their chests or backs ... men might just go and sit all day, eating crackers and sardines, and talk.[27]

Aside from the store itself, many of these towns offered a wide variety of other entertainment. Many miners, loggers, and family members had access to a YMCA, picture shows, swimming pools, bowling, and pool tables.[28] Some operators provided schools as well. Widen expanded the one room school it built in 1911 to two rooms in 1912. A school for black children was constructed in 1914, although it provided education only through the eighth grade.[29]

Gambling, alcohol, women, and trouble could be found in abundance as well, particularly in the very early days of the towns. During the pioneer stage of company town development, many single men worked not only in mines but on railroads and construction of the town itself. According to Shifflett, these men deservedly gained recognition as "a rough-and-tumble crowd that engaged in drinking, gambling, and violent brawling." One man who lived below a boarding house full of such men recalled their nature: "The thing I remember about the boarding house ... they'd get drunk, and there'd be more throat-cuttings there than anyplace you ever heard of. Just about every week, somebody would be stabbed, or shot, or have his throat cut. Throat-cutting was common and stylish."[30]

Some towns became well known for non-violent crimes as well. With a mixture of young single men, money, and new opportunities for women, prostitution became more prevalent, if not common, in some areas, and as a result many of the early mining towns had brothels. Keystone, in McDowell County, had a reputation for prostitution that rivaled any in Appalachia.[31] In an area of a little more than a block, "several dozen 'houses' ... each with 'eight or ten girls' did business."[32] Even while martial law was declared on Paint Creek in 1912–1913, several people were arrested for fornication, adultery, and operation of a house of ill-fame.[33] Sometimes arguments over women escalated into violence as well, such as the case in 1904 when John Boggs shot Fred Kale in a dispute over a woman.[34]

Racial violence also occurred. In 1896, Alex Jones, a black man, accidentally shot a bystander during an argument with another man on a train. County officials attempted to move him to Charleston, but his train was stopped by a mob and Jones was shot to death. Jones' killing was not the only lynching to take place during this period.[35] Racial and ethnically fueled violence such as this occurred in many areas outside the state. In Atlanta, a Jew was lynched while being held on charges of molesting and killing a fourteen-year-old girl.[36] A lack of effective law enforcement did not help the situation. With little policing available, some men occasionally reverted to traditional "mountain justice" when there was a perceived wrong, often acting as their "own law and protector."[37]

Eventually, the influx of families caused a decline in the crime and violence of the early towns. According to Ronald Lewis, this was the culmination of "a conflict in values and social norms [which] also emerged with industrialization in the mountains, which set law-abiding, sober, middle-class residents against saloon keepers, both legal and illegal, and those who preferred spending their free time in the bars and brothels rather than the churches."[38]

Despite the slack in crime, however, anger and the potential for violence were still boiling just under the surface in many towns.[39] In several towns, residents believed the biggest criminal in town was the company itself. While operators, and some residents, felt the towns were "an efficient and necessary institution," others believed that the icon of the town, the company store, was at the heart of an industrialist plot to keep the worker forever indebted to the company through unfair pricing. This feeling intensified after union activists began operating in the region. Bolstered by union agitators, many residents began questioning the pricing practices and use of scrip by the company store.

The question of company store pricing is complex. From the company's perspective, the availability of goods provided in their stores, while a great convenience to their residents and efficient in terms of location, was not a benevolent enterprise. Operators believed they had every right to earn a profit. In fact, stores provided as much as 10 percent of profit for the entire operation, including coal revenues.[40] This profit, as well as money from rents, actually made the difference between operating at a profit or loss in the first decade of the 20th century for many operations. And there was financial merit in their argument. Some operators argued the cost to produce a ton of coal in southern West Virginia was 5 cents more than it was selling for in 1904.[41]

This drastic price fluctuation continued well into the 1930s. The Greenbrier Coal Company (McDowell County) experienced drastic swings in pricing as late as 1932. In that year, the company posted a net loss of $524 in July and profits of $5,058 in October. The company store was much more consistent, however, with $1,026.10 in profits in July and $1,544.05 in profits in October.[42] While operators came to count on these additional revenues, many residents questioned the equality of pricing compared to more distant non-company stores. From their perspective, more than a few residents felt exploited by greed and the geographical monopoly held by the store.

Several commissions investigated the pricing practices of company stores throughout the first three decades of the 20th century, including the U.S. Senate investigation into the Paint and Cabin Creek Wars in 1913 and the Coal Commission Report of 1922. Their task was not an easy one. The U.S. Senate investigators questioned miners and company store managers.[43] Most miners spoke from memory, and while company store managers provided price lists and comparisons to independents stores, their reports were not always complete. In most cases, even from the residents' perspective, most prices were fair on a large number of items.[44] There were some interesting differences, however. One miner reported paying 8 cents a pound more for bacon and almost twice as much for a shovel at a company store, and others stated that some items were 40 to 60 percent higher in the company stores.[45] Another problem with the examination of pricing practices was that the documents provided by the company stores often had incomplete or no information on several items' pricing at independent stores.[46] Despite the possible subterfuge, the company store managers claimed their prices were fair "taking quality into consideration," and that some of their items were even cheaper than independent competitors, although the committee felt those cases were rare.[47]

In the end, just as with many of the problems surrounding the region, the issue proved complex to the point that one investigator grew frustrated at the "utter impossibility of comparing prices."[48] The final report of the Donahue Committee (ordered by the West Virginia governor prior to the Senate investigation), while generally placing the blame for the outbreak of violence on Paint and Cabin Creeks upon the UMWA,[49] provided ambiguous recommendations. The report stated that although some items in some stores were 10 to 25 percent overpriced, no widespread exploitation existed.[50]

The data seems to support the idea that prices for the vast majority of items in most stores were equitable, most companies did not expressly forbid residents from trading with independent stores, and many local farmers openly traded and did business with residents of company towns.

As such, the Donahue Report recommended that the companies try to approach pricing from a more altruistic perspective and for the residents to be more prudent in their financial endeavors.[51] The later U.S. Coal Commission report of 1922 seemed to have better luck at definitively comparing prices; they demonstrated a general price difference of 4 to 11 percent between company and non-company stores in southern West Virginia.[52]

Another major issue concerning the company stores was the use of scrip. The most common use of scrip was as a type of credit against the workers' labor if they desired goods between pay periods, which were generally once a month.[53] While the use of scrip varied significantly throughout the region, payment by scrip only was "uncommon."[54] The pros and cons of scrip often split along labor and management lines. The operators' perspective on scrip was that it provided a means for residents to obtain items of necessity from the company store between monthly pay cycles.[55] Residents had mixed opinions. Some believed the "aluminum money" did offer a stopgap between paydays while others thought the scrip to be yet another exploitive measure of company coercion. One former resident, Birdie Kyle, described the dilemma that some families faced in regards to scrip. He said, "You had to choose between two evils: draw scrip and have no cash on hand, or not draw scrip so that Dad could draw a payday."[56]

One of the largest problems with scrip was that it could only be exchanged for its full value at the company store in exchange for company goods. In the cases where company stores cashed in scrip, it was often at 90 cents on the dollar. Independent stores that accepted scrip did so at an even more reduced rate, sometimes only 25 cents on the dollar.[57] The Coal Commission report also raised concerns that it "tended to preclude housewives from reckoning what each item cost and whether the clerk had made the correct deduction."[58] As a whole, the scrip situation was handled in the same manner as company store pricing. It appears most families were cognizant of both company store pricing and the use of scrip and planned their finances accordingly.[59] Some families even excelled under this system; miners reported to Senate investigators having savings accounts of $1,000 to $2,000 and purchasing their own farms.[60]

The early company town environment was a complex society that challenged long standing norms and presented new opportunities and problems in regard to race, ethnicity, nationality, and gender, and generated heated debates over issues such as company store pricing and the use of scrip. These issues would not have existed, however, without the need for labor. It was the fundamental nature of early industrial labor, particularly mining, upon which both union and non-union elements stoked the fires of oppression and resistance. Tensions over the inherent dangers of mining itself, fair wage practices, and union encroachment compounded the societal aspects of the company town to create the volatile mixture that exploded into open warfare in southern West Virginia in the first decades of the twentieth century.

Mining is a dangerous profession. In the heyday of the Industrial Revolution profit often trumped safety and the mining industry personified this ideal. Between 1897 and 1928, over 10,000 people lost their lives in the mines and thousands more were left crippled, debilitated, and dying. In 1907 alone, over 499 miners died in West Virginia.[61] Death or injury could come in a variety of ways. Coal dust could ignite from a spark and cause violent and deadly explosions, such as the Monongah explosion in 1906 which killed over 300 men and still ranks as the largest loss of life in a single mining accident.[62] Walls could collapse or mines could be flooded. The accumulation of gas or misalignment of ventilation systems could also cause death. Even as mechanization began to remove some of the more difficult manual labor requirements of mining, it brought with it more dangers. Men could be crushed or have limbs torn apart by machinery. The increased use of electricity and machinery also enhanced the possibility of fires and explosions.[63]

Falling rock, small collapses, and other isolated accidents provided perpetual danger to miners and constant stress to their families, and accounted for the vast majority of deaths.[64] An example of this slow but steady loss of life can be seen in the fatalities of Kay Moor No. 1 between 1904 and 1940. Between those years, 21 men died in individual accidents that included electrocution, slate falls, and crush injuries.[65] Aside from injuries, countless miners were afflicted with pneumoconiosis or black lung, a disease caused by the chronic inhalation of coal dust. When the disease was finally recognized in 1968, it was estimated that over 125,000 miners were inflicted.[66]

The imminent threat of injury, illness, or death as part of everyday life must have had deep psychological impact on miners and families alike. Several recollections of mining accidents are reminiscent of combat veterans' stories. Retellings of the Stuart Mine explosion provide an excellent example. On January 29, 1907, over 50 men were killed when a miner's lamp ignited methane gas and powder and sparked a chain reaction of fire and death. One witness spoke of seeing 50 men lying dead, mules torn apart, and equipment strewn across the shaft bottom. Another saw a man with the top of his head taken off and another was found dead with his lunch box between his legs and a sandwich still held to his mouth.[67]

Stories such as these obviously impacted the ethos of miners, families, and the entire community. According to Shifflett: "Coal mining was a volatile industry and an insecure occupation. Danger and uncertainty had definite implications for the men and women who lived and worked in such close and constant touch with unemployment and death. Men could not presume anything so grand as a career."[68]

The enduring nature of this sense of impending death can also be seen in modern country music. Two examples are Dwight Yoakam's "Miner's Prayer" and Darrell Scott's "You'll Never Leave Harlan Alive," also recorded by Patty Loveless and Brad Paisley. Scott's song speaks not only of the danger of the mines but the sense of helplessness in escaping the mining culture.[69] Yoakam's verse is more direct and addresses the constant danger men faced each day as they entered the mines with a prayer to see the sun shine again.[70]

Nationality and race also played a role in mortality in southern West Virginia mines. Immigrants had a much higher mortality rate in the region compared to U.S. citizens. Between 1904 and 1908, 46 percent of miners were American whites, 22 percent were blacks, and 32 percent were immigrants. During this same period, American whites accounted for 35.5 percent of the fatalities while blacks and immigrants accounted for 16 percent and 48.5 percent respectively.[71] While immigrants made up one-third of the mining population, they accounted for almost half the deaths.

Operators often did not help the situation. One operator was reported to have said that the death of immigrant miners was not a serious thing, as they were "ignorant foreigners who can easily be replaced."[72] As accidents and deaths mounted, however, a few operators did urge increased caution and new ways of thinking as the mining industry rapidly expanded beyond its capacity to operate safely.[73] Reform-minded operators were few in number, however, and despite their efforts, "over time the concept of callous coal operators and/or companies certainly melded into the consciousness of mining labor culture."[74] It has remained there.

Several factors beyond nativism may have affected the high mortality rate of foreign miners as well. Immigrants worked more hours on average and also volunteered for more hazardous, higher paying jobs.[75] Inexperience and language barriers were significant reasons for accidents as well.[76] The language problems inherent with a multi-national workforce became such an issue that in 1908 the U.S. Immigration Commission report spoke specifically to this issue: "The mixture of several nationalities who do not speak the same language and understand one another with great difficulty is a disturbing condition and complicates this in the face of danger."[77] The Immigration Commission began to actively work against sending immigrants to West Virginia mines due to the high mortality rates of foreigners. By 1912, only ½ of 1 percent of European immigrants with mining experience went to West Virginia.[78]

Even today, each mining family lives with the quiet, but always present, anxiety of the dangers their husbands, brothers, sons, and now mothers, sisters, and daughters face each time they make their way into the earth to extract coal. Despite advances in mining technology, safety, and engineering, accidents still happen. The 2006 Sago and 2010 Upper Big Branch mine disasters provide sobering reminders of the dangers that exist below for the region's (and all) miners.

Miners face the daily threat of injury and death for cash wages. As such, one of most common causes for a labor strike in the industry's early history was the demand for increased wages. Southern West Virginia mine strikes were no different. Hoping to get their due, or at least subsistence in the company town environment, miners and union leadership struggled for concessions on workers' pay scales as well as what was deducted from their pay. Although several mine jobs were paid a set amount per day, loaders were generally paid per ton of coal. Questionable practices such as cribbing, which did not pay for all the coal loaded, and docking, which deducted money due to impurities, diluted the paychecks. The workers on set scales argued for pay that was both competitive with union camps and kept the pace with cost of living expenses. Set scale and per-ton workers alike had to keep a keen eye on what the company was subtracting from their pay in terms of scrip, rent, and other deductions.

The pay of miners fluctuated dramatically during the first decade of the 20th century, as the graph of West Virginia and Illinois pick miner annual wages demonstrates (Fig. 7).[79] Several factors likely played a role in this fluctuation, but the most significant cause was the dynamic nature of the coal industry during this period. As mines became unionized or signed contracts, wages generally increased. In West Virginia, particularly the southern fields, most camps remained non-union while at the same

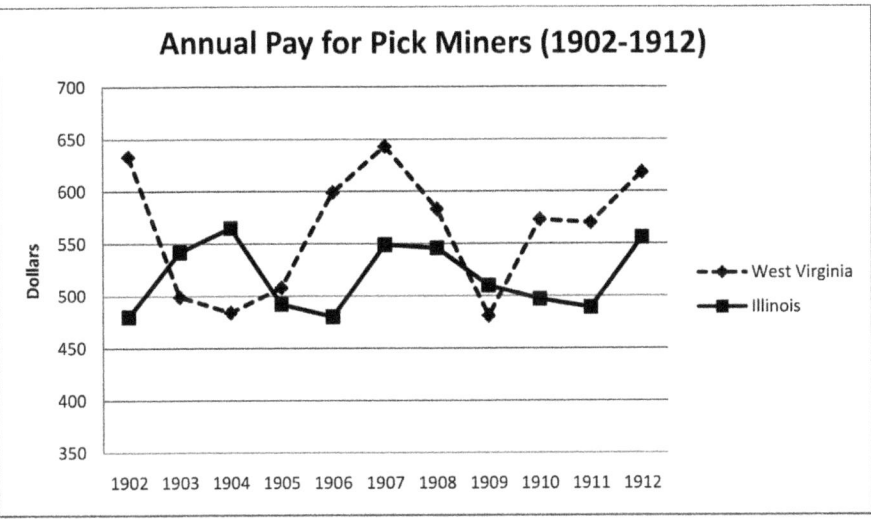

Fig. 7. Annual Pay for Pick Miners, 1902–1912, West Virginia and Illinois. Source: Report attached to *Conditions on Paint Creek*, p. 1657.

time many new operations sprung up. These new and non-union mines took in immigrants and blacks, who generally received a smaller per unit or day wage scale.

Mine workers, depending on jobs and skill level, made somewhere between just under a dollar and up to $6 per day, but typically made between $2.50 and $5 per day.[80] Wages varied depending on location, as most non-union mines in the region set their own pay scales. At the Paint Creek Collieries Co. from May 1, 1911, to April 30, 1912, average miners made between $3.05 and $4.93 a day. The best miners at Paint Creek Collieries made between $3.91 and $6.54, while day laborers averaged between $1.94 and $2.27 per day. From January through March of 1912, the three months prior to the Paint Creek strike, the best miners averaged a little over $4 a day.[81] During the strike, however, wages were significantly lower.

Skilled workers, such as blacksmiths, made between $2.50 and $3 a day, while laborers made less than $2 per day.[82] Hemuri Sandro was an exception. Sandro signed a contract with the George William Labor Contractors to work as a blacksmith at a coal mine for two years at $5.50 per day.[83] Loaders were paid by the ton. Their pay also had a high degree of variance. New River companies paid around 40 cents a ton in the first decade of the 20th century.[84] Mingo County mines averaged 41 cents per ton in 1912 and 50 cents per ton in 1916.[85] A study conducted by Nettie McGill provided the data on income for various jobs in 1920 for 11 company towns near Beckley seen in Fig. 8.[86] Many families handled their wages with financial acumen. One family left their farm for a coal town and over the span of forty years not only sustained themselves but put two children through college on a miner's pay.[87]

Earnings not only varied according to location and type of work but by nationality as well. Surprisingly, immigrants brought home the largest pay. In the U.S. Immigration Commission report of 1908, 4 percent of American whites earned over $3.50 compared to 8 percent of Slovaks. Among Bulgarians 35.6 percent earned more than $2.50 a day, while 27 percent of American whites earned that amount.[88] The average breakdown can be seen in Fig. 9.[89]

While immigrants seemed to earn more, it was not due to preferential pay scales. As discussed earlier, immigrants tended to work longer hours and volunteer for more dangerous jobs.[90] This was often due to the immigrant miner's desire to either send money to relatives in Europe, earn enough to purchase family members' passage to the U.S., or save enough to return themselves. In the areas of Fairmont and Monongah, immigrants

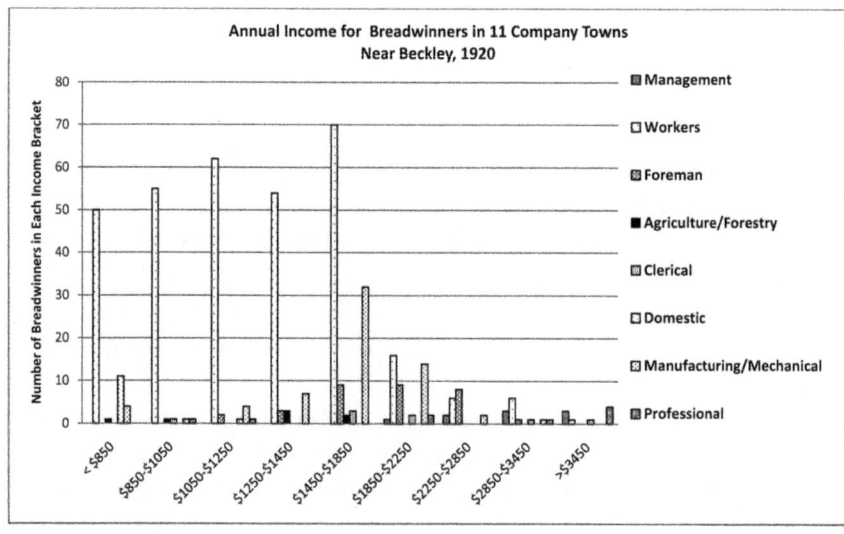

Fig. 8. Annual Income for Breadwinners in Company Towns near Beckley, 1920. Source: McGill, pp. 62–63.

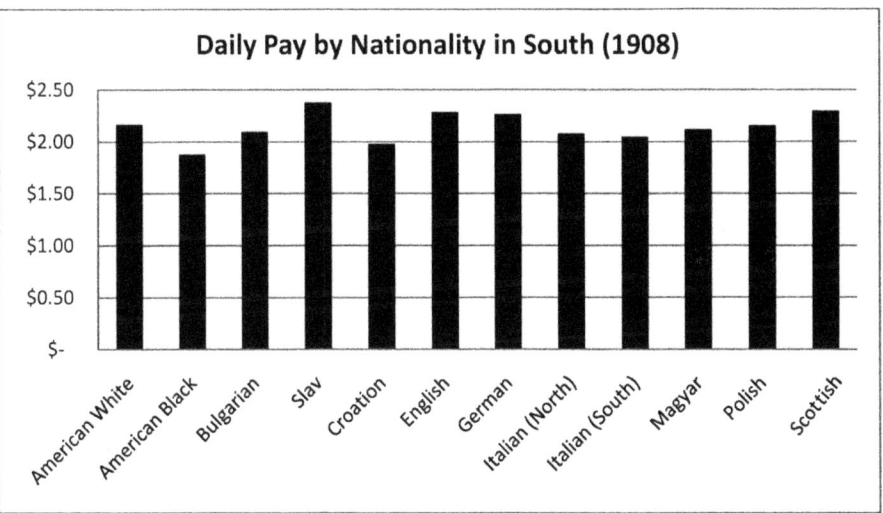

Fig. 9. Daily Pay by Nationality in the South, 1908. Source: Average daily wages by nationality in southern U.S. 1908. From Lawrence, p. 121, and Report of U.S. Immigration Commission 1908.

sent somewhere between $90,000 and $150,000 to relatives in Europe annually.[91]

Between the 1880s and the First World War, southern West Virginia company towns came to represent many things to many people. Early towns offered new opportunities to women, blacks, immigrants, and mountaineers hoping to escape life on the farm. Along with opportunities such as cash wages, modern conveniences, and more contact with the outside world, these people were exposed to an expansion of vices such as drinking, gambling, and sexual excess. With little in the way of law enforcement in the early camps, violence and decadence coexisted side by side with modernization.

The rough and tumble towns began to give way to more family oriented communities by the onset of the First World War. Central to the transformation of life in these towns was the company store. These stores and other company-directed community projects, such as theaters and bowling alleys, offered residents material goods and a lifestyle unlike any they had experienced in the remote Appalachian farms, southern fields, or European slums. As these towns continued to develop, however, many began to take a more critical look at the relationship between operators and their resident-employees. In some cases, the residents perceived programs and practices of the company to be unfair and in a few instances pure industrial slavery.

While residents of these towns were beginning to question the nature of life and death in company towns, two larger movements were taking place in the United States. First, the Progressive movement was challenging the seemingly unlimited power of the industrialists. This resulted in a backlash against excessive wealth and power that highlighted company town residents' concerns and encouraged further debate. Secondly, the continued rise of labor unions provided a vocal, and sometimes volatile, voice for the rights of workers on the national stage.

THREE

The Coming of the Unions and the Paint Creek-Cabin Creek Strike

By the end of the first decade of the 20th century, many southern West Virginia residents began to focus less on the opportunities offered by the company towns and more on the limitations and inequalities of camp life. Aided, or in many cases prodded, by labor activists such as Mary "Mother" Jones, people began to resist unfair treatment by absentee coal owners and their local surrogates — the often class, race, and ethnically conscious operators. It was this growing divide between the "haves" and the "have nots," spurred by both union and anti-union rhetoric, intimidation, and violence that would lead to the bloody "Mine Wars" of the first quarter of the 20th century. The legacy of these turbulent years in many respects still haunts the region and can be seen in a continuing history of corruption, distrust of outsiders, and ambivalence or abandonment of the political process by many southern West Virginians.

Issues regarding company store pricing and fair wages were driven as much, or perhaps more, by how they were perceived than by their true impact on the majority of residents. In many cases perception became reality.

Other organizations added to this constructed version of reality. One of the major influences behind how miners viewed their existence in relation to the company and its operators was the emotional and often inflammatory voice of the labor unions, namely the United Mine Workers of America.Despite the obvious merits of the workers' right to collectively negotiate fair and equitable treatment, wages, and benefits, it was often

UMWA radicals that provided the spark for the explosions of violence that occurred in the early decades of the 20th century.

Even before the tumultuous years of West Virginia's Mine Wars, echoes of criticism against absentee landowners and heartless operators could be heard in the region. In many cases, these early critics were local elites that had either failed to capitalize on early investment opportunities or had been pushed aside by wealthier, more powerful outside industrialists. One such frustrated investor was the editor of the Logan *Banner*, Henry Ragland. When it became known that the Norfolk & Western would not be connecting to the area in which he had invested, he quickly turned against speculation to become a voice for the small farmer: "The value placed on our lands by the speculators is no fair criterion of their value ... our home market for grains has enabled our farmers to live, but when the N&W is completed the present price for grain will be reduced by more than one half. We hope the prevalent custom of putting the small farmer in the clutches of the speculator will be avoided in the reassessment."[1]

Ragland, a Confederate veteran, accused the Republicans of plotting to "Africanize West Virginia" and blamed the railroad camps for creating "havens of vice, gambling, and drinking."[2] The former speculator drew distinct lines between industrialists and native West Virginians, saying, "Remember that in the fight ... one side represents a happy home and the other side a gilded hell."[3]

Criticism continued to grow. In 1890 critics of the industrialists found a champion in the UMWA. Organized from various failing and defunct labor organizations, such as the Knights of Labor and the National Federation of Miners and Mine Laborers, the UMWA sought to break the power of the coal operators.[4] By the turn of the century, the UMWA was poised to make a concerted thrust into anti-union territory. And southern West Virginia was the heart of anti-union power.

Several challenges faced the unionists as they infiltrated the mining camps in the region, however. Some miners had no problems with working in the non-union camps or had been able to negotiate terms at individual mines. The influx of immigrants and blacks also created unexpected barriers for labor advocates. With segregation, nativism, and ethnic tensions still strong, the inherent divisiveness of these elements often made it very difficult to form a consensus among the various subgroups of miners. Finally, and most importantly, the operators were not going to allow unionization without a fight.

Unionization efforts were even less effective in the lumber towns. Although lumber towns tended to be less diverse than coal towns, "the independent nature of woodsmen, their isolated experience in the forest, and great mobility rendered them poor candidates for unionization."[5] One of the few occasions of the lumbermens' attempt to organize took place when half the workers from the Greenbrier, Cheat, and Elk Railroad, a subsidiary of the West Virginia Pulp and Paper Company, struck in order to have their work day reduced from 10 to 9 hours. When the other half of the men showed up for work, "they were met with clubs, staves, and revolvers."[6]

In the power struggle over labor, operators held several advantages over the union. Almost all early miners in the region lived in company towns. In the ensuing clash, the town's infrastructure would become a powerful coercive mechanism. Whether for good or bad, company stores were a necessity for many residents. Not only did residents receive foodstuffs and other goods there, but the store also served as the area's post office and community center. Most miners also lived in company owned housing. If miners were to challenge the operators, they would be placing their access to necessities, mail, information, and even their homes at risk.[7] In addition to power within the confines of their own towns, many coal operators were very influential in local government, often carrying officials on their payrolls.

The UMWA also had strengths. Fresh off victories in the coalfields in northern states, the organization had momentum and a growing political and financial base. Even more important, however, were the UMWA activists' power of propaganda and speechmaking. Powerful and influential speakers, such as Mother Jones, would rebuke, inspire, and agitate miners in a way that would surprise and frighten not only operators but state and local officials as well.

The collision of UMWA agitation and the operators' backlash of coercive power tore asunder the very fiber of society and government in a series of mining wars that plunged the region into anarchy and resulted in several declarations of martial law between 1912 and 1921. In its drive to win the hearts and minds of miners, the UMWA leveled inflammatory speeches and provocation of violence against mine guards, local officials, and strikebreakers. The operators responded in like, first using the coercive power inherent in the company store and company housing system, then through intimidation at the hands of mine guards. In the end, UMWA rhetoric and operator coercion gave birth to widespread and often uncontrollable violence that overwhelmed local governments and law enforcement.

The Mine Wars of 1912–1913 and 1920–1921 not only bloodied the state but left a scar on the region that can still be seen today. The violence on Paint Creek and Cabin Creek, the Matewan Massacre, and the Battle of Blair Mountain highlight the social turmoil, lawlessness, and violence that became a way of life in many areas of southern West Virginia in the first decades of the 20th century. Many of the state's current problems, including distrust in or removal from the democratic process, fear or distrust of law enforcement, tendencies for extra-legal settlement of conflicts, and a general reluctance toward outsiders either grew out of or were enhanced during these violent and chaotic years.

When the mines along Paint Creek and Cabin Creek struck in 1912, they were the only non–UMWA mines in the Kanawha fields. All efforts at UMWA encroachment into southern West Virginia had failed, the one exception being its victory in the Kanawha fields.[8] There were many reasons behind the UMWA's limited success in the region. In addition to social, racial, and cultural differences which created barriers for organization,[9] some miners simply did not wish to join the union. Due to these factors, labor protests on Paint Creek were "sporadic, infrequent, unorganized, and local" from the 1880s until 1912. Shifflett further states, "Some non-Unionism was widespread enough to challenge as misleading the equation of the history of coal miners with a mass movement of class conscious labor workers rising up as one against an oppressive and exploitive labor system."[10]

Another explanation for the UMWA's limited success was the tireless work of the operators and their continued support from local and state officials. In southern West Virginia, the operators "employed practically every device known to antiunionists."[11] One of the most effective was the use of the legal system. In 1907, the case of *Hitchman Coal and Coke Company v. Mitchell* provided the perfect opportunity for the operators to legally gain the upper hand against the unions. The case upheld the right of a company to require its workers to sign "yellow dog" contracts, which in was an agreement between the company and the worker that the worker would not join a union.[12]

In Judge Alston Dayton, the operators found their champion. Not only did Dayton find in favor of the operator, but deemed the UMWA an unlawful organization as a monopoly in restraint of trade under both common law and the Sherman Anti-Trust Act. This decision, although overturned by an appellate court, was later upheld by the U.S. Supreme Court,[13] giving the operators legal grounds to refuse to deal with the UMWA.[14] The American Federation of Labor (AFL) deemed this decision to be "evidence of the growing arrogance and a greater and more flagrant usurpation of authority by the judiciary of our land."[15] Dayton did not limit his displeasure of the UMWA to the *Hitchman* case; during one case involving the UMWA, Dayton exclaimed in court that he would "not permit the United Mine Workers of America to exist" within his jurisdiction.[16] Dayton's support of capitalists extended to the lumber industry as well. When the Ritter Lumber Company admitted to peonage, Dayton fined the company $1,000, but stated that he "had no sympathy" for those who did not keep their contracts or fulfill their debts.[17]

Many operators truly believed they had a legitimate reason to fear the UMWA. The organized coalfields in the North believed West Virginia's non-union fields to be "a grave menace" to their operations,[18] and it was widely believed by West Virginia operators that when the bituminous fields of Pennsylvania, Ohio, Illinois, and Indiana were organized under the Central Competitive Field in 1898, one of agreements between the UMWA and operators was that the union would organize the southern West Virginia coalfields.[19] This mindset can be seen in a letter from Paint Creek and Cabin Creek operators to West Virginia Governor William Glasscock during the strike that accused the UMWA of standing in the way of law and order and being "dominated by the interests of the operators of [Northern] competitive states."[20]

Despite the lack of UMWA involvement, the workers on Paint Creek and Cabin Creek had established their own contracts with operators. When time came to renew the contract, however, Paint Creek miners demanded their pay scale be set to the same levels as union mines. Cabin Creek miners followed suit but asked for more. Their demands included: (1) union recognition, (2) free speech and peaceable assembly, (3) the end of blacklisting of union miners, (4) freedom to use non-company stores, (5) the end of cribbing,[21] (6) establishment of a 2,000 pound standard for a ton of coal, (7) verification of scales, (8) the employment of a checkweighman paid for by the miners, and (9) the concurrence on the docking of pay by both company and miners' checkweighman.[22] The operators refused and the miners struck.

When the miners struck, operators took steps to keep the mines running. These measures included the introduction of strikebreakers, eviction of striking miners from company homes, barring of access to company stores, and finally, establishing a coercive and intimidating environment through the use of the infamous mine guards. The operators' practices, however, failed to break the will of the strikers. Instead, striking miners turned to even more coercive, violent, and "extreme measures" themselves.[23] With this strike, a series of actions and reactions were put into motion that led to one of the most violent civil uprisings in American history.

As the situation escalated, more mine guards poured into the area. These men were hired, sometimes deputized, protectors of company property and enforcers of the operators' will. While the operators deemed these men (mostly Baldwin-Felts private detectives) good and courteous men,[24] many residents thought of them as hired thugs. The use of mine guards was not new, having grown out of the rough and tumble days of the early company towns. In response to the violence present in many early towns, operators had intermittently used private security to maintain order. On one occasion guards were instrumental in maintaining a quarantine which helped to limit the spread of smallpox at Kaymoor, near Fayetteville, in 1904.[25] More often than not, however, the guards were also used to protect company property during strikes. Such was the case when guards were used on the New River in 1902 and at Cabin Creek in 1904, but their numbers were small and there were few problems.[26]

This was not the case in 1912. Over 300 Baldwin-Felts guards were hired by operators in the Paint Creek and Cabin Creek coalfields in response to the strike.[27] Many residents and union activists saw the Baldwin-Felts men as "professional strikebreakers, all tried on a dozen industrial battlefields, [who] will to shoot with or without provocation."[28] These mine guards provided the spark that would ignite the firestorm of violence and death in the region.

Upon their arrival, the mine guards went about not only protecting company property but carrying out other duties as directed by the operators. One of the first tasks was bringing in new workers. Companies began transporting non-union workers, of which a large number were newly arrived immigrants and blacks, to replace the striking workers. These "transportation men" were offered transportation to the mine, the price of which they would work off in a predetermined period of time. Newly arrived immigrants, black sharecroppers, and down-on-their-luck men from northern cities piled onto railroad cars in New York, Boston, and other cities and made their way to the coalfields of southern West Virginia.[29]

Willam Veasly, a black miner who moved to West Virginia from Alabama as a transportation man, said the operators would use a "Negro preacher and give him $400 to $500 and send him to Alabama and tell him to bring back some people."[30] Some miners were even recruited in Europe and offered passage in return for their work, a practice reminiscent of indentured servitude. These men typically signed contracts that allowed for the deduction of their transportation from their wages or required they work a set period of time.[31]

Once they arrived at the mining camps around the region, many of these new workers found themselves in a situation quite different from the one explained to them by company recruiters. Cases of misrepresentation by agents and recruiters were common. Machinist Lawrence O'Brien believed he was being transported for skilled labor, but when he arrived he was given a shovel and told to dig coal. Others had similar stories.[32] When they raised questions, many were told they would have to work to pay off their transportation. One man was told, "If you don't go to work, we won't feed you."[33]

Many found working off this debt difficult. Transportation men began their jobs owing the company for their journey. The cost of food, tools, and housing were quickly added to the tally. One miner had been working from almost a month and still owed the company $4.74. Another told investigators, "I earned $25 when I was a cook and $20 for shovel work, but they told me I had only $10, and I don't know where the rest is."[34] Some transportation men claimed they were physically prevented from leaving by threats and intimidation at the hands of the mine guards. In Kayford, 150 men wrote a letter to the Labor Commission claiming they were being held against their will.[35] Several charges of peonage were made throughout the region as well. Examples include 350 Italians claiming they were being held and made to work without pay as were Bohemians in McDowell County. Although several reports were made between 1890 and 1920, only two cases were proven.[36]

Armed guards were also used against workers in some lumber towns as well. After complaints of peonage against the Ritter Lumber Company in Wyoming County in 1906, a U.S. marshal was sent to investigate. The marshal, Dan Cunningham, found that several employees were "compelled by force or otherwise, to work."[37] The superintendent himself conceded that "ten or twenty" men had been detained through armed men and threats.[38]

Companies also used armed guards against one another to retain their workers. Two representatives of the Babcock lumber company were attempting to find workers who had skipped out on their contracts and left to work with another company. On their way to the competing lumber company, the men were taken prisoner by guards and subjected to physical and mental abuse. The men were blindfolded and told they were to be shot while guards fired off pistols near them. The captives were then told they were to be hanged or dragged to death behind cars. They then had ropes attached to their necks with the other end attached to an automobile while the car was driven in short intervals to make them believe their captors were going to make good on their threats. Eventually the men were released with the warning "If you ever come back, we will kill you."[39]

In the struggle between strikers and strikebreakers, the strikebreakers were at a significant disadvantage. Most had arrived under dubious conditions and found themselves performing jobs for which they were not trained. Added to this tension was the fact that since a large number of the transportation men were immigrants or blacks, they also felt the sting of nativism and racism. An article titled "New Negroes Arrive in Southern Counties — Same Old Methods, Why Stand for It?," published in the Nicholas *Chronicle* on October 10, 1912, highlights the racial undertones of the time: "Strange Negroes are coming into almost every town in Mingo County. They are not being brought in by the carload, as they were brought at the time of the election two years ago, but they are coming in small gangs and being scattered about at the different coal works."[40]

Aside from Nativism and racism, strikebreakers were universally despised by striking miners and unions. Striking miners feared the permanent loss of employment, eviction from company housing, and restriction from the necessities offered through company infrastructure. Many strikers saw these transportation men as an embodiment of those dangers. Prodding and provoking the already agitated striking miners were UMWA activists. Typical of this saber rattling, Mother Jones called for the striking miners to "drive the damned scabs out of the valleys."[41]

Already a prominent labor advocate, the often profane Jones' speeches called for action. Many listened. The physician for Paint Creek overheard a striking miner proclaim that "they would make it so hot for them [strikebreakers] they could not stay there."[42] It was not long before things indeed became "hot" for the strikebreakers. Arriving workers were attacked at the train depots. One man suspected of scabbing was beaten and almost shot by a mob at Kayford. Others suffered worse fates. A group of men taking a wounded strikebreaker to the hospital came under fire at Holly Grove; the man later died.[43] In the caldron of labor unrest on the Paint and Cabin Creek coalfields, strikebreakers were caught between the coercion and exploitation of the operators and the threat of violence at the hands of striking miners. One man left the mines when a death threat came in a letter by mail. The author left the name of "Union Man."[44] Under the strain of threats of violence, many left if they could.

Operators also began to further exploit the coercive power of the company town. By this time, the unique nature of the company town in southern West Virginia created a condition where "in non-union counties, houses [were] owned by the companies. Justice [was] administered by the coal companies. Constitutional rights [were] interpreted by the coal companies.... The miners worship[ed] in a company church, [were] preached at by the company pastor; receive[d] treatment from a company doctor and hospital [and] die[d] on company land."[45] Even the clergy were not free of company influence and intimidation. A preacher who had mentioned wage issues to miners was beaten by the company employees in 1907.[46]

Striking miners, particularly in southern West Virginia, most likely lived in company houses. They also generally did their shopping, gathered for meetings, and received mail at the company stores. From the operators' perspective, the housing and stores were for working employees. As many men were no longer working, many companies began to prohibit gatherings at company stores and evict miners who had walked off the job.

During the Senate investigation into the Paint Creek and Cabin Creek strike, several miners reported they had been prevented from receiving mail and in some cases were barred from entering the company store. According to the witnesses, people were sent away by mine guards with oaths such as "[you don't] have a damned bit of business in there" and "we ain't got no use for you up here and you go on back down the road ... and stay there."[47] Most mine guards carried Winchester rifles and pistols to back up their words.

Mine guards also handled the evictions. Regardless of the legality of the practice, evicting people from their homes was obviously a heated issue on which both sides had strong arguments and feelings. From the company standpoint, the housing was effectively a benefit offered to their laborers. When a miner refused to work, he would forfeit the privilege of living in company housing. This process, according to the operators, was carried out in a professional, legal, and moral manner. Standard notices used by operators show the intent of professionalism and legality: "To _____: Having ceased to work for the undersigned company, you are hereby notified that you are no longer in the employee of said company, and you are hereby required forthwith to vacate and surrender to the undersigned company possession of the tenement house and premises of said company now occupied by you."[48]

Following a period between 10 days and two months, a notice such as the one below was then issued:

> _____ having ceased to work for the understated company, and having been properly and legally notified to vacate and having refused the offer ... to help you and your family to a location suitable to you in any union field in the State of West Virginia, it is our regret that we must exercise our legal right to forcibly evict you. This we will now do within the law and with no more force or injury to your household goods than you, yourself, or family make necessary.
>
> We again make you the offer to deliver your household goods to the depot or load in box cars and prepay freight on same to any point selected by you in any union field in the State of West Virginia, and to pay you and your family's railroad fare to the same point if you so desire.[49]

In many cases these evictions were carried out in accordance with such notices and families were offered transportation for both themselves and their property.[50] According to the operators these encounters were always conducted with the utmost "courtesy."[51] Despite the assertion of the operators, many striking miners saw things very differently. From the strikers' stories, evictions were conducted much differently. Between 15 and 20 armed mine guards would enter striking miners' homes and begin removing furniture to the street with no provocation.[52] Some miners claimed even more coercive and sinister actions were taken; Newt Gump told of mine guards removing peoples' property, under the protection of machine guns, while most were attending a funeral.[53]

Virtually every facet of the operators' plans to influence, if not coerce, miners was carried out by the mine guards. As mentioned before, these men were effectively a private police force under the control of the operators. Despite claims to their professionalism, courtesy, and tolerance, the

Evicted miners and their household goods. The forced removal of striking miners from their homes, legal or not, must have been intensely emotional and played a major role in the escalation of hostilities with mine operators (West Virginia and Regional History Collection, West Virginia University Library).

torrent of complaints regarding the mine guards must have had some basis in reality.[54] In fact, most striking miners and union activists blamed the escalation of violence on the ruthless behavior of the mine guards, who they believed had "openly, recklessly, and flagrantly violated ... the rights guaranteed by natural justice and the Constitution to every citizen."[55]

Gianiana Seville claimed that mine guards forcibly entered her home, struck her, and kicked her in the stomach while she was five months pregnant. The leader of the accused mine guards replied that no attack took place. He added that one of his men was detached to protect her at her own request.[56] Given the relations between miners, particularly foreign miners, and the mine guards during this time, the guard's story seems less believable. The Senate investigation into the strike is awash with complaints of intimidation and violence from both supporters of miners and operators alike. The miners and union activists spoke of rude, threatening, and violent mine guards ruthlessly carrying out the will of the despotic operators, while the operators and mine guards defended their actions as both legal and retaliatory in nature to the equally violent, illegal, and anarchist actions of the miners, done at the behest of the union bosses.

The UMWA quickly tried to capitalize on the situation.[57] Union funds helped to support striking miners and provided for tent cities that sprang up throughout the area.[58] The UMWA also provided copious amounts of propaganda. At the head of these efforts was Mother Jones. Playing on the growing concerns over mine guard intimidation and violence, Jones delivered inflammatory speeches to incite miners' retaliation. On the steps of the capitol she warned the governor that unless "he rid[s] Paint Creek and Cabin Creek of those goddamned Baldwin-Felts mineguards," there would be "one hell of a lot of bloodletting in these hills." She likewise told the miners to "arm yourselves, return home and kill every goddamned mine guard on the creeks" and to "blow up the mines."[59] To aid the strikers, it is believed the UMWA supplied the miners with over 1,000 rifles and 50,000 rounds of ammunition.[60] The UMWA also demanded the governor step in and order the mine guards removed. Governor Glasscock replied that under the current law, he had no authority to dictate private security matters to the operators, and the only way he would be able to control the situation was through a declaration of martial law.[61]

The sporadic violence soon erupted into open warfare. Train tracks were damaged, telegraph lines were cut, and many pitched battles sprang up around the area. A deputy sheriff was killed in Boone County while attempting to disarm miners.[62] Miners and guards clashed at Mucklow on Paint Creek in August 1912. Thousands of rounds were fired and 16 were killed. As the violence continued to escalate, 6,000 miners from union camps across Kanawha County gathered to challenge the mine guards on the first of September. At this point the governor's hand was forced. On September 2, Governor Glasscock declared martial law in the area of unrest and dispatched 1200 National Guard troops.[63]

With the arrival of state military forces, chaos gave way to military rule. Repairs were made to damaged rail tracks under the protection of state militia.[64] The tools of war were collected. The militia seized over 1,800 rifles, almost 500 pistols, six machine guns, and between 163,000 and 225,000 rounds of ammunition.[65] In most areas, Baldwin-Felts guards were replaced with West Virginia militia and the civilian court system was replaced by a military tribunal. Although the West Virginia Supreme Court upheld the governor's right to hold military tribunals during martial law, the issue was controversial, as throughout the periods of marital law, civilian courts remained open.[66] A major concern for civilian court officials was the ability for anyone in the area to receive a fair trial. In an area strongly divided over union and non-union lines and with corruption abounding, unbiased jury members would indeed be difficult to find anywhere in the region. Even the Kanawha County prosecuting attorney did not believe he could find a grand jury that had not already "taken sides."[67]

In southern West Virginia most people had indeed taken a side. Officials, law enforcement, and citizens alike were either staunch unionists or at least supported the miners on one side, or were anti-union or in the pockets of industrialists on the other. According to the judge advocate of the Military Commission, Lt. Col. George Wallace, "No indictments were returned [by the civilian court] and nobody was tried, and that was excused by the local officers on the ground of intense feeling on one side or the other." Wallace's frustration drove him to declare that "it has gone forth all over the world that West Virginia can not govern herself through her courts."[68] Unfortunately, the legacy of legal ambivalence, indecision, and outright corruption has continued even to present day.

The first period of martial law ended on September 15, 1912, but the peace was short-lived. Again, mine guard intimidation and UMWA agitation played major roles. As many mine guards were forced to leave the area once martial law was established, the operators simply hired National Guard troops once they were dismissed from duty.[69] This was much more than a convenient move for the operators. To many residents, these men represented the authority of the government as much as the will of the operators. When martial law would again be declared, these men, who had now become part of the problem, simply donned their military uniforms. The duality of the militia-mine guard situation would create a major question of impartiality in the second and third declarations of martial law.[70]

Mother Jones continued to inspire resistance throughout the period. During martial law, she stated, "I have had martial law declared more than once where I was, but I didn't stop fighting." She also directed striking miners to "bury their guns" because they would be needed again in the future.[71] Under continued prodding, unrest again flared up throughout the hills. Highlights of violence during the next few months included a second battle at Mucklow, the attack of unarmed mine guards by striking miners, and the shooting up of a tent town by an armed railroad car named the *Bull Moose Special*.[72]

Local officials seemed unable, or unwilling, to stop the escalating violence. Governor Glasscock reported to the Senate investigators that during the early stages of the conflict, "25 or 30 murders had been committed and nothing done."[73] As assaults, gunfights, and deaths mounted, county officials again sought the governor's assistance. The Kanawha County prosecuting attorney, T. C. Townsend, wrote to the governor:

> Since May or June, there has prevailed in Kanawha County, with but slight interruptions a state of insurrection and riot, accompanied by many acts of violence, including shooting from ambush into mining towns ... burning of portions of coal plants, the assassination of sundry persons and wounding sundry others from ambush, with sundry other killings and numerous assaults and woundings, the holding and firing into trains.[74]

Townsend's letter was supported by the sheriff, who believed there were between 500 and 1,000 armed miners and many outsiders who had moved into the area to support the miners after the strike began. Sheriff S. P. Smith painted a scene of chaos and violence, with reports of shooting, a train wreck and telegraph lines down: "The people were in a desperate condition. They were at the point of a mob, and one word there, I believe, would have started an uprising."[75]

Martial law was declared a total of three times along Paint Creek and Cabin Creek. Finally, a tenuous peace was brokered by newly elected Governor Henry Hatfield. The Hatfield Agreement resulted in a nine-hour workday, the right of miners to hire a checkweighman, and a semi-monthly pay system.[76] Although Hatfield's agreement did end the bulk of the violence in the southern coalfields, it had done little to address the root causes of the uprising. The actions of the government in response to the violence had perhaps only exacerbated problems in the long term.

During the periods of martial law hundreds of mine guards and miners alike were detained, charged, and sentenced in military courts. Mother Jones was found guilty of inciting a riot and sentenced to over 20 years. Although most, if not all, found guilty in the military courts were pardoned, bitter feelings remained regarding the conduct of the trials.[77] While the tribunals were upheld by the West Virginia Supreme Court,[78] Allen Loughry argues that the military judges often acted without adequate knowledge of laws and assigned sentences while "completely ignoring the state and federal Constitution."[79] Employment of militiamen by the operators in interims between martial law also severely damaged the image of impartiality on the part of the state government. The actions of some militia while in uniform likewise raised questions as to the state's unbiased position. On some occasions, militia was used to enforce evictions during martial law.[80]

Also damaging to public opinion were the raids on socialist newspapers, both in and outside of the areas declared under martial law. The Socialist Party of America (SPA) "had made strong inroads among West Virginia's industrial workers, especially its coal miners" during the first decade of the twentieth century. The 1912 election resulted in a 300 percent increase for Socialist Eugene V. Debs over 1908 and was the largest increase in the socialist vote in the United States.[81] Even following the agreement set forth by Governor Hatfield, the SPA inundated the region with pamphlets and fliers urging another strike.[82] The *Labor Argus* spoke out specifically against Hatfield's negotiated peace. Fearing another eruption of widespread violence, the militia was directed to raid socialist newspapers and arrest their editors.

Newspapers, including the *Labor Argus*, Huntington *Socialist*, and *Labor Star*, were raided. Warrants were not issued and some raids were undertaken outside the jurisdiction of the martial law.[83] These actions caused enough of a stir to warrant a visit by Debs. Debs' visit, however, did not result in the outcome many local socialists desired. Debs failed to publicly denounce the actions of Hatfield, which resulted in the alienation of local socialists and a drastic decline in SPA support in the region.[84]

For all of the bloodletting, little had been accomplished. The UMWA was still effectively blocked from the region. Even during a subsequent strike in June of 1913 in which the miners received most of their original concessions with minimal violence, the UMWA was not involved.[85] The labor movement was further weakened by the marginalization of local socialists. When the Paint Creek and Cabin Creek uprisings were over, the operators and mine guards still reigned supreme in the southern West Virginia coal fields.

Four

Profiles in Corruption and Failed Government
The Matewan Massacre and the Battle for Blair Mountain

In the years leading up to and during World War I, operators maintained their dominance over their employees, the unions, and most of southern West Virginia. This dominance was created not only by the victory at Paint Creek and Cabin Creek, but through legal decisions and growing fears of socialism. The Bolshevik Revolution in Russia and the wave of nativism cloaked in patriotism that swept the nation during World War I only provided more ammunition to the anti-union movement. In September 1913, operators formed the Coal Operators Protective Association and put $1,000,000 together to protect their property against "socialists, otherwise known as the United Mine Workers of America."[1] Even the UMWA promoted the need for production, prodding miners on the cover of its journal to "Dig Coal! Dig More Coal! Dig Still More Coal! The Success of the War Depends on the Coal You Dig!"[2]

Aside from war propaganda and patriotism, several legal victories also bolstered the operators' cause during this period. The West Virginia legislature passed bills giving the governor the authority to deputize citizens and call deputies into state service to put down insurrections and preserve peace. A law prohibiting idleness was passed, which required able bodied men to work thirty-six hours or more per week. "Those found guilty of violating the law were subject to a fine of $100 or more and a sentence of sixty days at hard labor."[3] Union activists were likewise targeted. The

Hitchman decision and Judge Dayton's ruling were used by a Charleston grand jury to indict UMWA President John P. White and 18 others. *Hitchman* was also supported by the *Red Jacket* injunction that further protected the operators' use of individual or yellow dog contracts.[4]

Sporadic violence continued as well. In 1914 the death of striker at the hands of a mine guard was ruled self-defense. In a striking example of the operator's political power, the hearing was held in a coal company office and union representatives were barred from the proceedings. Angered over the questionable nature of the proceedings, miners and labor activists paraded the miner's body through the streets. His corpse was followed by supporters carrying banners reading "This Man Assassinated At Colliers" and "Our Brother Murdered By Hired Thugs."[5]

Race tensions occasionally flared up as well. In 1916 a fight between a white man and a black man on election day resulted in the arrest of the black man involved and another who attempted to intervene. Later that night 30 armed blacks freed the two men in a subsequent shootout with Sheriff G. W. Thompson and a posse. George Wolfe, a nearby mine manager, had the following to say regarding the incident: "It will never do to let a matter like this rest. It shows the sentiment of the [Negroes] and that it is if you arrest some of their race, that it is proper for them to gather in a mob and kill white officers and turn the prisoners loose."[6] Wolfe believed the cause to be the Robinson-Lilly gubernatorial race, which had "seriously [affected] some of the colored people." He further stated, "You cannot send for a niggar and sit him down in the executive mansion and plot with him to overthrow the white people without evil results."[7]

Over 60 blacks were jailed as a result of the incident, even though no more than 30 were involved. Wolfe supported the move, stating, "If we white people want to conduct our business here in Raleigh County in peace, we will certainly have to handle this matter severely and put these Negroes in position to fear, for a while at least, to gather up a mob."[8] Jim Crow segregation may not have been a legal entity in southern West Virginia, but racism did exist in abundance. Although this incident highlights the racial tensions of the time, it also provides insight into southern West Virginia's brand of politics, which was often coercive, corrupt, and violent.

Perhaps no other official epitomized this form of "public service" more than Logan County Sheriff Don Chafin. In 1921, the Washington *Star* effectively summed up Chafin's role: "Everywhere one goes down in this country he hears the name Don Chafin, high sheriff of Logan County. One can see that he struck terror in the hearts of people in the union fields. Although a state officer, they do not trust him. Every kind of crime is charged to him and his deputies. He is king of the 'Kingdom of Logan.' He reigns supreme by virtue of a state machine backed by the power of the operators."[9]

Others have called Chafin a "hard-drinking, swaggering, bragging, bullying gunman" who ruled over Logan County as a "feudal barony."[10] Chafin was rewarded well for his service. The Logan County Coal Operators Association gave him $32,000 in 1919 and $46,630 in 1920 to provide salaries for the hundreds of deputies he employed. On a sheriff's salary of $3500 a year, Chafin was worth $350,000 in 1921.[11]

Matewan Chief of Police Sid Hatfield provided an opposing, but equally violent, model to Chafin. While Chafin championed the operators and fought labor organizers with a deadly zeal, "Smilin' Sid" Hatfield took up the banner for the miners' cause. Known as a skilled gunfighter reminiscent of the Wild West, Hatfield had killed a mine foreman and assaulted a former mayor but was never convicted of either crime.[12] Hatfield, along with Sheriff George Blankenship and Matewan Mayor Cabell Testerman, acted as buffer against operators in Mingo County just as Chafin provided muscle for the operators in Logan County. Sid Hatfield and Don Chafin would be at the center of a series of events that would again result in open warfare in southern West Virginian coalfields. One of them would be the catalyst for one of the largest civil uprisings in America's history outside of the Civil War.

As World War I ended, the UMWA again focused on the unorganized southern West Virginian fields. During the UMWA convention in 1919, the organization called for a 60 percent increase in pay, a six-hour workday, five day work-week, and nationwide contract with regional settlements. If the demands were not met, a nationwide strike would begin on November 1, 1919.[13] This move was part of a greater national labor movement that occurred in 1919 with over 3,000 work stoppages nationwide.[14]

There was merit in the union's requests. During the war, several changes occurred that adversely impacted miners' wages. Although between 1914 and 1917 the average pay had increased from 41 cents to 59 cents per ton, the number of operating days had been reduced from 243 to 220. Food prices had increased between 30 percent and 50 percent and overall inflation outstripped miners wages by as much as 400 percent. Before

World War I, Borderland investors received dividends between 15 percent and 30 percent. In 1918 they received 60 percent returns.[15] The growing disparity between the "haves" and "have nots" did not go unnoticed.

When the UMWA attempted to re-enter the coal fields in Logan County, Sheriff Don Chafin was ready. In September of 1919, local labor organizers attempting to meet with UMWA District 17 President C. Frank Kenney were "beaten back by the guards and operators." Chafin and his deputies immediately began "to arrest men and throw them in jail" and "evicted a few families."[16] As word of the Chafin's actions in Logan County spread, organized miners in nearby Kanawha County prepared to challenge Chafin's rule. Thousands of Kanawha miners armed themselves and prepared to march on Logan County.[17] In response, Governor John Cornwell activated the militia and warned the miners if they did not disperse, he would deploy the National Guard. Cornwell's threat, his promise to investigate activities in Logan County, and pleading from Kenney eventually persuaded the army of 5,000 to disband.[18]

Given the existence of widespread political corruption at the state and local level, little came of the promised investigation.[19] The UMWA eventually passed a resolution requesting a congressional investigation claiming Cornwell was biased and "not interested in determining the truth."[20] It was easy to see evidence of corruption with operator lackeys such as Wells Goody Koontz holding public office. Koontz, a state representative, stated that few miners actually supported a strike, as they were "the most happy ... independent ... and contented" of industrial laborers.[21]

Although the march on Logan had been halted, the strike deadline was rapidly approaching. Kenney warned Cornwell that the miners would take part in the nationwide strike that was to begin on November 1, 1919.[22] Cornwell did not wait for events to transpire; troops were called into the area two days prior to the deadline. UMWA efforts were further hampered by the legal system. On November 8, 1919, an injunction was issued under the auspices of the Washington Agreement and Lever Act (which made it a conspiracy to limit the supply or distribution of coal).[23] Having failed to organize in Logan County, the UMWA turned toward Mingo County in the spring of 1920.[24]

The operators again were standing ready for the union. By summer, 2700 Mingo County miners had been evicted from company towns and were living in tent cities similar to those created previously on Paint Creek and Cabin Creek.[25] Mingo County, however, was not Logan County. Pro-labor factions found support from local officials such as Sheriff Blankenship, Mayor Testerman of Matewan, and the always-ready-for-a-fight Matewan Chief of Police Sid Hatfield. On April 27, 1920, Blankenship arrested and temporarily detained Albert Felts, of the Baldwin-Felts agency, for conducting an illegal eviction.[26] Following the arrest, relations continued to deteriorate between the Baldwin-Felts men and Mingo County's pro-labor officials. They completely disintegrated on May 20, 1920.

On that day, Baldwin-Felts guards were evicting several miners from a nearby company town when they were confronted by Testerman and Hatfield. Felts claimed he had an eviction order from the circuit judge but could not present it to Testerman. Angered, Testerman warned Felts that he "would not get away with it." Following the threat to Felts, Testerman and Hatfield returned to Matewan. Upon their return Hatfield and Testerman received word through the county prosecutor that the evictions were illegal and warrants should be issued for the guards. All they had to do was wait for the warrants to be issued. Meanwhile, Albert Felts and a dozen other guards had returned to Matewan to wait for the 5:15 train to Bluefield, the same train on which the warrants for their arrest were to arrive. As events rapidly transpired, the warrants would become unimportant.[27]

The Hatfield and Felts groups met on the streets of Matewan. Hatfield informed Felts that he and his men were to be arrested. Felts in turn presented an arrest warrant for Hatfield which Mayor Testerman examined and determined to be "bogus." From this point, two general versions of the incident exist, both skewed by bias. The Baldwin-Felts version was that Hatfield then shot Felts in the back of the head and a gun battle ensued. Pro-union versions claim that Testerman was first shot by Felts while trying to intervene on Hatfield's behalf regarding the bogus warrant.[28] When it was over, two miners, seven mine guards, and Mayor Testerman were dead.[29] More intrigue was added when some witnesses claimed Hatfield had shot Testerman. The fact that Hatfield married the deceased mayor's widow only two weeks later did not help Hatfield's defense of the rumors.[30]

Justice was swift but typical for the region and the times. Hatfield was acquitted by a sympathetic Mingo County jury.[31] While Hatfield was basking in his victory and national fame, the operators were not idle. Hatfield and one of his deputies, Ed Chambers, were charged with destruction of coal company property in neighboring McDowell County. They would not be allowed their day in court. Hatfield and Chambers were themselves gunned down by Baldwin-Felts men while they made their way to the front steps of the McDowell County courthouse.[32] Finding a jury just as sympathetic in McDowell County as Hatfield had found in Mingo, everyone charged with his killing — although it occurred in daylight in front of the county seat of justice — was acquitted.[33]

The complete lack of an effective government was evident. In the first two decades of the 20th century in southern West Virginia, coal company influence, pro-union propaganda, and mountain justice often ruled over order, law, and democracy. Decades of intimidation, exploitation, frustration, and violence would reach a climax when an army of mine guards and state militia would come toe-to-toe with thousands of armed miners in the Battle of Blair Mountain.

As the previous events were transpiring in Mingo County, Chafin maintained his firm grip on Logan County. Dramatic changes were occurring, however. Motivated by Hatfield's stand against the operators in Mingo County, miners and labor activists doubled their efforts to organize the southern West Virginia coalfields. As more miners struck, violence increased, particularly along the Tug Valley. Miners clashed with two battalions of federal troops at Howard Colliery and Thacker.[34] The federal troops were part of a detachment of 500 men assigned to the area between August 29, 1920, and February 15, 1921. Mingo County also felt the need for more law enforcement; 780 men were deputized to help keep the peace. While many of these men were believed to be citizens of the county and were businessmen or other professionals, UMWA representatives and miners claimed several were former Baldwin-Felts guards.[35]

Between 1919 and 1921 martial law would again be declared four times in southern West Virginia.[36] Unlike the earlier Mine Wars, federal troops would be deployed at the request of the governor, as West Virginia National Guard troops had been federalized for fighting in World War I. The need for federal troops was warranted. The West Virginia attorney general stated during one of the declarations, "A state of war, insurrection, and riot, is, and has been for sometime, in existence in Mingo County.... Many lives and much property have been destroyed as a result thereof, and riot and bloodshed are rampant and pending."[37]

Similar to the situation earlier at Paint Creek and Cabin Creek, public order and security trumped individual rights as the military took control. Freedom of the press was suspended with the command that "no publication, either newspaper, pamphlet, handbill, or otherwise, reflecting in any way upon the United States, or the State of West Virginia, or their officers, may be published, displayed, or circulated within the zone of martial law."[38]

Violence continued throughout the summer. In May, a three day battle was fought between 2,000 miners and 1,000 mine guards and deputies. Four men were killed. In June, a tent city for striking miners was destroyed at Lick Creek in Mingo County. Spurred on by an inspiring and inflammatory speech by Mother Jones, more than 2,000 miners again formed to march on Logan County on August 21, 1921, only to be again talked into disbanding by the governor and threats from military officials. Most of the miners turned back and headed home.[39] At this point, when the crisis had seemed to pass, Don Chafin reignited the flame. Chafin sent between 70 and 100 men into the union portion of Logan County to arrest organizers of the march. In the ensuing shootout two men were killed.[40]

Hearing the news of battle, the miners re-formed and began their march again under command of UMWA leader Bill Blizzard. By the time they reached Blair Mountain their numbers had grown to over 6,000 men. The objective was a simple one; as the labor-army marched the men chanted, "We'll hang Don Chafin to a sour apple tree."[41] At Blair Mountain, the miners ran headlong into Chafin and 2,000 to 3,000 deputies, mine guards, and state police, now under command of Colonel William Banks of the West Virginia National Guard.[42] During the battle hundreds of thousands of rounds were fired, machine guns were deployed, and personal aircraft were used by the operators to drop makeshift bombs.[43] It is believed between 13 and 50 men were killed during the battle.[44]

President Warren G. Harding had seen enough. In addition to the 2,000 infantrymen, a chemical warfare detachment, and elements of the 88th Light Bombing Squadron, he dispatched the following warning: "Now, therefore, I Warren G. Harding, president of the United States, do hereby make proclamation and I do hereby command all persons engaged in said insurrection to disperse and retire peaceably to their respective abodes on or before 12 o'clock, noon, of the first day of September, 1921, and hereafter abandon said combinations and submit themselves to the laws and constituted authorities of the state."[45] Harding's warning did not deter the miners, but the sight of thousands of Federal troops deploying on their flanks did the trick. The fighting ceased after the Army arrived on September 3.[46]

Miners gave up their weapons and returned to their homes, or in some cases tents. UMWA activists and miners had been on the verge of making a brilliant assault on the power of the operators and their paid enforcers. In many ways, their cause was just. One union leader likened their cause with that of the Native Americans. "They played that game with the American Indian. They gave him the end of the log to sit on and then pushed him off that. We don't proposed to be pushed off."[47] Just as the Indian wars resulted in chaos and violence on the Great Plains and in the American West, the labor struggles of southern West Virginia tore communities apart as well. Perhaps the best measure of the anarchy and lawlessness that had beset the region can be seen in court records following the restoration of order. A total of 1217 indictments were issued for people involved in violence in Logan County. This included 325 murder and 24 treason charges.[48]

With their defeat at Blair Mountain, the UMWA's power in southern West Virginia was broken and would remain so for over a decade. Victorious in the courthouses through the *Hitchman* and *Red Jacket* decisions, operators were free to employ yellow dog contracts to prevent their workers from joining unions. Indeed, many legislators and jurists, following Judge Dayton's opinion, argued that the UMWA itself was an illegal organization and treated it as such. The nationwide fears of socialism and a renewal of nativism during World War I did not help the organization either.

When legal avenues failed, the UMWA and miners had tried the same tactics as their antagonists, with similar results. Not only were their efforts blunted at both the Paint Creek-Cabin Creek and Blair Mountain uprisings, but the state and federal government had stepped into restore order in both incidents, a move which inevitably favored the operators. Defeated legally and militarily, "union organization in the southern fields was dealt a death blow from which it would not recover until the passage of the National Industrial Recovery Act [NIRA] of 1933."[49] Until then, the operators would run virtually unchecked in the region. As one operator during this period warned, "You tell the union that when it sends its organizers in here, I'll get an army." The operator's superintendent quickly added, "And I'll lead it."[50]

An Era Ends, But Problems Do Not

From the end of the Civil War through 1929, profound changes occurred throughout southern West Virginia. With few exceptions the region had been relatively isolated from commercial and industrial endeavors taking place in the rest of the nation. The rapid influx of industry, based off northern and European industrialists' desire for southern West Virginia coal and timber, caused rapid and often cataclysmic changes. New towns sprang up all across the valleys as the number of mines and logging operations exploded. These towns did not signal the death of longstanding power bases and social norms, but rather presented a new and complex challenge to the patriarchal oligarchy of mountain clans. This oligarchy, founded on patriarchal dominance of kinship groups, land ownership, and a long history of subsistence farming, had to find a way to deal with this new challenge. The way these patriarchs dealt with this challenge, much more than how they were dominated by it, played a profound role in the development of new power structures in the state. The results would prove to be complex, lasting, and often negative.

Company towns offered alternatives to the longstanding structure of subsistence farming. And they provided excitement not found on the farm. In an area still mired in remains of an antiquated bartering system, cash meant power and cash could be found in the company towns. Others sought to free themselves from the yoke of their parents. For many their inheritances had been whittled down through generations of land division. These parceled inheritances divided not only the land but families as well. Some came for more illicit reasons. Gambling, alcohol, and prostitution prevailed in many company towns in their early stages. Women were also drawn to the coal and lumber camps to escape domineering fathers or husbands, to supplement their families' income, or to experience freedoms not available on the farm.

The new towns likewise caused a massive demographic shift. Even though thousands of farmers left the field to work for coal and lumber companies more, workers were needed than the area could provide. European immigrants and blacks from the Deep South made up the bulk of these additional laborers. For a region that had been relatively homogeneous, ethnically speaking, for close to two hundred years, there were obvious growing pains. Racism and nativism combined with the already volatile mixture of sex, gambling, and alcoholism to create a culture that not only brought new opportunities to poor farmers, immigrants, blacks, and women, but at the same time made them susceptible to exploitation and violence.

The rise of these towns did not mean the end of subsistence farming.

In fact, some areas actually saw an increase in the number of farms during this period. What company towns did represent was a shift in power from local elites to absentee landowners. With the mineral and timber wealth of southern West Virginia a hot commodity, many landowners jumped at the opportunity to exchange land for money. Local professionals, particularly lawyers, were also more than willing to broker these deals or scoop up land for themselves to later sell at immense profits. Although definite cases of trickery and shady dealings robbed southern West Virginians of their land, many were more than willing to let it go. Through a desire to increase capital, to enhance local influence, and in some cases due to fraud, hundreds of thousands of acres of land, and therefore power, shifted from the hands of West Virginians to absentee landowners.

The company towns also became a tool for operators to exploit labor, circumvent the law, and create miniature feudal estates from which they controlled or at least influenced virtually every aspect of their citizens' lives. In many cases these operators were aided by local and state officials who gladly forfeited their responsibility to their constituents for the coal operators' money.

Miners, prodded by UMWA support (and propaganda), eventually began to resist what they believed was unfair, unlawful, and un–American treatment. As tensions rose, the region exploded into civil war on more than one occasion. These civil uprisings were large, violent, driven by intense emotions, and involved significant corruption of public officials. As a result, these insurrections could only be brought under control through multiple periods of martial law. In the end the operators held the upper hand. Through wealth, legal victories, and pure physical strength, the industrialists fended off multiple attempts of labor advocates to organize southern West Virginia coalfields. Throughout the period, events took place and norms were established that still play a role in the region's society and culture.

Four outcomes are of particular importance. The domination of local affairs by absentee landowners and industrialists left a bitter taste in many residents' mouths. As a result, an innate resentment of absentee ownership was created that tied outside financial investment with economic, and eventually legal and social, domination. As many local officials were paid surrogates for the operators, a distrust of local and state officials, particularly law enforcement, became endemic. This distrust of law enforcement has also created a willingness to undertake extralegal means of solving disputes. Mountain justice circumvented a slow and often defunct legal system and was supported by a tradition of independent farmers dealing with such matters on their own terms. Finally, a resilient kinship structure not only survived company towns and coal operator influence, but exists today in many areas of the region.

FIVE

FDR's Legacy
The Great Depression and Continuing Problems with Public Welfare, Agriculture, and Unemployment

Southern West Virginia was facing economic peril well before the Great Depression. Therefore the Great Depression only highlighted and exacerbated the precarious economic condition the region was already experiencing. Fostered by a weak local economy still operating at least partially on remnants of the barter-borrow preindustrial system, land misuse, and the dominance of a coal industry that had used too many workers to produce too much coal, "the nature of the state's economy and society made it especially vulnerable to the wrenching changes of the Depression."[1]

Once the country was in the throes of economic collapse, recovery efforts took several forms. Private venture programs supported by conservative West Virginia governors, direct public aid managed by federal authorities, work-related aid through programs under the Works Progress Administration (WPA), agricultural rehabilitation programs, land use and management incentives, and homestead and relocation experiments were all tried at some point between 1929 and 1940. The majority of these programs had little to no success. Some even made matters worse. The factors affecting the ultimate outcome were complex, multi-faceted, and, unfortunately in many cases, enduring.

This chapter, while addressing several programs, will focus on two aspects of New Deal politics that still challenge the region. These challenges are the development and effectiveness of public welfare and relief programs and the difficult nature of dealing with rural rehabilitation, relief, and improvement in an agriculturally-minded society living on land with poor agricultural potential. Before these challenges can be addressed, a discussion of agricultural, environmental, economic, and legislative issues unique to the region just prior to and during the Great Depression are necessary. These factors, and how government addressed them, are key to understanding the enduring legacy of both agricultural and welfare reform in the region.

Agriculture, in the form of subsistence or small commercial farms, provided the backbone of southern West Virginia's economy prior to the major industrialization of the late 19th and early 20th century. When the mining and lumber companies came to the region in force, they found an agricultural society already feeling the weight of several social, economic, and environmental stressors. Wholesale timber removal and mining operations further damaged the land and limited economic diversity. Devastating droughts and floods, aided by widespread deforestation, caused even

Devastating flooding helped set the stage for economic, social, and environmental turmoil that turned the Great Depression into a humanitarian disaster in southern West Virginia (Library of Congress).

more damage to an enfeebled agricultural area and for many tipped the scales between subsistence farming and destitution.[2]

Social stressors that existed prior to the coming of the Great Depression included a patriarchal inheritance system that divided land among all descendents (generally male) and therefore limited productive agricultural lands with each generation. Between 1850 and 1880 alone, Appalachian Plateau farm size fell by one half.[3] Most farms were also purely subsistence enterprises, or garnered very small profits. A WPA study determined that throughout Appalachia, farmers consumed 42 percent of the agricultural goods they produced — more than twice the national average. Additionally, 85 percent of Appalachian farms made less than $1,000 in gross income in 1929.[4] During the same year, a study recommended that for a farm in Nicholas or Webster County to be successful, it needed to bring in $1,200 annually.[5] An enduring barter-borrow system also existed that was ill-prepared for the overwhelming push of capitalism that came with industrialization.[6] The precarious condition created by the fragile agricultural system and antiquated barter based economy weakened regional stability.

The limited availability of local cash investment also intensified economic instability as well as opened the door for wholesale outside investment. Following the Civil War, federal leaders sought to solidify national authority over many facets of government once controlled at the state level. One such element was financial. The prohibition of state currency and the 1865 tax on non-federal banks worked to "inhibit local control over the [Appalachian] region's capitalist transformation and favored its control by outsiders."[7] Two additional economic factors resulted in further destabilization of the regional economy. Inflation and the combination of overemployment of miners and overproduction of coal set the stage for drastic wage cuts, massive unemployment, and growing numbers of poor when the full weight of the Depression hit the nation.

As mentioned in Chapter 4, inflation outstripped miners' wages by as much as 400 percent in the years following World War I.[8] With unions effectively blocked from the coalfields of southern West Virginia, miners' wages were generally determined by operators' profit margins and fluctuated wildly during the 1920s. At times, some miners would receive pay much higher than that in union camps, and at other times they earned less than $1 a day.[9] Such huge shifts in daily wages generated continuous instability in mining families' financial status and subsequently local economies.

The largest economic problem was the fact that during the 1920s there were "too many mines and too many miners."[10] In 1920, the United Bituminous Coal Commission reported that the U.S. needed less than 500,000 tons of coal annually and approximately 350,000 miners to mine it. In the 1920s, national mining employment peaked at 750,000 (1923), 121,000 of whom were working in West Virginia, and national production peaked at 573,366,985 tons (1926).[11] Several other events were underway that would further undermine the coal industry. The mechanization of mines was picking up pace and would eventually negate the need for massive numbers of laborers. Other energy sources such as natural gas and oil were likewise beginning to challenge coals dominance.[12] As 44.6 percent of the total wages in West Virginia came from the coal industry between 1925 and 1936,[13] the impending decline of the industry would have devastating effects on the region.

In addition to social and economic components, southern West Virginia also faced environmental devastation. Generations of overuse and misuse of farmlands, including slash and burn farming practices, had seriously impacted the soil's capacity to produce volume and quality, particularly of corn. This problem only grew worse as land was divided into smaller tracts by inheritance and sale to speculators, causing farmers to use land that was less fertile and without proper rotation. Industrialization sped up the environmental destruction. Mining communities built operations and towns over the most level and fertile lands along river valleys. Lumber companies stripped entire mountains. Through this process, "millions of acres of agricultural lands were removed from agricultural use."[14] By 1900, the over 1.5 million acres of spruce forest native to the West Virginia had been reduced to approximately 225,000 acres.[15]

These actions accelerated the erosion of already-depleted topsoil and the siltation of waters. By misuse, overuse, and destruction of the environment, many regions of southern West Virginia were left extremely vulnerable to droughts and flooding.[16] Aided by these conditions, a series of environmental and weather related disasters beginning in 1929 did more to ravage southern West Virginia's economy and imperil its families than the stock market crash of 1929. Droughts in 1930 and 1932 not only destroyed crops but generated massive forest fires that destroyed over 350,000 acres.[17] Flooding along the Kanawha River valley in 1932 caused much damage, and widespread flooding in 1937 created even more hardship for residents.[18] A devastating chestnut blight impacted farmers who used the nuts for fodder and families who used them for sustenance and income.[19] The overall economic downturn, when combined with these disasters, worked to reduce the purchasing power of farmers by more than half.[20] Average income from livestock and crops fell from $725 in 1929 to $233 in 1932.[21] With reduced income, small farmers had little luck of receiving loans for feed and seed from the weakened and ultra-conservative banking system.[22] These events left many subsistence and small farmers on the brink of failure.

As the coal industry declined under the weight of the national Depression, mine closures increased and unemployment soared. Between 1929 and 1933 coal production fell by 40 percent. In McDowell County alone, one-third of the mines closed, resulting in the unemployment of 5,000 miners with the remaining 14,000 only working part-time.[23] As these mines failed and miners lost their jobs, many returned to family property to "try to coax a living from the land."[24] Sixty families returned to agriculture on land provided by a coal company on the Poca River. They "cleared the land, built log cabins, and started homesteads."[25] In all, 43,000 families participated in ad hoc "back to the country" endeavors which were often supported by coal operators and railroads.[26]

Between 1930 and 1935, rural farm population increased by 114,000.[27] In a region where a government-sponsored state guide commented that "the most remarkable thing about West Virginia farming is that is carried on so extensively under such difficult handicaps," the land could not effectively support these numbers.[28] As the majority of land was often infertile, steep, or just not available, many unemployed miners were simply stranded in failed coal towns. Webster County alone had 15 such communities.[29]

Some West Virginians reverted back to the barter-borrow system to meet their needs. Kanawha County coordinated such a system in which people requested such barters as a house and lot in town for a farm, a fur coat for vegetables, and a pig for a shotgun.[30] A man in Fayette County traded the convenience of a 1932 Chevrolet for the income of a paper route.[31] A return to this economic system would not prevent the region from spiraling into economic and social destitution, however. The combination of failed agriculture, limited land, massive unemployment, and an already weakened economy created conditions in southern West Virginia that were among the most precarious of any region during the Great Depression. In February of 1935, the Beckley *Post-Herald* reported that the number of Raleigh County residents on direct relief had risen from 617 in January 1934 to 2,034 in October of the same year.[32]

Under these conditions, poverty, malnutrition, homelessness, exposure, and starvation were real threats. Reports of people living in caves, mothers drowning their children and themselves, parents leaving children, and children forced to share beds with elderly strangers in overcrowded county poor houses abounded.[33] One woman died of starvation and exposure rather than ask for aid.[34] West Virginia had the highest infant mortality rate in the United States and the typhoid death rate was four times the national average.[35] In March of 1931, Kanawha County Welfare Secretary D. E. Shaffer appealed to the public for relief funds for families on Cabin Creek. He feared that if help was not soon provided to the 215 families stranded in the region that "many persons, particularly children, [would] die."[36] The mayor of Beckley made a similar plea, asking all salaried men to contribute three days' pay, as it "may be the difference between life and starvation."[37]

Such requests were typical in times of need prior to the New Deal. Under President Herbert Hoover and a series of conservative West Virginia governors, the onus of humanitarian relief was placed upon the private sector.[38] In fact, when a contingent of leaders from a hunger march on Charleston met with Governor William G. Conley, he told them that he did not have the "power or the means" to help and let them go with a promise that things would improve and a private donation of $10.[39] Conley's successor, Herman Kump, was a conservative Democrat and believed in the duty of the individual, as seen in a comment he made during a speech at a Safety Club meeting at Kelly's Creek Colliery in 1935: "While the government can do much, and should be every possible and proper thing for the relief of those who are in distress during periods of depression, our emancipation from the thralldom in which we are held depends upon ourselves as individuals."[40]

As conditions grew worse, West Virginia legislators continued to promote private donations and conservative government spending. In the early 1930s, West Virginia legislators made drastic cuts in government programs while refusing to allow deficit spending or approve relief programs. Roads decayed due to lack of maintenance, teacher salaries were cut by 12 percent in 1933, and graduate education plans at West Virginia University were put on hold.[41]

One major action taken by the legislature, and a disastrous one at that, was the Tax Limitation Act (TLA). According to Jerry Thomas, this act, which greatly reduced an admittedly high land tax, "would haunt the state throughout the Depression years and beyond."[42] In an attempt to lower the tax burden on farmers, the legislature effectively destroyed its revenue base. When federal relief projects finally became available under New Deal programs, the TLA "inhibited the efforts of the state, counties, and municipalities to deal with the Depression and to cooperate with the New Deal."[43] The TLA would complicate, bog-down, and confound West Virginia's political and therefore social welfare and infrastructure progress throughout the Depression. With over $15 million in shortfalls due to the bill in 1933, legislators were forced to generate additional revenues through other taxes that eventually exceeded the original land tax burden.[44]

In the end some funds were made available to the state through increased, but still insufficient, revenues from new taxes and the political work of West Virginia governors. Some counties and municipalities, however, were very effective at obtaining matching funds on their own. Charleston Mayor Daniel Dawson obtained funding for projects that provided jobs in improving or building up city infrastructure, such as the Kanawha Boulevard and Southside Bridge projects and the construction of auditoriums, schools, fire stations, sewer systems, and public housing.[45]

A lack of tax revenue, due to a "failure of the property tax system," has continued to significantly impact regional development.[46] Due to these continued problems, "although values of mineral properties have escalated rapidly in Appalachia, local governments have not experienced a corresponding increase of property tax revenue" well into the 20th century.[47] In 1979, the top 25 percent of landowners paid less than 25 percent of the tax burden while the bottom 25 percent paid 85 percent. A 1979 land ownership study found that "decades of absentee corporate ownership ... have failed to produce adequate water, sewer, transportation, health and educational facilities."[48]

In addition to taxation practices limiting development and diversification, corporate and absentee land owners themselves have compounded the problem. Fearful of potential roadblocks to future mining operations, corporations have been reluctant to support development and economic diversity. Housing has also been affected, not only in southern West Virginia but throughout greater Appalachia: "From the tightly packed valleys of West Virginia to the open plateau and rolling hills of northern Alabama, the picture looks the same. Local residents cannot obtain land for housing because it is closely guarded by its corporate and absentee owners."[49]

Limited land for housing has resulted in a lack of development, only made worse by poor infrastructure. With few new homes and limited financial capacity for down payments, many residents have resorted to either renting older homes in poor repair or buying mobile homes. In a 6 month period in 1979, 76 percent of occupancy permits issued in seven West Virginia counties were for mobile homes.[50]

Individual tax issues are still a major problem for West Virginia as well. In 2005, state taxes per capita were 15th highest in the nation while the tax burden as a percent of income is 4th highest. The state tax, at 8.02 percent, when compared to neighboring states, is even more drastic. Every neighboring state has a lower tax burden, the lowest being Virginia at 2.79 percent and Kentucky being the closest at 7.49 percent. As such, a condition still exists in which in "almost every measure of tax burden ... West Virginia puts itself at a competitive disadvantage in attracting business."[51] Likewise, for residents on the borders of Kentucky and Tennessee, moving a few miles, and thus out of the state, can reap significant rewards in terms of reduced tax burden.

Tax problems are also indicative of a general over-involvement of government in the economy and the markets. According to a recent study, "West Virginia intervenes into our economy to a greater extent than any other state in the nation. With over 52 percent of all spending in West Virginia controlled by the government, it is no wonder the state ranks last in terms of free-market/capitalist economies in the nation.[52] Russell Sobel provided a framework of the government's role in economic matters (Fig. 10).[53]

According to Sobel, in order to have effective outcomes in jobs, new business, wage and income growth, and increased goods and services, the government, through tax codes, business regulations, and the judicial and legal system must promote new business. Mired by political corruption, cronyism, and poor political involvement from the citizenry, the "rules of the game" often work to fatten the pockets of politicians and already established corporations (namely coal) instead of promote new business and therefore employment. Although it will be discussed later, the fundamental aspects of this mechanism, a skilled labor force, infrastructure, and financing, are also wanting in many cases in southern West Virginia.

Federal legislation occurred during the Depression and beyond that dramatically impacted southern West Virginia as well, in both positive and negative terms. The National Industrial Recovery Act (NIRA) of 1933 resulted in the creation of the National Recovery Administration (NRA)

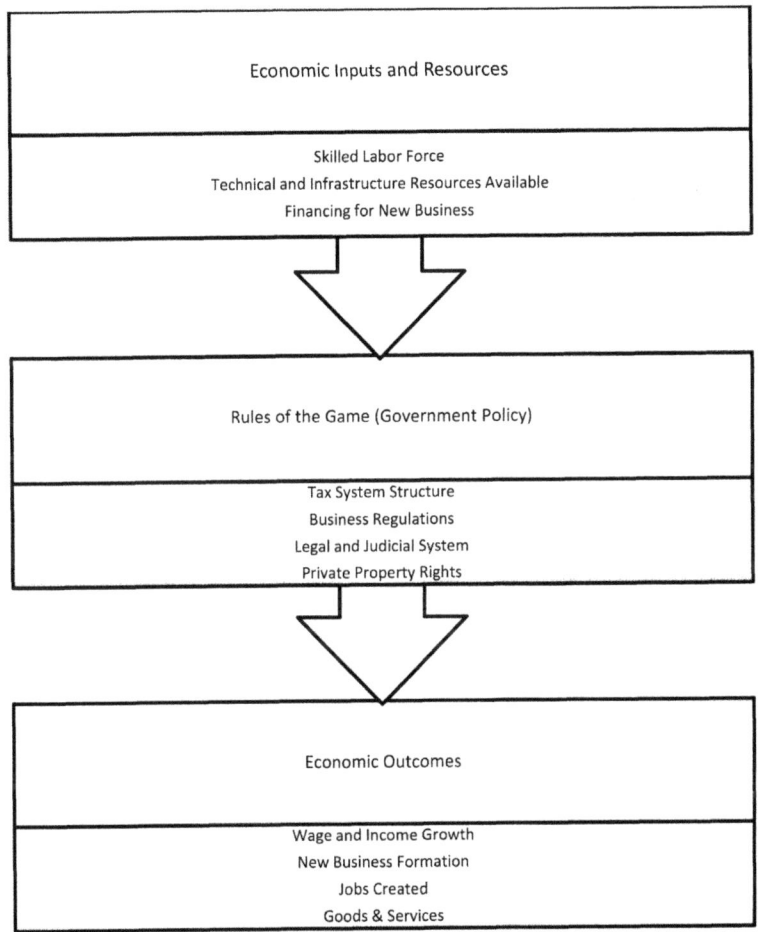

Fig. 10. Mechanisms of Economic Outcomes. Source: Sobel, p. 16.

and the Public Works Administration (PWA). The Federal Emergency Relief Act of 1933 established the Federal Emergency Relief Association (FERA) and its state-level component, the West Virginia Relief Association (WVRA). FERA provided direct payments to unemployed people to "prevent physical suffering and to maintain living standards."[54] The creation of the Civilian Conservation Corps (CCC) that same year also provided for much needed jobs, forestry and conservation projects, and training for young adults.[55] The Emergency Relief Appropriation Act of 1935 resulted in the creation of the WPA, and the Social Security Act of 1935 provided a number of public support programs, including unemployment insurance and Aid to Dependent Children (ADC).[56]

NIRA would help to simultaneously revive the coal industry and improve the conditions of miners while also providing funds for public works programs and resettlement experiments. NIRA provided for a suspension of anti-trust laws for businesses that accepted minimum wages, maximum hours, and collective bargaining. UMWA membership, having fallen to dismal numbers during the 1920s, increased by 160,000 in one month. Southern West Virginia membership rose from only seven in 1933 to 87,764 by 1935.[57] Although NIRA was struck down by the Supreme Court in 1935, the stopgap Guffey-Snyder Act and later the Guffey-Vinson Act maintained the initiatives at the core of NIRA legislation. With the passing of the Wagner Act (National Labor Relations Act of 1935), employees and unions were granted even more protection.[58]

While operators in Kentucky resisted the legislation and violence occurred there, it seemed that southern West Virginia operators and miners had bled enough in the 1910s and 1920s. With the prodding of President Franklin Delano Roosevelt, the operators and miners forged the Appalachian Agreement, which included: (1) an eight-hour workday, (2) a 40 hour work-week, (3) checkoff of union dues, (4) selection of checkweighman by miners, (4) prohibition of scrip, (5) the end of required shopping at company stores and residence in company housing, (6) minimum age for employment, which was 17, and (7) an agreed upon grievance procedure.[59] The infamous mine guard system ended in 1935. Effective legislation against the practice was passed, and Governor Kump ordered Sheriff Maginnis Hatfield of McDowell County to disarm all mine guards in the county, clearing out the last stronghold of armed mine guard intimidation and coercion.[60]

Paul Salstrom has criticized the NIRA and the NRA for causing several problems that linger in Appalachia. He argued that high wages and NRA codes caused pressure for higher prices and mechanization, sabotaging employment. He also claims the Appalachian operators were denied a competitive edge and blames the resultant mechanization for an increase in the prevalence of black lung disease.[61] Despite the fact that mechanization did occur and black lung cases have been tied to increased use of automated mining equipment (due to increased dust), mechanization would have occurred eventually with or without the NRA.

Jerry Thomas focused on the positive aspects of NRA and subsequent legislation in *An Appalachian New Deal: West Virginia in the Great Depression*. According to Thomas, these elements allowed the coal industry to stop "its slide and begin to recover" and included increased employment and wages, increased profits for mining companies, improvement of labor-management relations, an increase in industry-wide stability, and set hours and wages.[62] Most importantly, disputes between labor and management in the future would be addressed in the form of negotiations instead of open warfare.

Although labor relations between miners and operators improved during the 1930s, Depression Era southern West Virginia was still home to perhaps the most deadly and drawn out industrial disaster in U.S. history: the Hawk's Nest Tunnel tragedy. The Hawk's Nest Project involved the creation of a dam across the New River, the digging of a massive 3.7 mile tunnel, and the building of a hydroelectric plant. The project, which was undertaken between 1930 and 1936, had initially promised to bring jobs to the region. Unfortunately, the company contracted to perform the work did not hire locally, wages were much lower than normal for the area, and safety conditions were atrocious.[63] In addition to deaths from accidents that kept a steady stream of ambulances leaving the site, silicosis weakened and killed hundreds if not thousands. While published reports count the total deaths (mostly blacks) at 476, unofficial reports attribute somewhere between 700 and 1400 deaths to the project.[64]

In 1933, President Roosevelt moved to provide more direct aid to the needy. The Federal Emergency Relief Act established FERA, administered in West Virginia through the West Virginia Relief Association, and was soon followed by the establishment of the Civil Works Administration (CWA). FERA/WVRA, while providing direct relief to the unemployed, also pressed for work relief programs as a means of mitigating the natural development of sloth that many thought would occur under direct government handouts.

Interestingly, while the work relief movement grew, West Virginia was getting help from the federal government to fund its own relief activities. The FERA funding at the state level came with a 3 to 1 matching requirement from the state. Due to its desperate financial status, mostly resulting from revenue shortfalls caused by the TLA, West Virginia could not supply the matching funds. Through pleading by Governor Herman Kump, and a sympathetic FERA program director, Harry Hopkins, FERA carried 95 percent of the cost for West Virginia relief.[65]

Some programs funded by FERA/WVRA, if not widely successful, made positive impacts on the lives of thousands of West Virginians. Nurses were hired to improve public health programs and over 500 teachers were employed for adult education. By 1936, then under the WPA, the program employed 800 teachers and helped to provide education to over 33,000 adults.[66]

The number of southern West Virginians on relief was massive. In 1933, 20 percent of Kanawha County residents were on relief rolls. With such large numbers, relief payments were often not enough. Over 6,000 children in McDowell County alone could not attend school for lack of adequate clothing.[67] As the winter of 1933-1934 approached, officials feared disaster, as FERA relief payments were not fully meeting the basic needs of many. As a result, the CWA was established. The Civil Works Administration, in conjunction with the Civilian Conservation Corps, provided much needed income and work. Although the CWA was shut down in 1934 due to costs, it provided valuable insight into conducting relief work programs.[68]

Over 80 CCC camps operated in West Virginia.[69] The CCC, with obvious military overtones and often administered on the operational level by military officers, paid workers $30 a month, $25 of which was required to be sent home.[70] The camps not only provided employment and wages and carried out important forestry and conservation work (including fighting forest fires), but sought to improve the character and skills of the program enrollees as well. Camps provided various sporting activities, dances, and educational opportunities.[71]

Education and character development were key elements of the CCC program. The director of Camp McDowell, an Army officer, "impressed upon each boy his responsibility to his camp and himself, emphasizing cleanliness, courage and kindness as essential of self-improvement."[72] The emphasis on education can be seen in the CCC regulations:

1. To develop in each man his powers of self-expression, self entertainment, and self culture.

2. To develop pride and satisfaction in cooperative endeavor.

3. To provide as far as practicable an understanding of the prevailing social and economic conditions, to the end that each man may cooperate intelligently in improving these conditions.

4. To preserve and strengthen good habits of health and mental development.

5. By such vocational training as is feasible, but particularly by vocational consoling and adjustment activities, to assist each man better to moot his employment problems when he leaves camp.
6. To develop an appreciation of nature and of country life.
7. Eliminate illiteracy.
8. Raise the [skill] level of enrollees deficient in school subjects.[73]

In many ways, the program was effective. Conservation projects not only worked to conserve the nation's natural beauty but made it more accessible to the general public. Men often received letters of recommendation, highlighting both their skills and character, for future jobs once released from the program.[74]

Despite their success, CCC programs generally provided only basic skills and were for men only. Another program, the National Youth Administration (NYA), was also active in southern West Virginia. The program sought to provide full-time training augmented by part-time employment. Thousands of West Virginia youths enrolled in the program, which paid between $6 and $20 and taught skills such as farming, auto repair, soil conservation, and carpentry in addition to completing various construction and defense related projects.[75]

The Federal Emergency Relief Appropriation Act of 1935 demonstrated the federal government's desire to move from direct relief to work relief. The act provided $5 billion for work projects and employed not only unskilled laborers and blue collar workers but professionals, including writers and artists.[76] The key mechanism of this work relief was the Works Progress Administration. Although political in-fighting between West Virginia's governor, U.S. Senator Matthew Neely, and federal officials negatively impacted relief and work relief programs, including FERA, WVRA, and WPA, several programs provided much needed work to many, including artists, educators, and women. WPA projects resulted in not only infrastructure improvements, but cultural and education benefits as well. WPA funds were responsible for establishing the Huntington Orchestra, the making of the movie *A Better West Virginia*, and the publication of *West Virginia: A Guide to the Mountain State*.[77]

WPA and other public work programs had their critics. Some believed the majority of programs provided no actual skill training. Another problem with WPA projects was the sheer magnitude of people involved and the resultant logistical and management problems. Poor planning and a lack of supplies often left many workers standing around waiting for transportation, materials, or directions. To casual observers the program seemed both a waste of resources and a haven for loafers. Popular nicknames for the WPA were "We Pay for All" and "We Piddle Around."[78] A combination of this growing stereotype, no doubt supported by at least a small amount of truth, led many to think the WPA was not a mechanism of recovery but machine that produced sloth with a dole. A Bureau of Agricultural Economics representative in West Virginia echoed this sentiment while complaining about agricultural workers: "We have very little shortage of men but they will not work for the farmer as long as they can get direct relief and commodities or in other words sit around and wear out the best part of their pants and let the government feed them. In fact, they only want a job where they only have to draw their breath and wages [and] would rather draw their wages if someone else would draw their breath for them."[79]

Aside from direct relief and work relief initiatives, other programs to address rural poverty were implemented as part of New Deal policy. At the heart of many of these programs was the desire to maximize the region's potential for agricultural production. Many believed that if the land could be fully utilized or if the right mixture of agricultural and manufacturing could be reached, the problem of rural poverty could be solved. With this in mind, resettlement, rehabilitation, and land use programs were undertaken. Unfortunately, none proved to be completely successful. The attempts, however, highlight several elements vital to understanding the region's past and current experiences.

Small, private resettlement and homestead programs had resulted in limited success at improving the condition of those involved. In addition to the Poca River homestead and other programs supported by coal operators and railroads already mentioned, other communities were meeting with some success. Under President Hoover's administration, the American Friends Service Committee (AFSC) had experimented with cooperative programs that aimed to teach small scale manufacturing skills by which subsistence farmers and unemployed workers could earn money. Following the model of a furniture making program in the Mingo County lumber town of Duty, AFSC undertook programs in northern West Virginia to teach skills in shoemaking, furniture making, carpentry, and sewing.[80] One of the better known cooperatives was the Mountaineer Craftsman Cooperative Association, in northern West Virginia. Initially, the cooperative received limited funding and saw a net loss of over $500 while only paying $1 a day in wages. In 1933, however, the government supplied additional funding, resulting in a net profit of over $1900 by April of 1934.[81]

With a few small success stories, such as those under the AFSC, funding was obtained through the Division of Subsistence Homesteads (later transferred to the Resettlement Administration in 1935) and three experimental West Virginia homestead projects were undertaken. These projects were the Red House community in Putnam County, the Tygart Valley community in Randolph County, and the Arthurdale community in Preston County. Even though the location of the Arthurdale community places it outside the scope of this study, its role as the model for all such programs and involvement by Eleanor Roosevelt make all three homesteads relevant topics of discussion.[82]

The focus of the homestead movement was to select quality people and develop a self-sustaining community which provided most of its own sustenance while using cooperative manufacturing skills and jobs in nearby industries (which had not yet fully materialized) to provide spending money. At Red House, which was sponsored by FERA, 150 families were chosen from the relief rolls and were provided an acre of land, a house which they would rent to own, a barn, pigpen, chicken coop, two hogs, and chickens. The community itself also included common pasture land, a canning plant, and various small manufacturing shops.[83]

Despite the high hopes and media attention placed on the homestead projects, none could be classified as a success. Arthurdale start-up costs skyrocketed. The initial setup cost was estimated at $2,000 to $3,000 per family. Due to logistical errors and construction delays, including the ordering of summer cottage-style housing unsuitable for West Virginia winters, the cost rose to more than $10,000 per family.[84] Arthurdale and Tygart Valley had poor transportation lines and were plagued with irregular wages.[85] Thirty percent of homesteads in Tygart Valley could not pay their monthly rent by January of 1937. At Red House, residents found it difficult to earn enough cash for farm supplies, and no industrial supporter materialized.[86]

Even though personal attention from Eleanor Roosevelt resulted in General Electric establishing a plant in Arthurdale, the project did not provide enough jobs and soon shut down.[87] In fact, the publicity brought to the project by the president's wife only highlighted the shortcomings. Political opposition grew and the administrators themselves soon starting calling the homestead concept "a headache."[88] By 1936 proactive efforts regarding the homesteads were stopped and they became yet another economic burden on the government. An AFSC field worker admitted the program had been reduced to "little more than a federally financed housing program."[89] In 1937 the remnants of the program were handed over to the Farm Security Administration, which was more concerned with farm rehabilitation than resettlement.[90]

Adding to the public and political failures of the program, many residents themselves were left with a bitter taste in their mouths over the entire experience. As the programs began to falter and pressure was placed on administrators, the homesteads began to look more like coal company towns than an experiment in cooperative community. One homesteader relayed his frustration with not only the resettlement experiment but the government in general. He said, "What is the use of trying so hard? The government is going to run this thing as they want to no matter what we think about it."[91] His frustration was not unfounded. One of the local homestead officials in Arthurdale (the principal) refused to allow the Homesteader's Club to hold a beer and oyster supper in celebration because she believed them to be too "socially immature" and that they "could not properly handle themselves." In fact, few public gatherings, such as square dances, could be held without her attendance.[92] In addition to complaints that officials "impose[d] their will on the homesteaders," the situation deteriorated further when the Farm Security Administration began evicting homesteaders in Red House for failure to pay rent and utilities.[93]

Although the homestead program had started with much promise, it had devolved into another marginal-at-best program that placed a drain on government funds. Mismanagement, underfunding, and the overbearing behavior of administrators turned the noble experiment into a mirror image of the oppressive and unstable company towns many residents had hoped to escape. Many participants not only lost faith in the government but soon returned to relief rolls.

With the homestead experiment producing less than expected results, resettlement plans were scrapped in favor of rural rehabilitation. Several barriers existed to effective rural rehabilitation, however. As mention previously, the land itself was overused, misused, and growing more unproductive each year. A 1939 study determined that over 90 percent of West Virginia land had serious soil erosion.[94] Added to these problems was a rapidly increasing farming population that further stressed an already burdened system. If pre-existing conditions were not damaging enough, the ambiguous nature of rural rehabilitation itself doomed the program from the beginning.

A major organization involved in the restoration of U.S. agriculture during the Great Depression was the Agricultural Adjustment Administration. Unfortunately for subsistence and small farmers, the administration believed the key to recovery was ensuring the security of large commercial farms, few of which existed in southern West Virginia. Although there was merit it this concept, such thinking did little to help the rural poverty problem that had existed prior to, and was only exacerbated by, the Great Depression.[95] A report sponsored by the WPA highlighted the government's true feelings of long term agricultural success in the region: "The non-commercial, self-sufficing character of most of the farms and the remoteness of many of the mountain valleys have created an economic and social structure almost completely lacking in dynamic factors."[96]

Efforts were made to improve the conditions of subsistence and small farmers, although the government was never fully behind rural rehabilitation as a means for national agricultural recovery. FERA provided low-interest loans and created farm-home management plans as well as provided emergency grants. Farm debt adjustment also provided relief for some. The West Virginia Rural Rehabilitation Corporation established a five man council to review and adjust farming debt in each county. The council consisted of a banker, a lawyer, and three farmers and, according to Kevin Cahill, was probably one of the most successful rural rehabilitation tools using during this period.[97]

A major contributor to the ultimate failure of rural rehabilitation was, as with most programs, a lack of money. Between 1934 and 1941, 7,823 farmers received normal rehabilitation loans but this was only a portion of the 60,000 farms considered low-income. Even though farmers on the program did see an increase in income, it very rarely corresponded to an increase in net worth.[98] Several reasons existed for this disparity. First, many subsistence farmers received money through part-time mining, direct relief, or other forms of income. Secondly, what extra money was made was often re-invested into the tragically inefficient farms run mostly by part-time farmers.

This practice established a vicious cycle in which a marginal farm would invest money from loans or additional income in livestock. If crops were poor (which they often were) or no other money was made available, feed and fodder could not be grown or purchased. Unable to maintain their livestock, the farmers often sold or ate their investment. This cycle drove small farmers deeper into debt.[99]

Even when money was made available, many farmers had physical limitations. As most farmers had spent time in coal mines or cutting timber, many carried injuries, illness, and a body aged beyond its years into the difficult task of mountain agriculture. The Farm Security Administration calculated that 15 to 20 percent of farms failed rehabilitation due to health problems of farmers.[100] Health concerns are still a major barrier to employment and a burden on the government in the region; in 2005 West Virginia led the nation in the percentage of residents receiving federal disability payments.[101]

Legislative decisions also worked against the subsistence farmer. The Bankhead-Jones Farm Tenancy Act of 1937 required supervisors of rehabilitation programs to focus on farms in which greater than 50 percent of the total family income was received. Only after all such farms were assisted could funds be directed to those not meeting the requirement. This blocked the majority of southern West Virginia farms from obtaining loans.[102] For those that could obtain loans, many suffered the same vicious cycle previously discussed. Even for the farmers who managed to cover their loans, repayment itself was not necessarily a sign of success. In Nicholas and Webster Counties, income from WPA work projects and the CCC provided the means for repayment in most cases, not effective farming.[103] Other reasons for failure included inadequate farming knowledge, poor education, and subpar management skills.[104]

The next effort in agricultural and rural relief was land use management and reclamation. Concerns of soil erosion, overpopulation, and environmental depletion were not unknown at this time. The logical solution seemed to be to stop trying to squeeze blood from a turnip. The Bureau of Agricultural Economics laid the blame on the carrying capacity of the land and overpopulation.[105] Other officials saw "no suggested means to stop erosion except by terminating agriculture." R. G. Ellyson, the director of West Virginia's rural rehabilitation program, came to the conclusion that resettlement out of the region was the only answer.[106] Neither option, however, proved universally feasible, given the strong ties to land felt by many residents and the generations old belief that subsistence farming would provide enough to get by. By providing additional relief to failing farms, the government had only helped to perpetuate this mindset.

A novel, and perhaps ingenious, alternative was presented by economic geographer J. Russell Smith. Smith proposed that farmers quit failing crops, such as corn, and instead plant tree crops that would provide fodder for livestock. He suggested planting chestnut (the type not affected by the blight), persimmon, oak, and mulberry. The planting of trees would not only provide food for farmers and livestock, but would halt devastating erosion problems caused by timber removal. The Agricultural Adjustment Administration already had a program under which farmers could quit traditional agriculture and plant trees. The option provided for a one-time payment of between $5 and $35. However, the AAA program was created to foster new growth for the lumber industry and placed restrictions on which type of trees could be planted. The AAA-approved trees were pine, spruce, poplar, black locust, and walnut. With the limited exception of black walnut, none of these trees supplied adequate fodder for livestock, and because of government miscommunication and red tape, the Smith plan never materialized.[107]

As the Great Depression was lifted by rapid production and mechanization of World War II, large farms completed their ascendance over small and subsistence farming in the eyes of the government. Throughout the 1940s, conservative legislators in Congress fought against continued support for rural farms, and by 1943, the FSA, operating "more like a bank loan officer seeking good risks than an agency carrying out a broad attack on rural poverty," cut rural rehabilitation program funding by 43 percent.[108] Additionally, the FSA was prevented from purchasing land or supporting cooperatives.[109]

Despite half-hearted and poorly coordinated efforts, millions of dollars had been thrust into the rural rehabilitation programs of the 1930s. Inefficiency, politics, and in some cases lack of solid logic had worked to inhibit government aid to small and subsistence farms in terms of increasing productivity. There were some bright spots, such as the debt adjustment program and the Rural Electrification Administration (REA), which doubled the number of farms with electricity between 1937 and 1940.[110] In the fight against rural poverty, relief mechanisms only left many farmers dependent on government aid and public work to subsist.[111]

Perhaps the most enduring and controversial piece of legislation impacting southern West Virginia was the Social Security Act of 1935. In addition to unemployment benefits, old-age insurance (Social Security), and aid to the blind, the act also established Aid to Dependent Children

(ADC).[112] ADC, initially focusing on direct aid to at-risk children, over the years developed into programs that sought to provide aid, education, training, and employment opportunities to the entire family. The benefit to many families is undeniable, but to some, the programs have become either long-term replacement for work or a bureaucratic mountain of red tape preventing both effective employment and adequate assistance. In each instance, underlying conditions of rural poverty, combined with cultural and economic factors prevalent in southern West Virginia, have been key contributors to continuing problems in public welfare in the region.

In addition to federal social security programs, the West Virginia Compensation Act began dispersing benefits in January of 1938. Some of the program's goals included providing security to unemployed families to "guard against the menace to health, morals, and welfare" caused by unemployment, maintaining purchasing power, and preventing the debilitation consequences of poor relief assistance.[113] Several aspects of the program were not well suited to the reality of conditions in southern West Virginia. A large portion of contributions to the program (37 percent in 1939) were through miners' wages and benefits paid out were to unemployed miners (44 percent), so the program was susceptible to industry trends. Secondly, the program did not allow for payments during labor disputes and did not recognize that looking for "suitable work" in other jobs was not viable in company towns. Finally, the program did not account for widespread part-time employment that was common throughout the region.[114]

ADC was the primary vehicle for welfare from 1933 until 1962. In the 1960s a renewed focus on both Appalachia and rural poverty sprung out of John F. Kennedy's presidential campaign and President Lyndon Johnson's War on Poverty. These events brought not only national attention to the region and its problems but resulted in a series of new welfare, social, and employment related programs as well. The attention was well founded. During the 1950s mechanization of the mines continued, small farms were further marginalized, and other energy sources such as oil and gas dug into coal's portion of the market.[115] The 1950s and 1960s also saw the final dismantling of the majority of company towns.[116] As the towns closed and jobs disappeared, homeless and unemployed families left for the few regional industrial bases, moved into nearby towns when possible, left for other states, or just stayed on in ghost towns. In 1960, average income in Appalachia was 65 percent of the national average and unemployment was 40 percent above the national average.[117]

West Virginia had begun the shift to family centered care in 1961 through the Emergency Employment Program. This program focused on unemployed fathers, and required the enrollees to be involved in some type of work-related program to receive benefits.[118] In 1962, ACD was replaced by Aid to Families with Dependent Children (AFDC) as welfare reform continued to shift focus from children to the family in an attempt to prevent adult welfare dependency.[119] The Economic Opportunity Act of 1964 resulted in several new efforts as well. Through this act several programs, such as Youth Corps, Job Corps, Head Start, and work study programs, were created, as well as the Work Incentive Program (WIN) and WIN-II, which began in 1969–1970.[120] WIN provided training and structural job searches on a voluntary basis until it became mandatory in 1971.

The Area Development Act of 1961 and Area Vocational Education Program provided for government sponsored retraining of long-term unemployed people. Between 1959 and 1964 such retraining programs resulted in some success. Trainees who completed the program saw increased employment and slightly higher income than those not enrolled. Additionally, the extra income paid back the cost of the training in 13.3 months for men and 18.8 months for women.[121] Other initiatives, such as the expansion of the Food Stamp Program and increased flexibility in Medicaid, allowed many on welfare to increase their income slightly and still receive other assistance benefits.[122] Even though these programs demonstrated a positive impact on employment, purchasing power, and income, many were left in poverty. As one mining town resident said, "Just look up any hollow and you'll find hungry, unemployed people."[123]

The 1970s saw a reduction in two-parent welfare caseloads in West Virginia, reaching an all time low in 1974. This decade also saw an increase in employment opportunities due to the resurgence of the coal industry.[124] Additionally, between 1964 and 1976, federal social welfare spending increased from 5 percent to 11 percent of the GDP. Due to this additional spending and inflation, welfare grew faster than wages during the 1970s.[125] As a result, although many took advantage of increased employment opportunities, others chose to remain on welfare rolls.

Jack Weller discussed some of the reasons behind this preference for receiving aid over working, especially when the benefits of both are basically equivalent. Weller's argument goes beyond the basic "dole breeds sloth" concept but, while providing an insightful window into social and cultural factors common in the region, should not be applied wholesale.

Weller believed that due to the cultural and social strength of subsistence farming, there was not an initial understanding of the value of vocational training. To Weller, the mountaineer considered the "concept of choosing a vocation, becoming trained in that field, and traveling wherever it calls him" to be "largely foreign to the mountain boy."[126] Under this construct "because work's only purpose is earning a living, the mountaineer when unemployed has a different attitude toward unemployment insurance from that middle class leaders envisioned when they set up payments in the law.... The mountaineer, however, sees the insurance as a legal substitute for work."[127]

To some welfare recipients, decades and generations of existence in poverty had become institutionalized by the 1970s. The concept of "poverty as a way of life," once entrenched into social paradigms, often "inhibit[ed] social adjustments and economic changes."[128] This mindset continues to exist in some areas, much to the dismay of local officials, conservative taxpayers, and many others.[129]

Even with improving job availability and increased assistance throughout most of the 1970s, West Virginia still lagged behind the nation as a whole in many areas, as seen Fig. 11 and Fig. 12. By the late 1970s, the coal boom had began to bust, jobs again became scarce, and those currently on assistance were faring just as well as those working low paying jobs. When a national recession hit and a conservative federal government took steps to reduce domestic spending, southern West Virginia fared poorly.

The Omnibus Budget Reconciliation Act of 1981 imposed stricter limitations on welfare recipients. This included a maximum asset limit, excluding home equity and one car, of $1,000. This reduced the national case load by over 700,000. Unfortunately many of those removed from the program were mothers working in marginal jobs. During this period, 46 percent of working mothers reported childcare as their only barrier to work.[130] The tighter asset limits, in addition to cuts to childcare programs, adversely affected working mothers throughout the region and the nation as a whole.

The 1980s also saw the creation of new work programs. This included the Job Opportunities and Basic Skills Training Program (JOBS) and Community Work Experience Program (CWEP). JOBS focused on work preparation and employment training programs while CWEP provided work experience through placement in public and non-profit organizations. The CWEP option was used extensively in West Virginia, as it was difficult

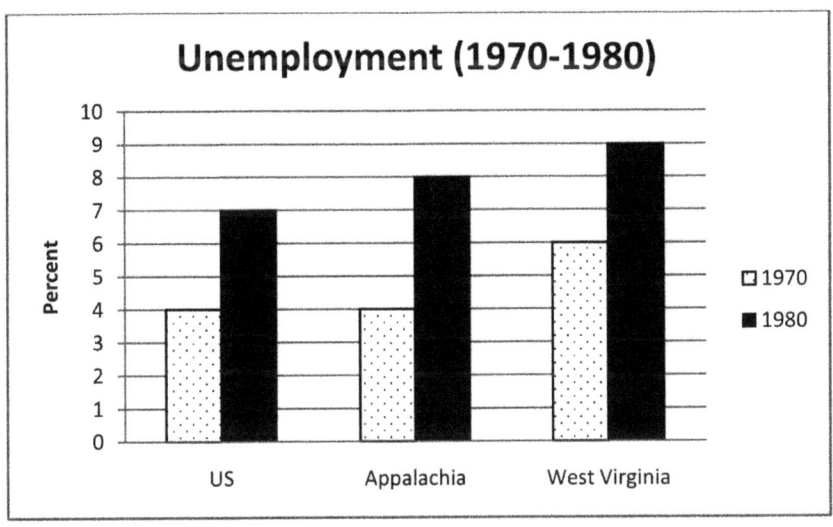

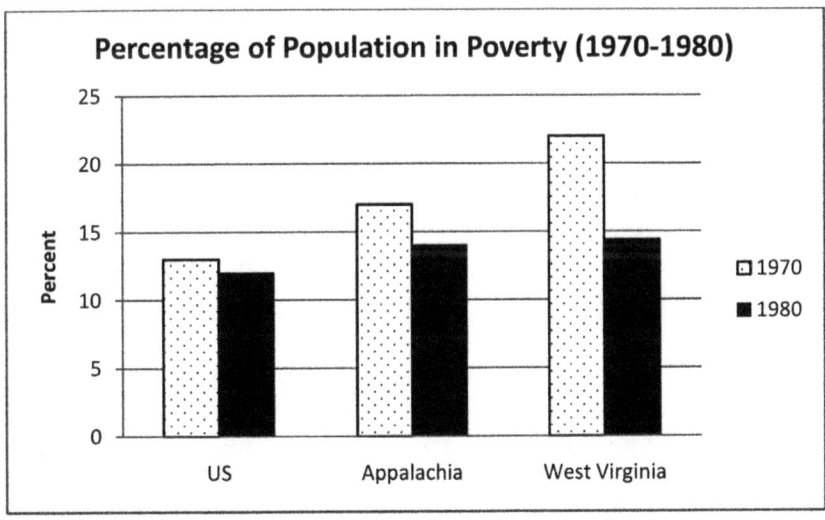

Top: Fig. 11. Unemployment, 1970–1980. Source: Sousa, p. 8. *Bottom:* Fig. 12. Poverty, 1970–1980. Source: Sousa, p. 8.

to find private sector work due chronic job shortages. CWEP also sought to improve the image of recipients through community involvement and gaining new skills.[131] A study of CWEP outcomes, however, showed that although some skills were gained, most did not lead to higher wages and increased employment.

Subsistence living in the region existed to levels where "public attitudes toward welfare [were] ambivalent."[132] In general, CWEP itself did little to change opinions, positive or negative, of welfare in southern West Virginia. Although Chang Fisher has demonstrated an 8.5 percent decrease in two-parent welfare caseloads during the 1980s, other factors also came into play that could have impacted case numbers.[133] These factors include a shift from specialized or higher paying jobs to part-time retail and service related employment and massive outmigration from the state during the decade.[134]

In the 1980s, the coal industry faced another downturn. Mechanization continued to replace higher paying employees with technology, and a large shift in the type of jobs available took place in the 1980s. Fig. 13 shows the drastic changes in employment type that took place between 1980 and 1990 in many southern West Virginia counties.

With over 1600 mines closing in the late 1970s and early 1980s, mining jobs rapidly declined.[135] Many looked toward the only types of employment available — retail and service industry jobs. Unfortunately, the shift from manufacturing or mining to retail and the service industry resulted in a loss of income between $10,000 and $15,000 per year.[136] Generally, three options were left to the growing numbers of unemployed. One could find a lower paying job in the service or retail industry, go on welfare or other assistance, or leave the region in hopes of finding employment elsewhere.

For those unable to find employment which kept them above subsistence levels, public assistance was the next option. Fig. 14 shows the increase in households receiving income through public assistance between 1980 and 1990. This chart demonstrates the inability of retail and service related jobs to replace higher paying salaries once made by miners and a few other industries such as manufacturing and construction which became, and generally remain, scarce in the region. The limited earning capacity in retail and service industries, when combined with the availability of benefits for unemployed, sometimes worked to limit motives to find a job. For those on the fringes of the wage scale, employment sometimes did not outweigh the benefits of aid, as seen in Fig. 15. A mother of two earning less than $10,000 a year from a low-paying part-time service or retail job could receive almost the same, or in some cases more, in aid benefits for not working at all.

Others simply left. In the 1980s, southern West Virginia saw a population decrease in excess of 8 percent. This decade was preceded by a 7.2

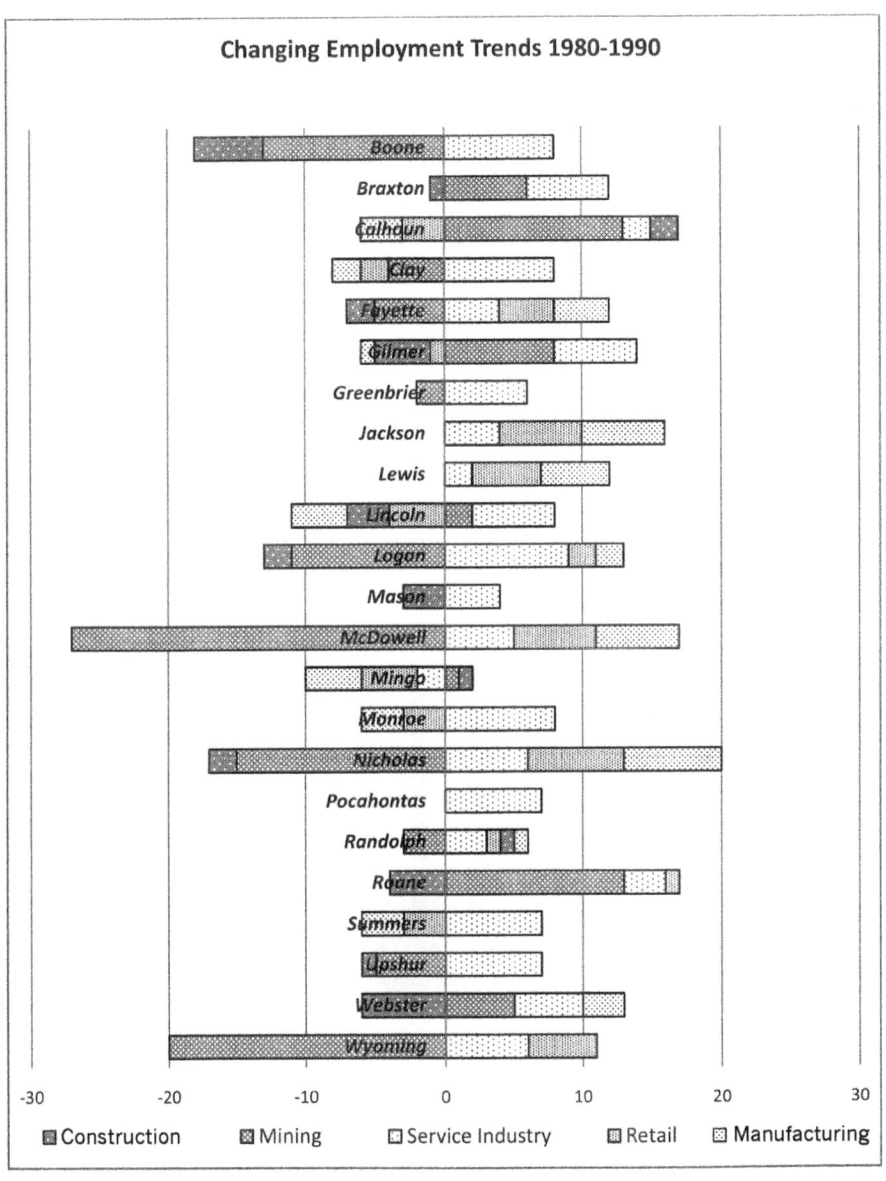

Fig. 13. Changing Employment Trends, 1980–1990. Source: Sousa, p. 115.

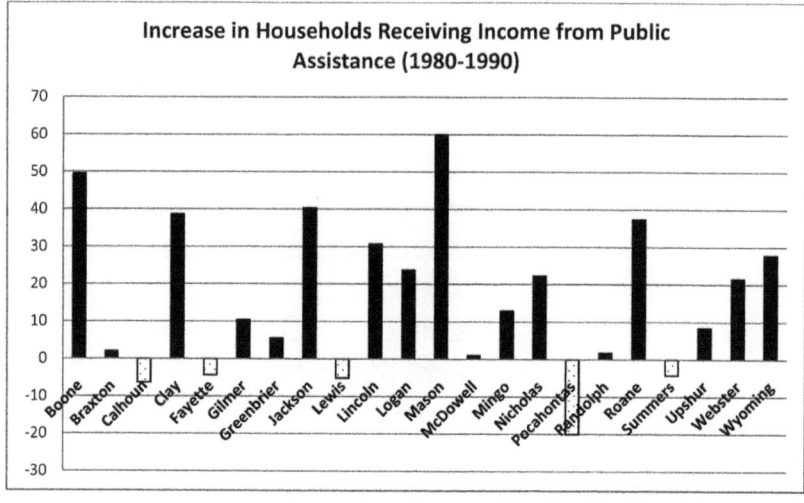

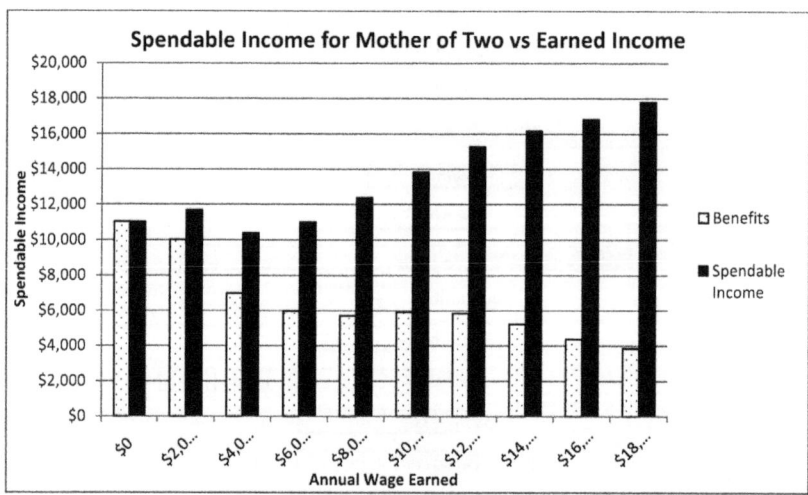

Top: Fig. 14. Households Receiving Public Assistance, 1980–1990. Source: Sousa, p. 60. *Bottom:* Fig. 15. Spendable Income for Mother of Two versus Earned Income. Source: Sobel, p. 178.

percent reduction in population between 1950 and 1960, and the loss of 116,184 residents (6.2 percent) between 1960 and 1970.[137] Some of those leaving made their way to northern West Virginia counties that were closer to industry in Ohio, Pennsylvania, Maryland, and northern Virginia. Most of those who left the state moved to Virginia and North Carolina.[138] Of these out-migrants, 63 percent were between the ages of 20 and 34. Additionally, 18 percent of the college-educated population left the state. To make matters worse, almost half of those who came into the state during this period were living below the poverty level.[139] Fig. 16 and Fig. 17 show the loss of population for many southern West Virginia counties.

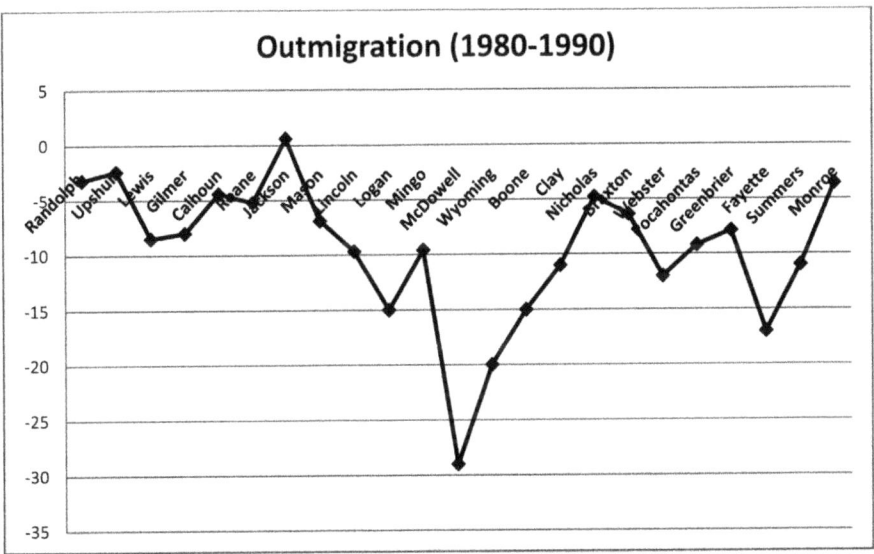

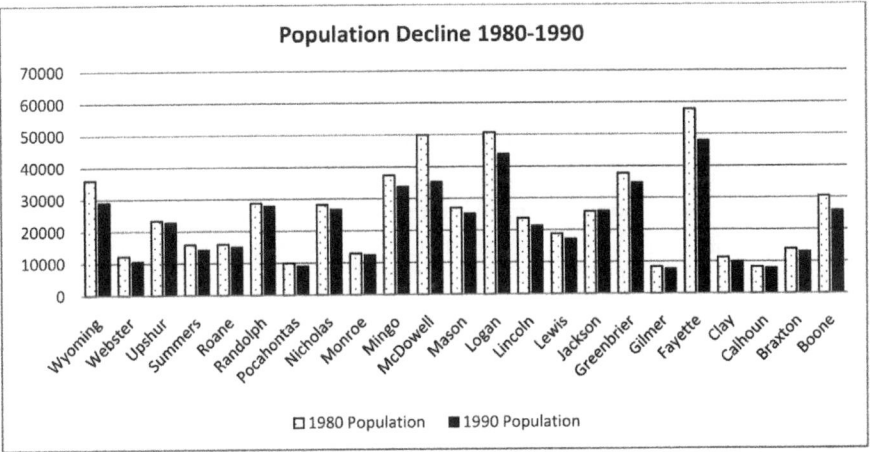

Top: Fig. 16. Outmigration, 1980–1990. Source: Sousa, p. 67. *Bottom:* Fig. 17. Population Decline, 1980–1990. Source: Sousa, p. 67.

The conditions in southern West Virginia put many in a difficult situation. Higher-paying jobs were replaced with lesser paying jobs requiring fewer specialized skills but more basic education. Welfare programs, even when effective at providing job training and experience, were hampered by a dismal job market. Those people unable, or in some cases unwilling, to find gainful employment often found that benefits from public assistance programs often provided as much or more than part-time retail and service jobs. The region also saw a massive exodus of young, educated residents to areas that had more to offer. At the same time some of southern West Virginia's best and brightest migrated elsewhere, over half of those moving to the region were themselves living in poverty.

This transfer of educated youth for ready-made welfare cases worked to limit the base of educated persons necessary for regional reform and added to an already burdened welfare structure. It is no wonder that the Appalachian Regional Commission (ARC) designated over half of West Virginia's counties as "distressed" due to unemployment rates, poverty rates, and per capita income.[140] The majority of these 26 distressed counties were in southern West Virginia.

In 1996, the Personal Responsibility and Work Opportunity Reconciliation Act (PRWORA) replaced AFDC with Temporary Assistance to Need Families (TANF). At the heart of TANF was the desire to place more responsibility upon the recipient of aid.[141] The program's goal was to "diminish household dependency on government cash assistance programs and shift the focus of public assistance from welfare to work."[142] TANF created a lifetime limit of 60 months of aid and placed additional pressures on states to meet TANF requirements or lose funding.[143] West Virginia's response was the WV WORKS program. The WV WORKS administrators, facing a lack of administrative capacity, quickly took advantage of exemptions and loopholes in TANF regulations to maintain their funding and provide aid to a population that did not fit the model under which TANF was created.[144]

WV WORKS utilized incentives such as the following:[145]

- Disregarded 60 percent of working parents' earned income for eligiblity
- $100 marriage incentive
- Child support incentive — provided $50 a month when child support was paid

- Support Service payment for items such as tools, professional certifications, relocation expenses and other costs related to involvement in approved WV WORKS activities
- GED and aptitude testing
- Access to WV Education Program (WVEP), which provided cash assistance for education costs.[146]

Other program elements that WV WORKS administrators utilized to continue aid were a 24 month exemption from work activities and an exemption for up to 20 percent of caseloads in cases of hardship.[147]

TANF's major problem was that it did not account for the reality of conditions in southern West Virginia, such as the scarcity of jobs and the ability of those jobs to provide adequate wages.[148] WV WORKS administrators, fully aware of this condition, were faced with the loss of funds for failure to meet minimum work participation requirements and employment options laid out in TANF regulations. In response to these requirements, WV WORKS undertook two endeavors, the widespread use of CWEP to make up for the lack of private jobs and the increasing pressure to reduce the number of people receiving benefits.[149]

With limited private employment options available, WV WORKS took full advantage of CWEP, as seen in the breakdown of average monthly work activity for TANF enrollees in fiscal year 1999 in Fig. 18. Although CWEP kept enrollees active and receiving benefits, few new skills were learned and jobs remained hard to come by. The second element of WV WORKS response to PRWORA requirements was the pursuance of case load reductions. Between August of 1996 and June of 2000, WV WORKS had reduced its case load from 89,039 down to 31,500 (a 65 percent decrease).[150] The case reduction program was so effective that West Virginia lowered its workforce requirement to 15 percent in 1997 and 0 percent in 1999.[151] Elizabeth McGaha identifies four reasons that aided this reduction. First was national economic growth. A decrease in real benefits as well as the expansion of Federal Earned Income Tax Credit may have played a role. Finally, other public assistance programs, such as Medicare and the Food Stamp Program, were expanded during this period.[152]

Although a reduction in enrollees would seem to be progress at a glance, the reality is actually alarming. A ticking time bomb has been set in motion from often well meaning attempts to provide services to the needy and maintain federal funding. Although the mid–1990s and early

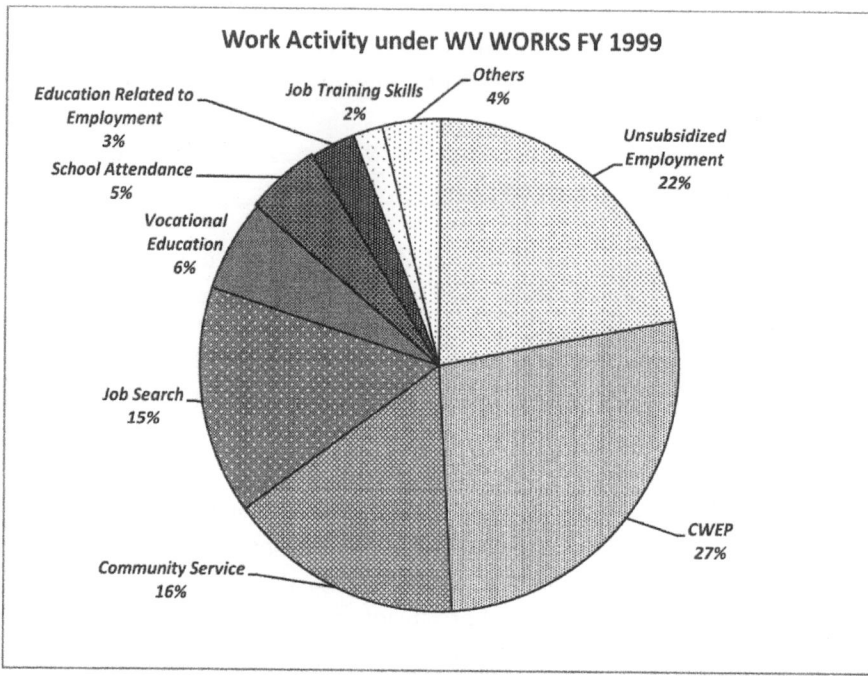

Fig. 18. Work Activity, WV WORKS, Fiscal Year 1999. Source: Plein, p. 18.

2000s saw massive case load reductions, the true problem of rural poverty was not adequately addressed — that being the limited job availability and economic opportunities supported by an entrenched culture of poverty. A review of how those leaving TANF during this period demonstrates the very limited success of the program.

A survey of WV WORKS program leavers in 2000 showed that many still faced the same barriers to success they faced when entering the program (Fig. 19). Many times barriers were numerous; over 54 percent of leavers surveyed faced more than three.[153] In addition to barriers that had not been effectively addressed, many were still faced with the daily hardships of poverty (Fig. 20). Multiple hardships were experienced by 84 percent of leavers, with 54 percent facing more than four.[154] Many leavers taking the 2000 survey were unaware of the full benefits offered by WV WORKS, particularly in terms of health care, dental, and educational opportunities.[155]

The region's welfare program was further limited by a 2002 budget

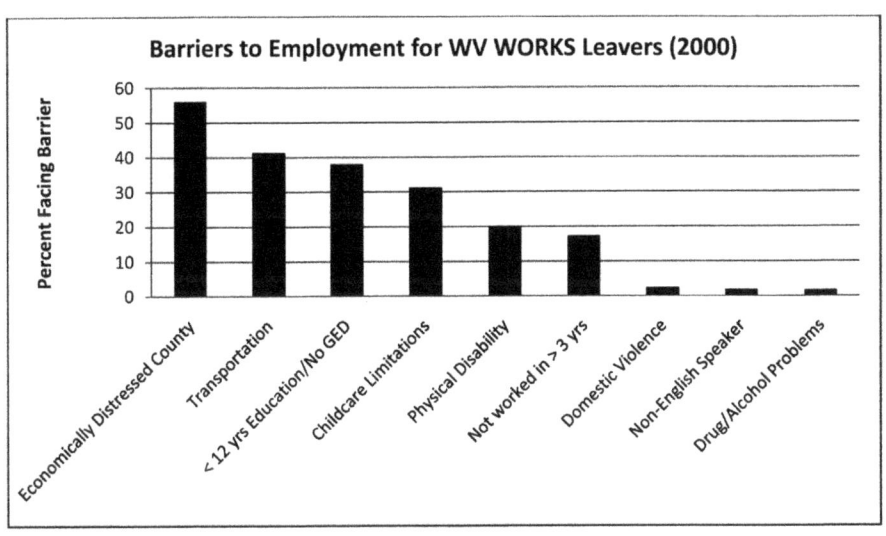

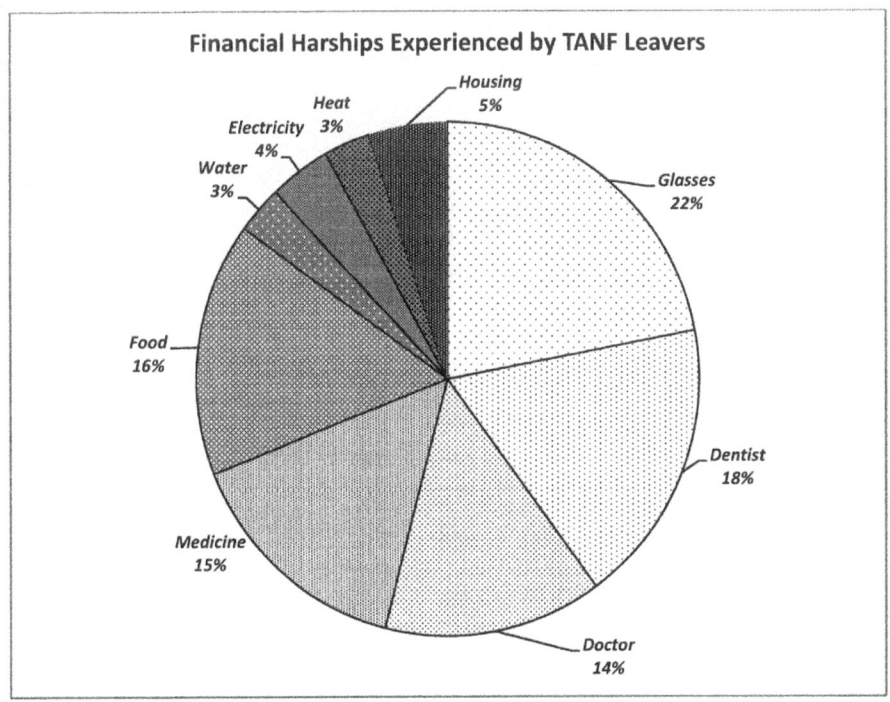

Top: Fig. 19. Barriers to Employment, 2000. Source: Dilger, et al., p. 274.
Bottom: Fig. 20. Financial Hardships. Source: McGaha, p. 36.

shortfall that resulted in smaller cash payments, a reduction of the 60 percent income exemption to 40 percent, and reduced funding of support services. This trend was expected to grow worse as those leaving WV WORKS still faced barriers to employment and financial hardship. As these leavers re-enter the system, the case load reduction benefits will evaporate, and with jobs still scarce, the state will face penalties for not meeting work participation requirements.[156]

Social welfare programs have always faced the dilemma of becoming a mechanism for government handouts to those who could work but choose instead to remain on assistance. While "personal responsibility, or lack thereof, may be at the root of some families' dependence on public assistance," there are also those for whom "economic circumstances beyond their control bring many families into the welfare system."[157] Under these conditions, more and more residents have come to rely on public assistance or other forms of social insurance. According to L. Christopher Plein, "Retirement benefits, disability insurance, medical payments, veterans' benefits, unemployment insurance, food stamps, and cash assistance have become an important economic foundation for local economies," accounting for over 26 percent of the state's total personal income.[158]

This is particularly true in southern West Virginia. Sustained generations-long poverty, the instability of the state's mono-industry (coal mining), and limited economic opportunity have created a vicious cycle in which those on welfare often have few viable options of earning enough to escape the pit of poverty, at least while remaining in the region. Barriers such as a region-wide lack of public transportation and limited childcare availability only make the problem worse. A Congressional investigation in 1988 concluded that "most families do not even think about how things look down the road because they are exhausting every thread of energy confronting the day-to-day struggles of making ends meet."[159]

Out-migration is also still a major factor of regional demographics. Between 2000 and 2008, while West Virginia as a whole saw a marginal population increase of 0.3 percent, the southern West Virginia counties involved in this study saw an average population decrease of 2.6 percent. The county facing the largest population loss was McDowell, with a 16.9 percent reduction.[160] The current conditions of welfare and employment opportunities in the region demonstrate the continuing struggle for economic security. In the end, this security can only be achieved by improving economic opportunities or by continued out-migration.

Six

Health and the Mountaineer
Perspectives on Public and Occupational Health

When it comes to health and medical care, West Virginians have undergone a significant transformation over the generations. The traditional robust, free-spirited, hardworking, nature-loving miner, railroad worker, and lumberman who spent his free time climbing the mountains in search of wild game had been supplanted in mainstream American thought. In his stead is a lazy, overweight, diabetic with tooth decay.[1] Unfortunately, in some ways the stereotype reflects a painful reality of public health in the region. Adding to the problem is the growing dependence on pain killers, namely Oxycontin, which not only damages the body but undermines long established kinship bonds.

This chapter will examine the region's public and occupational health experience from the days of the early company towns to modern day. Through this process one can see how southern West Virginia residents' perspectives, understanding, and use of public and occupational health initiatives, as well as the field of medicine in general, have been impacted by many of the same factors which have shaped other elements of the region's society and culture. Four elements played a key role in the development of residents' perspectives on medicine and occupational and public health; these are poverty, traditional kinship bonds and family ties, cultural paradigms, and an acceptance of hard living, work related dangers, and other health issues as a norm. Before these topics can be developed in more depth, a brief review of the history of public health and the growth of the medical profession in southern West Virginia is necessary.

Just as the growth of company towns resulted in a coming together of races and ethnicities, farmer and industrialist, patriarchal landowner and capitalist developer, it also brought together an isolated mountain people, steeped in traditional medical remedies and a marginal medical profession, with a rapidly advancing medical science and a new generation of scientifically-focused medical practitioners. Even the limited number of formally trained practitioners in the area before the coming of industrialization received their training from conservative, and therefore slow to reform, institutions such as the Medical College of Virginia, the University of Louisville, and the College of Physicians and Surgeons in Baltimore.[2] As the old and new came together, this flux in medical thought and theory caused conflict between the old-guard mountain doctors and their more formally educated young challengers.[3] Not unlike the struggle between patriarchal landowners and industrialists which disrupted the mountain society, this battle between local practitioners and new medical professionals over issues such as public health and sanitation often led to confusion and exasperation among residents.[4] The confusion between tradition and modernization created a situation in which the implementation of public health initiatives became a long, as some would still argue ongoing, process in southern West Virginia as residents resisted replacing the old, comfortable mountain healer with the educated, scientific doctors and nurses who touted methodologies and theories alien to many mountaineers.

The early to mid–19th century mountain practitioner most likely received training through an apprenticeship program which involved minimal formal medical training. Aside from the familiarity of these practitioner-healers, who had existed in the region for generations, they were often a more economical choice for the cash strapped miner and subsistence farmer. Particularly popular were the myriad of elixirs and tonics sold by these healers.[5] Given the choice of health care options, many subsistence farmers and company town residents chose the advice, cures, and other goods offered by the mountain practitioners. To the region's residents, such a choice was financially sound, tradition-based, and easier to accept and understand than complicated and more expensive procedures promoted by the new generation of medical professionals. The state itself initially helped to promote the legitimacy of these healers; although West Virginia began licensing doctors in the 1880s, a grandfather clause was included for those who had practiced for greater than 10 years. Under this system, two men who listed themselves as illiterate were allowed to continue practicing medicine in Logan County.[6]

Eventually, however, modern practitioners gained a foothold, particularly as employees of coal and lumber companies. Between 1886 and 1917, the number of West Virginia medical practitioners reporting legitimate medical degrees increased from 45 percent to 99 percent.[7] By 1915, the landscape of the medical profession in the region had taken on a much more scientific and professional appearance. The West Virginia State Medical Association published the *West Virginia Medical Journal*, which discussed a variety of medical topics. Between July and November of 1915, the *Journal* had published articles, papers, procedures, studies, and discussions on topics such as cancer, diabetes, eye diseases, dental care, the use of X-ray technology, suicide prevention, caesarian sections, pediatrics, orthopedics, surgical methods for gunshot wounds, infectious disease, and mining injuries.[8]

By the 1920s, the new generation of professionals was poised to make significant changes to the nature of public health in southern West Virginia, as well as greater Appalachia. Doctors, public health nurses, and concerned women's clubs made a concerted assault on prenatal care, child health, sanitation, and public health in general.[9] Their efforts were given a major boost by the Sheppard-Towner Act, with goals of better infant care through teaching of mothers, care for mothers in need of skilled supervision during pregnancy, childbirth, and postnatal stages, and more widespread medical and nursing facilities.[10]

In many cases reformers had their work cut out for them. In a 1920 study of Raleigh County coal communities, 300 of 316 children examined were determined to have one or more health defects (Fig. 21).[11] Key elements necessary to the success of health care reform were preventive measures in sanitation, hygiene, and nutrition.[12] This fact became obvious to all as doctors and nurses made their way out to the lumber and mining camps and the remote farms throughout southern West Virginia.

Sanitation practices, or lack of them, were often the first thing visiting medical professionals noticed. A practitioner visiting a tuberculosis patient on a remote farm found the home, which held 10 occupants, "unpainted, uncarpeted, unswept, unscrubbed, and unsanitary in every way."[13] Others saw settlements where "waste matter entered the creeks flowing through the center of the town, privies were tumble-down, and incredible amounts of garbage and rubbish lay on the ground."[14] Few families had running

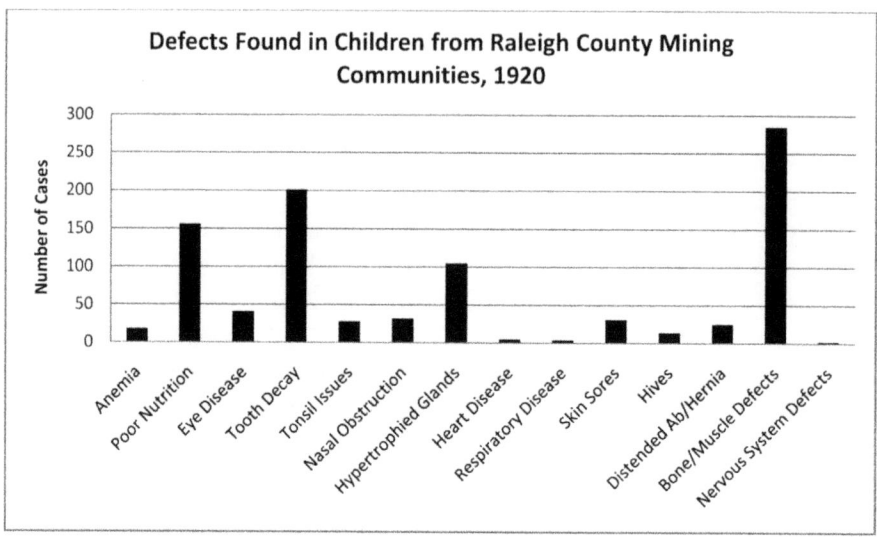

Fig. 21. Defects in Children, Raleigh County, 1920. Source: McGill, pp. 55–56.

An example of the rural health centers found in company towns and planned communities of the New Deal (Library of Congress).

water, and water sources were shared by between 3 and 20 families; only 136 of 1,928 children in the Children's Bureau study had access to a bath in their homes.[15] Even when access to water was available, regular analysis was uncommon.[16] Analysis was often not necessary, however, as springs "were contaminated by chickens and stock, or by dishwater, drainage, and garbage; many were situated in hollows on a lower level than surrounding privies."[17] The following comments were also included in the study:

- Chickens, flies, and hogs had easy access to privies
- Dead hogs were left lying in the streets
- Privies were "seldom and insufficiently cleaned"
- Some families waited for nearby creeks to rise, then simply overturned privys into flood waters
- In some places, sewage stood with surface water in stagnant pools, and
- "Flies abounded, mosquitoes also were numerous."[18]

With conditions such as these, "typhoid fever and other diseases connected with an impure water supply and the careless disposal of waste matter [were] likely to be a menace."[19] In 1917 the Metropolitan Life Insurance Company found Appalachian mining families to have exceptionally high rates of typhoid, scarlet fever, tuberculosis, and diphtheria.[20] Correcting the problems would be difficult and take decades. Similar conditions existed in some areas 20 years later in Logan County. Due to "so many deaths in mining accidents, starvation, and the spread of pneumonia and typhoid," coffin making was chosen as a job for relief projects during the Depression.[21]

The efforts by health care professionals, and particularly public health nurses, in the mid–1920s to correct these issues were significant. In 1925, the Children's Bureau reported the following activities for the previous year in West Virginia:

- 265 children's health conferences servicing 3,341 children
- 19 prenatal conferences servicing 92 expectant mothers
- 260 mothers' classes servicing 9,432 attendees
- "Mother's craft" courses for 7,253 girls
- 220 community health organizations
- Correspondence courses, and
- Several public health surveys.[22]

In 1927, the following activities were likewise reported:

- 306 child health conferences servicing 2,330 and finding 1578 defects
- 34 prenatal classes servicing 46 expectant mothers
- 26 nursing conferences servicing 278 children and 13 expectant mothers
- "Little mothers" courses for 582
- 12,629 home visits by nurses
- 12 new child health care centers
- 425 lectures
- 324 group demonstrations
- Midwife surveys in eight counties
- Child health surveys in 13 communities
- 372 midwives permits issued
- 85,355 pieces of literature prepared and distributed
- 2861 correspondence courses conducted, and
- 19 public health exhibits held.[23]

The Sheppard-Towner Act, along with its funding, was lapsed in 1929 after the American Medical Association asserted that it was a threat to their professional autonomy.[24]

Aside from the nursing jobs created under New Deal projects, the next major health care movement came in the 1960s as part of President Lyndon Johnson's War on Poverty. Sponsored by the Appalachian Regional Commission (ARC) and West Virginia University's Center for Appalachian Studies and Development, nurses again deployed to the front lines in the battle for public health and basic medical understanding. In many cases, these nurses faced some of the same problems as their predecessors in the 1920s and 1930s. Nurses again taught the importance of sanitation, basic household safety, dental care, care for the chronically ill and elderly, and answered questions such as, "Do I have to have all these babies?"[25] At the top of the list of problems was limited education and enduring poverty. Fifty-two percent of families involved in the project made less than $3,000 per year and two-thirds had less than a 9th grade education.[26] The nurses also found many still clinging to home and traditional remedies. Vanilla was used on burns, mustard for cuts, and bleach for sores. One resident reported that "when Chessie cut her foot something awful, we packed it in hot sheep's manure."[27]

Despite setbacks such as the lapsing of the Sheppard-Towner Act, the decaying of New Deal initiatives as America ramped up for World War II, and the gradual decay and graft in War on Poverty programs, the experiences and information gained by these pioneering groups of rural health care professionals, with public health nurses as the workhorses, laid the groundwork for the growth of modern-day medical specialization of rural medicine. In a specialty pioneered by Appalachian universities in the 1990s, a new generation of doctors and physicians' assistants has focused their studies on rural medicine and some of its cultural intricacies.[28]

An example of these programs is East Tennessee State University's Appalachian preceptorship. This four-week elective course in the Department of Family Medicine includes not only practical experience but introduces students to cultural aspects of Appalachian communities. Elements of the program include lectures from Native American healers, Appalachian storytellers, ministers, and anthropologists. Between 1985 and 2004, over 225 medical students from 95 different medical programs have taken part. Those completing the program were three times more likely to practice in rural communities.[29]

One such professional is Dr. Paul Conley, who, after completing his medical training in the North, returned to his hometown of Summersville and is on staff at Summersville Regional Medical Center. Dr. Conley hosts a local radio show titled "Doc Talk" where he discusses local and national health issues. Although he was often called "hillbilly" by his colleagues during residency, Conley performed superbly, winning honors as the top graduate at St. Luke's Hospital just outside Philadelphia.[30] He has also partnered with the community television station, SCTV, where "Doc Talk" has expanded to provide medical information, including videos of actual procedures, through an additional medium to local residents.[31] Practicing what he calls "big city medicine with hometown care,"[32] Conley and others like him are again facing the challenges of rural health care head-on. Their work is very much needed, as the region's residents still suffer from many health issues at a much higher rate than the national average.

Among the myriad of health care concerns in southern West Virginia are heart disease, some cancers, arthritis, obesity, hypertension, not to mention a rate of lost work days to injury that is "exceptionally high."[33] Of the 55 counties making up West Virginia, 48 have higher than average prevalence of obesity. Fifty-two have higher than average cases of hypertension, 49 have higher than average occurrence of smoking, and 54 have a higher than average use of smokeless tobacco.[34] This data supports why the state ranks among worst in the nation (1st or 2nd) in diabetes, obesity, heart attacks, strokes, and self-reported health.[35]

The high prevalence of smoking also supports the historically high number of lung and bronchus cancers in the state. While the national average for incidents of lung and bronchus cancer between 2002 and 2006 was 69.0 per 100,000, the state average was 90.4, with Mingo and Logan Counties having rates of 133.1 and 127.5 respectively.[36] A study conducted from 1950 to 1969 also showed a relationship between mining towns and lung cancer. Twenty-three mining communities in seven states were involved in the study, and a 20 to 30 percent increase in the prevalence of lung cancer was seen in these areas.[37] Fig. 22 provides data for several southern West Virginia counties chosen randomly to present a more in-depth look at factors impacting health.[38]

Why does the region still lag behind in so many aspects of public and occupational health? While some problems are reflective of greater American and Western trends, such as increases in caloric intake and sedentary lifestyles,[39] other aspects of southern West Virginia culture still create barriers to healthy living. Likewise, the dangerous nature of industrial labor (namely coal mining) is only made more precarious when profit is placed

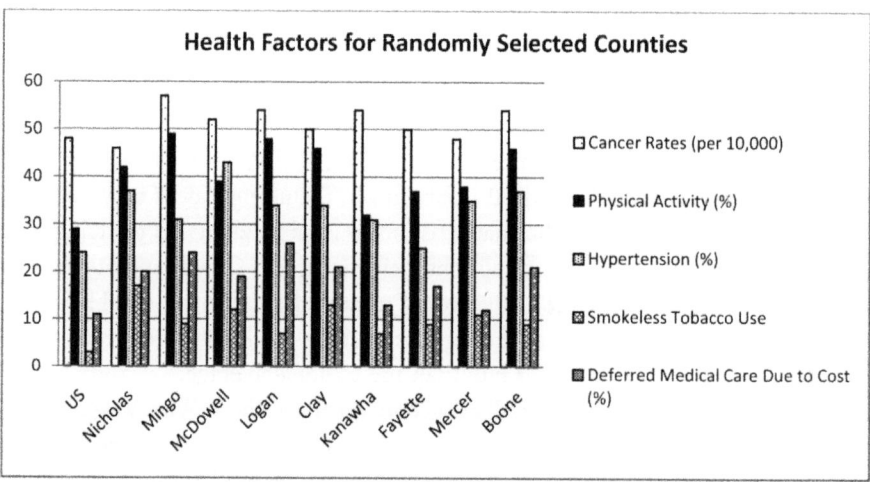

Fig. 22. Health Factors for Randomly Selected Counties. Source: West Virginia Bureau for Public Health. Cancer data from 1996 to 2000. All other data from 1999.

before safety. A prime example is the likelihood that a failure to take prudent safety precautions played a role in the death of 29 miners at Upper Big Branch Mine in Raleigh County in April 2010.

One of the major, and perhaps most significant, factors relating to public health and overall attitudes toward the medical field is the role parents, and particularly mothers, play in developing attitudes toward personal health, doctors, and the use of preventive health care.[40] Many parents fully embrace modern medicine, including healthy lifestyle choices. Tracy LeGrow discussed this increasing trend in her dissertation on health care decision-making among women in Appalachia. According to LeGrow, the realization of maternal roles and the availability of the Internet have resulted in a new group of health-conscious mothers. This group has shifted their primary concern toward their children, educated themselves via the Internet on basic medical symptoms, treatments, and methodologies, and brought this information and child-focused approach to the table when dealing with medical professionals. These women have effectively created a paradigm shift regarding medical care in the region, one in which they have became consumers versus recipients of health care — at least for their children.[41] While this group has taken a proactive approach (although child, not whole family oriented), others have not. This rejection of modern approaches to the medical sciences occurs in varying degrees and for many different reasons, such as economic and social barriers and well as cultural paradigms.

In 2006, 17.2 percent of West Virginians surveyed reported they could not afford health care, compared to 13.3 percent nationally.[42] Although the ultimate outcome of President Barak Obama's health care reform is yet to be fully evaluated (and peripheral arguments aside), the new legislation will have a significant impact on availability of health care for marginalized Americans. As 17.2 percent of West Virginians live below the poverty level in 2008,[43] however, other aspects of poverty will continue to impact their utilization of health care. Even if health care is made more available to the poor, those living on the margins or worse may have difficulty obtaining time off from already low-paying jobs and obtaining transportation to and from medical facilities.[44] In some cases, financial limitations beyond that of actual health care expenses may prove prohibitive despite the availability of public health care itself.

Social perspectives relating to patients and doctors also play a role in the utilization of medical care in southern West Virginia. Just as in the early days of industrialization, professionals, including doctors, generally make up local-level elites due to their higher education and income levels. This social status often impacts the doctor-patient relationship. An inferred superiority in some cases creates an intellectual and educational intimidation of patients.[45] Although rarely intentional on the part of the medical professionals, many patients automatically defer to the medical advice with little questioning or thoughts on second opinions.[46]

Another legacy is an underlying distrust of outsiders. As many doctors are from outside the region, including a large number of foreign born practitioners, communication issues and lack of cultural understanding only add to residents' trepidation.[47] In addition to economic and social concerns, lasting elements of kinship relations, religious faith, and a heritage of mountain medicine also play a role in health care choices in the region.

Familial bonds and faith can be positive or negative. Close bonds among family members allow for a broader range of support and assistance during illness, injury, and stressful situations. Likewise, spiritual faith also provides avenues for personal and family strength during trying times. Other aspects of spirituality and kinship ties, however, work to build barriers to effective medical care. While an attack on faith-oriented healing is not the purpose of this argument, avoiding available care and relying on faith can, and often does, result in poor outcomes for the patient. One resident told of many occasions in her youth when instead of utilizing available medical care, the local preacher was called to pray over her father.[48] Some in the region, however, have found a balance between faith and science. As the author's grandmother has often said, "I believe God can heal people; that's why he made doctors."

While religious faith, generally in the form of Protestantism, remains a key element of the region's cultural and societal makeup, several scholars have taken a more analytical and psychological look at religion. In a region where financial woes, dangerous jobs, and political and financial helplessness persist for a noticeable portion of the population, some scholars associate fundamentalist religious perspectives with "psychological catharsis and personal escape."[49] According to these scholars, "Rural and lower socioeconomic status persons need emotional religion more because they have become increasingly alienated in a rapidly changing society."[50] Photiadis and Schnabel argued that the resultant "bewilderment and confusion" are in turn related to both a need for "religion as a buffer" and "fundamentalistic beliefs."[51] Sari Tudiver likewise noted the power of religion in greater Central Appalachia, saying "in their churches, mountaineers find the joys of fellowship, protection from intrusive institutions and ultimately, the chance of salvation from an imperfect world."[52] In addition to element of escapism, religious faith can also act to embolden residents against what they determine to be negative aspects of modernization, or in other words, "act as a social and ideological force functioning to galvanize oppositional cultures, foment dissent, and solidify group identity."[53] In this manner, religion has been used to encourage resistance to coal company oppression and the perceived and real attacks on Appalachian society and culture throughout the region's history.

Although there is some merit in the role religion plays in tension, grief, and stress management from a psychological viewpoint, the resilience of many Appalachian families in the face of financial difficulties or even great family tragedy demonstrate a positive, tangible perspective which cannot be denied. This resilience, specifically related to Appalachian women, was researched by Joy A. Butcher-Winfree in her dissertation, "Portraits of Resiliency: A Qualitative Study of Appalachian Christian Women." Butcher-Winfree's study, admittedly biased by the author's religious views, looked at the lives of five Appalachian Christian women who had faced more than their share of adversity.[54] This study, along with countless examples of anecdotal evidence, demonstrates the viability of Appalachian spirituality. When faith is used out of fear or sloth, however, it not only corrupts the perpetrator but the entire community. This is the fine line both traditionalists and those mired in the culture of poverty mentality must walk. Otherwise, religion becomes a divisive tool rather than a support mechanism for traditionalists and an excuse for the poor for inactivity instead of a foundation from which to advance.

Just as faith has continued to be a strong element in lives of southern West Virginians, so has the practice of home remedies. Due to financial and social factors, as well as a strong heritage of mountain medicine, home remedies still carry much weight in many families. Passed down from grandmothers and mothers to the next generation of women, many practices have survived for generations. Home medical treatments such as onion poultices used to sweat out a cold and vinegar soaks for sprained ankles are still in use by some southern West Virginians.[55]

Occupational health and safety are also major areas of concern for the region. As always, coal mining plays a significant role. Despite advances in mining practices over the decades, the business is still dangerous. In 2007 the fatality rate for all coal mining was six times higher than the rate for all private industry. This rate was actually a 57 percent reduction from the previous year, which included the Sago Mine disaster.[56] With 29 deaths at Upper Big Branch Mine, 2010 was another grim year.

Catastrophic accidents with multiple deaths in mines are often sensationalized in the media. Nonfatal injuries, however, occur much more often and rarely make front page news. Between 1978 and 2008 the annual percentage of employees injured at underground mining operations ranged from a low of 7.4 percent in 2008 to a high of 15.7 in 1988 (Fig. 23). During that same thirty year period, an underground miner averaged an 11.4 percent chance of being injured each year.[57] While not as sensationalized as major mining fatalities, nonfatal injuries still exact a toll on miners, families, and the communities.

These injuries also result in a longer than average time away from

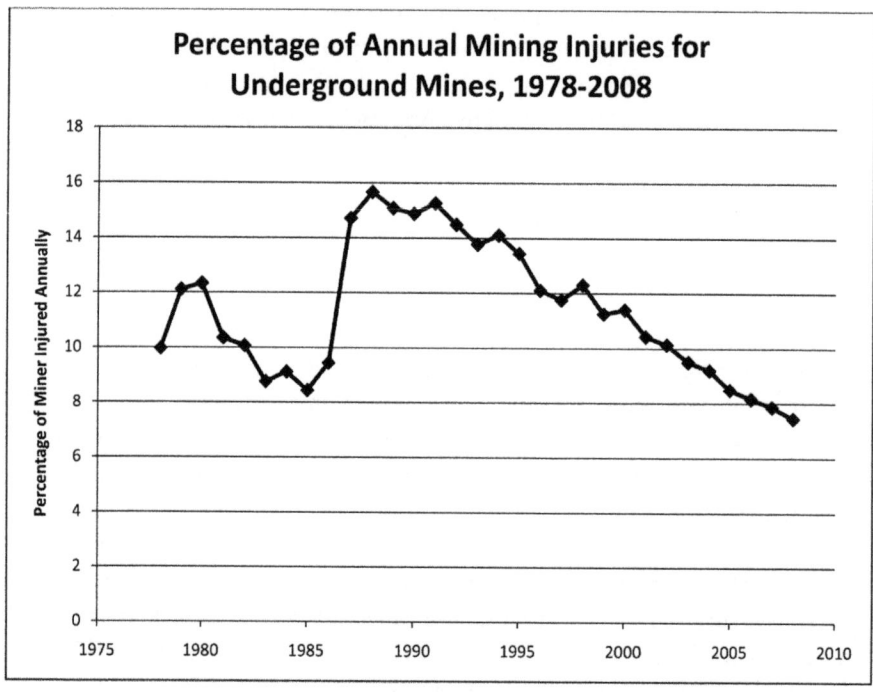

Fig. 23. Percentage of Annual Mining Injuries for Underground Mines, 1978–2008. Source: Mine Safety and Health Administration.

work.[58] Even though miners' wages are among the highest in the region, lost work from injuries can mitigate the financial gain. When serious injuries do keep miners out of work for long periods or indefinitely, few options exist for employment due to physical limitations and limited education, which many are left with after years in the mines. Likewise, as a lifetime of more minor injuries are accumulated, miners are faced with a myriad of chronic, debilitating conditions later in life which again limit further opportunities to maintain an adequate income. Although a slight decrease has occurred in the last few years, the rate of nonfatal injury, illness, and lost days due to injury for underground bituminous coal miners remains much higher than the national average (Fig. 24).[59]

With such a large number of work-related injuries and chronic pain, addiction to pain killers has become a major problem in the area. Called "hillbilly heroin" due to the similar effect if abused, Oxycontin has not only resulted in widespread addiction in many areas of southern West Virginia, but acted as a catalyst for rising crime as well.[60] With a street value that at times reached up to $160 per pill, the drug was not cheap.[61] Shoplifting, theft, and prescription fraud skyrocketed as addicts sought money to obtain the drug. In many cases, the power of addiction trumped the power of kin-

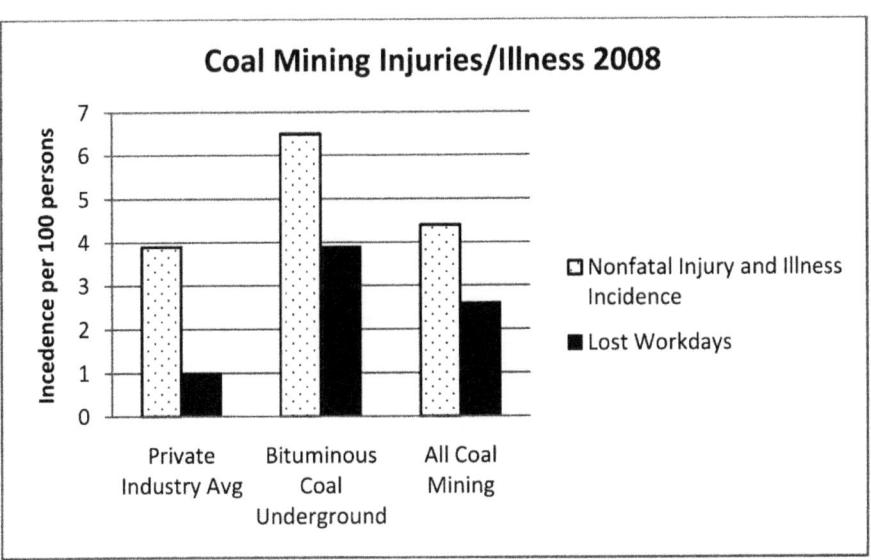

Fig. 24. Coal Mining Injuries and Illnesses, 2008. Source: U.S. Dept of Labor, Bureau of Labor Statistics.

ship as addicts robbed not only strangers but family members as well in order to feed their addiction.[62] The problems became so bad that the state sued Purdue Pharma, the manufacturer of the drug, in 2001. By then addiction had reached a level which "led to a dramatic increase in social problems, including drug abuse and criminal acts to obtain Oxycontin," and "public health [has been] substantially and negatively impacted" due to its abuse.[63]

In addition to work-related injuries, miners are also at risk for unique lung conditions due to the nature of their work. In 1979, a study determined that one-third of all underground miners were affected by respiratory conditions.[64] The most significant of these is coal worker's pneumoconiosis (CWP). The disease, given the common name black lung, has become synonymous with mining. Caused by long-term inhalation of coal particles, the disease can manifest itself in various ways. This includes simple CWP, complicated CWP or progressive massive fibrosis (PMF), and rheumatoid pneumoconiosis (Caplan syndrome). In both simple CWP and PMF, lung function is reduced due to fibrosis and emphysema. In PMF, it is believed that additional accumulation of other inorganic minerals and silica aid the process. Once the PMF stage has been reached, it may continue to progress without further exposure. In some cases (although more prevalent in European mines) a rheumatoid aspect of the disease, Caplan syndrome, can present itself.[65]

Silicosis is another disease which miners, particularly those involved in tunnel drilling, roof bolting, and transportation, may contract. As silicosis is indistinguishable from CWP by radiograph, autopsy is the best differential methodology. Examination of 4115 deceased miners involved in the National Coal Worker's Autopsy Study from 1972 to 1996 showed that 23 percent of the sample had pulmonary silicosis while 58 percent had lymph node silicosis.[66]

Although improvements in regulations and technology have worked to limit the exposure of miners to dust generated by the mining process, some operations, such as long-wall mining, still generate large concentrations of coal dust. This threat can be seen in a recent increase in black lung cases among both younger miners and those with greater than 20 years of experience, according to data taken in the 1990s.[67] Even if the dangers of respiratory conditions were completely mitigated, generations of miners would still have to deal with the debilitating symptoms of previous exposure.

Public and occupational health conditions in southern West Virginia are improving and will likely continue to do so, although overall growth is stunted by the adverse effects of widespread poverty. Rural medicine programs and aspects of modernization (such as the Internet) being developed by and injected into the region, regardless of resistance, have led to new advances in public health practices and knowledge. Better informed themselves, and treated by professionals specializing in rural medicine and building upon earlier public health pioneers, residents have access to ever-increasing knowledge, programs, and care. Problems still exist, however, as poverty and a propensity for home remedies still negatively impact the ability or desire to access modern medical care.

As this book is being written, the debate continues regarding President Obama's massive health care reforms. Although it may be years before the constitutionality and effectiveness of the reforms are accurately evaluated, it will likely have similar outcomes as FDR's New Deal. While some will undoubtedly and rightfully benefit, others will likely see the program as simply another support mechanism by which their marginalized and government funded existence can be maintained. Only time, effective administration, and future legislation will tell the final story.

Occupational health may also improve, particularly as response develops to the disastrous and highly publicized Upper Big Branch mining accident. Even if changes do occur, however, thousands will be faced with pre-existing conditions ranging from nagging chronic injuries to black lung. Even if sweeping reform does occur in mining safety, the job will always carry a certain degree of danger.

Seven

Democracy Lost
Political Corruption and the Impact on Political Involvement

Thomas Paine wrote that government "in its worst state [is] an intolerable one; for when we suffer, or are exposed to the same miseries by a government, which we might expect in a country without government, our calamity is heightened by reflecting that we furnish the means by which suffer."[1] James Madison also wrote: "It is essential in such a government [republic] that it be derived from the great body of the society, not from an inconsiderable proportion or of a favored class of it; otherwise a handful of tyrannical nobles, exercising their oppressions by a delegation of their powers."[2]

Southern West Virginians have too often suffered from tyranny (or at least neglect) at the hands of their own government for generations. While obviously the entirety of West Virginia government is not to blame, the region has suffered far more than its share of exploitation and the loss of benefits considered the norm for American citizens. In extreme cases citizens have suffered misery and violence at the hands of the very people tasked with representing their interests. In fact, the prevalence of political corruption in the state's short history was the sole focus of Allen Loughry's dissertation and subsequent book, *"Don't Buy Another Vote. I Won't Pay for a Landslide": The Sordid and Continuing History of Political Corruption in West Virginia*, from which much information for this portion of the study was obtained.

According to Loughry, "In spite of [the state's] wealth and beauty, the citizens of West Virginia have been subjected to never-ending corruption and money dominance of government that have pervaded the culture of national, state, and locally elected officials."[3] This "money dominance" was highlighted during the 1960 Democratic primary when Senator John F. Kennedy chose West Virginia as a proving ground that a Catholic candidate could win in Protestant country. And he did, by a huge margin.[4] Following his victory, however, many questions were asked as to the methods employed by the young senator from Massachusetts in his Appalachian victory. Aside from massive polling campaigns and skillful politicking,[5] Kennedy spent an amazing amount of money on the campaign and accusations of vote buying abounded.[6] JFK himself joked that he had received a telegram from his father which read: "Don't buy another vote. I won't pay for a landslide."[7]

Although this election brought political corruption in West Virginia into the national spotlight, it had existed for years. The wealth, power, and influence of coal operators, railroads, and other industrialists dominated the political scene in the state during the Industrial Revolution and to some degree continue to do so today. This legacy, combined with a tradition of dominance by elite mountain families and an often apathetic population, have paved the way for corruption and in-fighting that have limited the effectiveness of modernization initiatives, impacted any educational and health care improvements, siphoned much needed funds from state and local coffers, and at times coerced and intimidated its own citizenry.

As a result, many southern West Virginians have "expressed great disillusionment with politics generally and said they had "given up" on politicians and brushed aside any attempt to discuss them seriously," often using the term "crook" to describe them.[8] In the wake of a history of corruption and growing apathy toward the political process, some citizens simply continue to either vote for those with familiar names or just remove themselves from the democratic process completely, figuring their vote would not matter anyway. This chapter will address the history of political corruption, some of the resultant barriers to modernization that have evolved from this legacy, and the continuing atrophy of the individuals' role in the democratic process.

West Virginia's politico-legal problems began early. In 1870, a wave of ex–Confederates won election as part of the broader Redemption movement against Reconstruction, and a constitutional convention soon followed. The new 1872 Constitution highlighted the ideals of its ex–Confederate drafters and resulted in a drastic change to state tax and land policies.⁹ The new regulations "provided a generous delegation of power to private decision makers, but the official machinery for enforcing the regulations governing corporate franchises in the public's interest was dramatic in its absence."¹⁰ It is under this same politico-legal landscape which Henry Gassaway Davis and Stephen B. Elkins were granted a charter which allowed a route from any point on the B & O Railroad on the North Branch of Potomac to any land or mine owned by their company in several counties, including the "right to condemn land or material necessary for the construction of the railroad should it encounter resistance from reluctant landowners."¹¹ This expanded, and one-sided, nature of eminent domain was not practiced by Davis and Elkins alone, to the dismay of many local landowners.¹²

The 1872 Constitution also resulted in the removal of judicial barriers to democratic power. With re-elections required for all Supreme Court and circuit court judges, the state saw all but one (a Democrat) of four justices replaced and all but one of nine circuit court judges replaced by Democrats.¹³ With the changing of land and tax regulations and a more "modern, positivist legal philosophy" coming for the state's highest court, there was an almost immediate shift of legal favor from agrarian to industrialist power bases.¹⁴ Ronald Lewis calls this sea change in position so dramatic "that [the court's] decisions can only be interpreted as the judicial subsidization of industry to the disadvantage of other segments of society."¹⁵ With its earliest existence steeped in a seemingly symbiotic relationship with industry, almost every facet of state and local government has been touched by corruption.

Sheriff Don Chafin and his almost feudal control over Logan County, while perhaps the best known, was not the only case of corruption and abuse of power by law enforcement in southern West Virginia. In 1904, the Mingo County sheriff's election had to be determined by the State Supreme Court. major irregularities included armed men stationed at polling sites, the barring of people from voting, the distribution of whiskey at election centers, and other acts that contributed to a general state of "fraud, trickery, and corruption."¹⁶ During the 1926 election, the Charleston Mayor and several law enforcement officers were arrested on charges of intimidation of election officials.¹⁷ In 1933 the Bluefield *Daily Telegraph* reported intimidation of voters by deputy sheriffs under direction of coal operators in McDowell County.¹⁸ In 1913, Logan County Sheriff Joe Hatfield installed over 200 slot machines to recoup money he had borrowed to win his election.[19]

During the Depression, Logan County's law enforcement problems continued. The Logan (town) chief of police was killed in December of 1930 for trying to shut down gambling parlors and slot machines. In the ensuing investigation it became known that state police officers had supported local authorities in an attempt to keep gambling and speakeasies open. The corruption was so prevalent that Circuit Court Judge Naaman Jackson feared the murderer of the chief of police would be acquitted due to intimidation by the Logan County sheriff's office. Eventually, the West Virginia attorney general brought in a jury from Monroe County and the killer was found guilty. He also took control of the Logan County sheriff's office and dismissed several officers, many of whom were doubling as mine guards. The involvement of the state police in the gambling scandal eventually forced the resignation of the superintendent.[20] Reforms were short-lived, however. In 1932, Senator Mansfield Neely was again investigating cases of intimidation and false arrest in Logan.[21]

Unfortunately this trend of corruption has continued. The Charleston Police Department became embroiled in charges of accepting bribes in order to support illegal activities such as prostitution, gambling, and the running of illegal private clubs.[22] In 1982 the Mingo County sheriff position was sold for $50,000. The impact on law enforcement was obvious; a pot dealer, his wife, and 13 children lived across the street from the police office and even left signs reading "out of pot, be back in 30 minutes."[23] A Delbarton (Mingo County) chief of police demanded a $1,000 bribe from a prisoner and bilked the residents out of $5,600 in phony charity funds while another officer on the force was convicted of bribery.[24] A Mingo deputy sheriff was also found guilty of insurance fraud.[25] Between 1984 and 1991 alone, six sheriffs, eleven deputies, eight police officers, and two county prosecutors were convicted of crimes.[26]

Cases of misuse of power and outright criminal behavior seem to occur too often in southern West Virginia. According to the West Virginia Advisory Committee to the U.S. Commission on Civil Rights, as late as 2004, "incidents of police misconduct continue unabated in West Virginia." Lawsuits and court expenses alone have cost the West Virginia State Police millions over the last decade.[27] Misconduct, abuse of power, and intimidation by law enforcement officials result in two distinct conditions that often build upon one another. First, the history of police corruption, misconduct, intimidation, and violence has turned many local citizens against law enforcement. Fostered from southern West Virginia's history of company town violence and mountain justice, a distrust of law enforcement has led some to deal with slights, petty crimes, and other injustices with extra-legal retaliation, generally causing an escalation of violence among civilians. Secondly, the publicity attached to so many cases of misconduct often overshadows the honorable (and difficult) work the honest and ethical law enforcement officers in the region carry out on a daily basis. The heightened distrust of law enforcement and the use of extra-legal responses to personal slights or injuries only make their job more difficult and dangerous.

Local and state elected officials have also committed more than their share of abuses of power. From the coming of the Industrial Revolution to the area following the Civil War, local elites have practiced a form of power patronage and subtle (usually) coercion in their small spheres of influence. Drawing on land as the source of financial strength, and with backing and direction from absentee industrialists, many prominent local landowners and professionals have improved their own status but often done little to bring true change to the populations they represent.[28] The long and dubious list of offenders includes prosecuting attorneys, treasurers, state legislators, judges, and even governors. While the corruption of law enforcement robbed many citizens of a sense of security and impacted civil liberties on occasion, the problems (while occurring frequently) were specific to isolated incidents or situations. The corruption of elected officials, however, has had a much more pervasive outcome. Through bribes, extortion, embezzlement, and outright greed and lust for power, southern West Virginians have not only lost a significant amount of faith in government itself but have missed out on improvements to infrastructure, education, and other modernizing initiatives due to the misconduct of several politicians.

Some West Virginia governors have been at the forefront of this list. In 1968, former governor W.W. "Wally" Barron was indicted on bribery and conspiracy charges for kickbacks he received while governor from 1961 to 1965. Although acquitted, he was later convicted of jury tampering and sentenced to 20 years by a federal court for conspiracy, bribery, and obstruction of justice. He served four years. Barron's own attorney stated that his client had stolen as much as $7 million from the state during his years of "public service."[29]

When Governor Cecil Underwood's term ended in 2001, taxpayers were again left wondering where money had gone. The Governor's Contingency Fund, which six months earlier contained $22.36 million, had a balance of $22,000 when Underwood left office. Apparently the money did not go to pay the state's bills; the incoming governor was left with a state phone bill of over $5 million. In addition to obvious concerns over embezzlement and misappropriations, Underwood also received criticism for failing to pursue lawsuits against coal companies for over $200 million in unpaid premiums. Coal operators were major contributors to Underwood's campaign.[30]

Perhaps no West Virginia governor epitomizes corruption and "good ole boy" politics more than Arch Moore. Moore, a congressman and three time governor of the state, was implicated in corruption cases for decades prior to his eventual conviction. In 1975 he was indicted for extortion but acquitted. In 1977 Moore signed a settlement with Pittston Coal Company for $1 million which absolved them of further crimes. One week prior, the U.S. Army Corps of Engineers had registered a $3.7 million bill to the company and informed the state it would sue if necessary. Although several witnesses, including Moore in his deposition, claimed the governor knew of the impeding bill, Moore claimed at trial he was unaware.

In 1987, West Virginia was ordered to pay the $3.7 million, plus $10 million in interest.[31] The law finally caught up with Moore in 1990. He pled guilty to mail fraud, extortion, filing false tax returns, and obstruction of justice. He admitted to obtaining the 1984 governorship through use of illegal contributions and bribes. He also extorted $573,000 from a coal operator for a promise to gain refunds from the West Virginia Black Lung Fund. The operator, H. Paul Kizer was expecting a $2.3 million refund, and Moore promised to 'slice through the red tape' for 25 percent. He was sentenced to over 5 years in prison.[32]

Beyond the millions of dollars lost to the state under Moore's watch, many believe he was responsible for allowing coal operators to openly flaunt safety regulations. The most horrific of these instances was the Buffalo Creek Disaster, which occurred February 26, 1972. On that day, a coal refuse bank gave way and flooded the communities below, killing 125, injuring 1,100, and leaving more than 4,000 homeless.[33] While state regulations required that dams of that sort be no higher than 15 feet, the Buffalo Creek Dam was 70 feet high.[34] During the resultant investigation, locals leveled charges of a general lack of safety regarding the dam.[35]

Although Moore denied government knowledge of the lax attention to safety, reports from other officials, including a 1967 letter from former Secretary of Interior Stewart Udall warning of weak coal refuse banks, were presented.[36] Many survivors thought little of Moore's actions following the disaster as well. Aside from being filled with flood waters, one man stated that Moore had "filled our valley with promises."[37]

The list of corrupt lesser officials could, and has, provided enough fodder for a book (based on Loughry's dissertation). The few examples below are provided to demonstrate both the prevalence and variety of corruption in the region:

Officers of the court:

1. Logan County Judge James Grubb was convicted of corruption charges in 1992 for aiding and abetting the payment of a bribe, mail fraud, conspiracy to commit fraud, witness tampering, and racketeering.[38]

2. Logan County Magistrate Danny Wells was charged by the U.S. attorney in 2003 for taking sexual favors, money, and labor in exchange for freeing defendants from jail.[39]

State legislators:

1. State Senator Randy Schoonover accepted bribes from a wrecking service in order to get West Virginia turnpike business. Schooner claimed to be drawn into the scheme by Summersville Mayor Steve LeRose. The LeRose family, a former prominent family in Nicholas County, has been implicated in several questionable activities and will be discussed later.[40]

2. State Senate President Earl Ray Tomblin's family was involved in illegal gambling in the state for years.[41]

3. State Senate President Larry Tucker has been imprisoned twice on charges of extortion, lying to a grand jury, and obstruction of justice.[42]

4. Tucker's replacement, Dan Tonkovich, was found guilty of extortion, attempted extortion and racketeering.[43]

Other state officials:

1. Treasurer A. J. Manchin resigned in order to avoid impeachment. An audit had found $300 million missing from state funds.[44]

2. Treasurer John H. Kelly pled guilty to mail fraud, bribery, and banking violations.[45]

3. Attorney General Charlie Brown resigned for involvement in extortion, illegal fund raising, and paying a secretary $50,000 to have an abortion.[46]

4. Attorney General Donald Robertson pled guilty to federal charges involving bribes to a contractor.[47]

Mayors:

1. The Jefferson mayor (Kanawha County) was charged with 21 counts ranging from tax evasion to embezzlement in 2001.[48]

2. The Summersville mayor (Nicholas County) was found guilty of executing, aiding, and abetting to defraud a financial institution and filing a false income tax return.[49]

The case of Summersville Mayor Steven LeRose bears further discussion for two reasons. First, it receives little treatment in Loughry's work. Secondly, it provides an example corruption in the region as well as demon-

Former State Treasurer A.J. Manchin (seated, with unidentified associates) in a posed photograph, while attempting to demonstrate cooperation, can likewise symbolize the history of political patronage, excess, and abuse which has haunted the region (West Virginia and Regional History Collection, West Virginia University Library).

strates both the public's ambivalent response to corruption and the sense of entitlement that many convicted felon-politicians in the region have felt toward their continued bilking of its citizenry.

The LeRose family was typical of prominent county-level families in the region. One brother, Steven, was the mayor of the Summersville from 1985 to 1999 and one time West Virginia GOP leader. The other, Rodney, was the owner of several car dealerships and involved in several other business ventures. As is too often the case in local politics, the prominent LeRose family took advantage of their position both in the local government and the community. Grand jury evidence indicated that the LeRose brothers frequently used corporate funds to pay for extravagant personal expenses. As the family businesses became less profitable, the LeRose brothers resorted to a check-kiting scheme, involving personal and business checking accounts, in order to keep the businesses afloat.[50] In addition to Steve and Rodney, the remaining brothers, Tim and Mark, were charged with filing false tax returns.[51]

Over $64,000 in insufficient funds fees per year in one of the three banks used in the plan demonstrates the magnitude of the scheme. Unaware of the scope of the scheme and relying on the family name, the chief executive officer of the bank did not press the LeRoses over their irregular banking practices. The kiting scheme was eventually uncovered by accident when an employee from another bank involved in the scheme incorrectly coded a LeRose check, which led to an internal review. This bank, United National Bank, and Bank One returned checks written on other LeRose accounts, primarily accounts at First Community, therefore protecting them from loss. In the end, First Community suffered a loss of $3,364,958.[52]

The troubles began for the LeRose family when the Evergreen Federal Savings bank, of which Steven was the president, failed in 1991. LeRose and other bank officers had loaned themselves (at interest rates lower than public levels) over $2.2 million for other businesses ventures. The failure of the bank cost taxpayers $2.6 million. Additionally, by 1998 Ford Motor Company and Chrysler were pursing the family for almost $5 million from revenue from car sales made by LeRose dealerships. The family filed for bankruptcy and sold off various possessions, including 4 homes, several dealership lots, and 24 tracts of land.[53] In 1999 the family's financial woes were compounded by legal ones. Eventually, Tim and Mark LeRose were fined $5,000 for filing false tax reports. Rodney was sentenced to 12 months and 1 day, the one day so he could spend his sentence in minimum security state facility instead of a county jail. Steven's final sentence was set by a court of appeals at 2 years and 3 months in August of 2000.[54]

The LeRose family typifies the corruption discussed in detail in Loughry's work. What is perhaps more fascinating than the amount of corruption is the degree to which it has become if not tolerated at least expected. Only days before LeRose pled guilty to federal charges and amid a storm of controversy, he received 26 percent of the vote and came in second in his bid for re-election as mayor of Summersville.[55] Even public figures had no problems defending the family; a former city councilman called the LeRoses "good boys, even though they went wrong."[56] Such public sentiment has emboldened other convicted felons to attempt to regain their former positions of power.

Former Senate President Larry Tucker and Mayor Steven LeRose both have run for office (Tucker for Nicholas County commission and LeRose for mayor) following their release from prison.[57] Comments posted by residents on a blog related to LeRose's mayoral bid, while enlightening, highlight fundamental problems in the region's political process. Although several commented on not only the ethical, but legal, ramifications of having a convicted felon hold a public office, others were much more sympathetic:

- "Steve has done his time. Let's give him a chance and focus on all the good that he did for our community."
- "Steve has always expressed love, hope and concern for the people of Summersville. The world is better because he is here. He was convicted of a crime, did his time and is ready to get back to what he does well — serving us as mayor. He has always been competent in this capacity and that's what the election is about."
- "And I think you'll see that the citizens will say it's okay as well. Everyone has to admit that Summersville would not be what it is if it weren't for Steve LeRose. Yes, he's a convicted felon, and yes, he did his punishment. As a person, many people may not like Steve (I'm still up in the air on this), but as a mayor I think he's the only practical choice. He knows the job, does the job, and does it well. Something that I personally respect about Steve is that although he had criminal troubles in his personal life, he NEVER dragged his position of mayor nor did he include the

city in his criminal endeavors, unlike our neighbor city of Richwood."[58]

LeRose did not win his bid for election, nor did Tucker. The level of support garnered for these men, however, highlight the willingness of many citizens to forgive political and criminal transgressions and rely on the power of a family name when election time comes. In addition to misconduct of officials while in office, the election process itself in southern West Virginia has been plagued with fraud, intimidation, violence, bribery, and other irregularities. Just as police misconduct has damaged civil rights perceptions and political scandals have squandered resources and negatively impacted peoples' faith in government, the questionable history of elections has further damaged residents' trust in the democratic process.

Election scandals have occurred for generations in the region. Elections have been wrought with bribery, extortion, intimidation, vote-buying, and outright violence. In 1926, the Bluefield *Daily Telegraph* wrote, "The spectacle of petty violations of election laws, and corrupt practices have always been before us, and yet nothing is ever done about it."[59] During the 1926 election Representative J. Alfred Taylor complained that "votes were openly trafficked at the rate of $5 apiece and that intimidation was rampant."[60]

By the 1920s, vote buying was an entrenched practice in the region. According to David Walls and John Stephenson in *Appalachia in the Sixties: Decade of Reawakening*, "As early as the 1940s, elder statesmen of both parties conceded that votes had been bought in their state for as long as they could remember."[61] If votes could not be bought, they were sometimes fabricated. At one point in Mingo County the number of registered voters was higher than the number of eligible citizens.[62] Logan County elections were just as bad in 1960. According to *Life* magazine, "anything from $2 to $5 buys a vote on election day, and sometimes they are delivered in wholesale lots. Moonshine is still used as a payment for a vote, but it is now a risky business."[63] Despite the Logan *Banner*'s editor calling the 1960 primary the worst in his experience, the Charleston *Gazette* called it the most honest election ever held in Logan County. The *Gazette* qualified its comment by stating, "This is not to say that there were no votes bought with money or whiskey."[64] Regardless of the editorial opinions, both papers provided an indication of the level of corruption inherent in the political process. Even more troubling, a local judge said he was "encouraged by the conviction that with crooks operating on both sides, the honest voters ... really decide the elections."[65]

It was under this blanket of excepted corruption the Kennedy campaign entered into the 1960 primaries. Many believed the huge victory realized by JFK was due to political factions, selective slating,[66] bribes and organized crime.[67] According to Loughry, at typical vote would be bought in the following manner: (1) voters willing to sell their vote would ask an election commissioner for assistance, (2) the election commissioners would "assist" by casting a ballot in favor of a specific political slate, and finally, (3) the commissioner would then signal an outside organization to make payment for the vote.[68] Vote buying or not, a local Democrat said, "The biggest thing that turned West Virginia for Kennedy was U.S. currency, at least in Boone County."[69] Another editorial claimed that Kennedy spent at least $50,000 in McDowell County alone and that it "would have been a very close race" but Kennedy "wasn't taking any more chances ... he took the rubber band off the bankroll. Or maybe it was Pappa's."[70] Elections often went beyond simple vote buying, however, often involving intimidation and violence.

One former "Appalachian boss," Raymond Chafin, described pre–1960s politics as "fist-and-skull back then. If you didn't go out there and risk getting shot or killed, you didn't work an election at all." Facts backed up Chafin's claim. In 1925 citizens in Mingo County were shot at while trying to vote.[71] The 1927 Charleston mayoral election was also noted for several "certain disorders and acts of intimidation." These "irregularities" included the shooting of a Republican election commissioner, the threatening of a Democratic official at gunpoint, the assault of Democrat attorney W.E.R. Byrne, and the shooting of an election worker. A court ruled that these actions had no impact on the voting in the precinct in which they occurred.[72] By the 1930, election violations were growing so prevalent that a Republican newspaper in Logan "exposed and tried to correct some of the rottenness and corruption" of their own party.[73] In 1933 charges of fraud and conspiracy were brought against A.G. Rutherford for incidents occurring during the state senate election. Claims included placing armed men outside of polling places, the removal of ballots, changing voting areas, and general intimidation of voters.[74] Even as late as 1968, voters in Lincoln County were ordered by armed men to vote for certain candidates.[75]

Concerns over coal power influence have even reached the highest court in the state. The most recent example was the *Caperton v. Massey* case. In August of 2002, a Boone County court ruled in favor of Hugh M. Caperton in a case involving unsavory business acts by A.T. Massey, which resulted in the closing of Caperton's Harman Mining Company. The court found that Massey had acted out of "fraudulent misrepresentation, concealment, and tortuous interference with existing contractual relations" and awarded Caperton $50 million. Massey filed post trial motions against the decision. In 2004, the motions were denied and the court additionally found that Massey "intentionally acted in utter disregard of [Caperton's] rights and ultimately destroyed [Capterton's] business."[76]

Massey, namely through CEO Don Blankenship, continued to work to have the decision overturned. Blankenship's beliefs on the judicial process became quite obvious during a court case involving the death of two men during a fire at a Massey mine in January 2006. The Massey CEO stated that "in the West Virginia court system, you have to measure the potential outcomes and make a settlement based on business rather than fairness."[77] Blankenship acted upon this business over fairness mantra in order to stack the judicial cards in his favor at the first opportunity. As West Virginia, along with 38 other states,[78] elects state Supreme Court justices, Blankenship focused his efforts on replacing sitting Justice McGraw with Brent Benjamin. Blankenship donated $1,000 directly to Benjamin's campaign, then donated $2.5 million to the "And for the Sake of the Kids" organization which opposed McGraw and supported Benjamin, and spent an additional $500,000 on expenditures such as letters and television and newspaper ads. Benjamin won the election by a slim margin.[79]

Trouble arose when Justice Benjamin provided the deciding vote in a 3–2 reversal of the Boone County court decision. Even more alarming, photos of another justice, Maynard, vacationing with Blankenship on the French Riviera, also surfaced. The dissenting opinion highlighted these concerns; Justice Starcher, who had pled for Benjamin to recuse himself, stated the majority's opinion was "morally and legally wrong."[80] Starcher further raised concern that "Blankenship's bestowal of his personal wealth, political tactics and 'friendship' [had] created a cancer in the affairs of the court."[81]

Eventually, the case was heard before the U.S. Supreme Court, which found that "Blankenship's campaign efforts had a significant and disproportionate influence in place justice Benjamin in the case," and it was returned to the West Virginia Supreme Court of Appeals.[82] Once back in West Virginia courts, however, it was coal politics as usual. The case was again overturned in favor of Massey in a decision which dissenting Justice Workman wrote "turned West Virginia jurisprudence on its ear."[83] A case such as this, taken from the 21st century legislative and political landscape of southern West Virginia, shows that the political might of coal power is much more than a lingering memory.

In preventing citizens from even conducting fair elections, corrupt officials and politicians took a third component of constitutional rights away from the citizens of southern West Virginia. Misconduct, intimidation, and corruption by some law enforcement officials took away many citizens' sense of security and damaged an already fragile relationship between law enforcement and the average citizen. This relationship, strained by years of coal company influence and coercion, mixed with strong feeling of individual freedoms and private reciprocity, worked to alienate law enforcement from the public in some cases. Finally, many elected officials further weakened the citizenry's connection with government by committing abuses of office that robbed the region of valuable resources, limited true political power to a small group of unscrupulous elites, and embittered many residents who came to see politicians as crooks and not representatives of community needs and concerns. The state's history of corruption and the over-involvement of government in the economy have created a situation where "the political allocation of resources is problematic. When the government is heavily involved in activities that provide favors to some at the expense of others, people will be encouraged to divert resources away from productive private-sector activities and toward lobbying, campaign contributions, and other forms of political favor-seeking."[84]

Even for those that kept faith in ethical politicians (they did, and do, exist), there was no guarantee such people would receive a fair opportunity at election due to rampant vote buying, ballot tampering, and outright intimidation. In its inability to provide security, a truly representative government, or fair elections, the political process in southern West Virginia for almost a century has failed its people. As James Madison warned: "In framing a government which is to be administered by men over men, the great difficulty lies in this: you must first enable the government to control the governed; and in the next place oblige it to control itself."[85]

Unfortunately, many southern West Virginia politicians felt 'obliged' to almost everything except self-control. The crooks alone cannot be blamed, however. As Loughry argues, a nonchalant attitude toward government in southern West Virginia "demonstrates that this was simply a way of life for politicians throughout various communities." Loughry also put forth an explanation of such widespread corruption:

> Corruption in the West Virginia political arena originates in part from the societal attitudes toward [the] formal political process. Moreover, governmental attributes that encourage corruption in the state include wide authority of the elected officials along with minimal accountability [or] corruption for corrupt activities. Societal attitudes fostering such corruption include compliance to personal gain over the rule of law, while it is also true that political corruption has persisted as a way for members of poverty-stricken social groups to ascend the social ladder.[86]

Although Loughry mentions several factors enabling government corruption, root causes lie in: (1) a tradition for individualism and reciprocity that existed in the region prior to the Industrial Revolution and was reinforced by the lack of, weak, or corrupt law enforcement in early company towns, (2) the influx of outside industrialist capital into the capital-starved region following the Civil War which allowed outside interests to obtain disproportional influence in local politics, (3) the failure of subsistence farming and weak local economies based on coal and lumber industries, which created widespread poverty and made cash even more important, and (4) the combination of outside influence on the political process, weak law enforcement, and a sense of helplessness attached to poverty that in turn fostered an ambivalence toward political corruption.

This ambivalence has been extremely detrimental to the region's development. In some cases, people have simply given up and removed themselves from the process altogether, refusing to vote because "regardless for whom they vote, candidates do not really care about their concerns."[87] Aside from the impact on the democratic process, untold damage has been done to state infrastructure, including education, healthcare, and development, due to the loss of millions of dollars in not only cash but other resources as well. Loughry ably sums up this intangible loss when discussing the abuse of position (and trust) committed by former State Treasurer A.J. Manchin: "While school budgets do not allow some children to go on educational field trips, thousands of tax dollars were available for chartered flights, awards, certificates, key chains, and magnets. Just as coal companies kept the miners isolated out of greed, this state treasurer because of his improper and illegal use of state money kept a generation of West Virginia children less educated, less advantaged, and less prepared for the world they were about to enter."[88] In the end, too many government officials have worked to shift "resources away from production and toward plunder."[89]

Eight

Culture, Identity, and Modernization

As a result of my military duties, my oldest daughter has lived in many different regions of the country. I choose her for this brief discussion because unlike other family members (and myself), she has been more completely socialized into the areas we have lived through the influence of schools and other children. She has lived in southern California, South Carolina, upstate New York, and the Pacific Northwest. After our last visit to southern West Virginia, she informed me it was like visiting a different country. Obviously this was not an academic, or even necessarily a negative, assessment. Her statement did, however, remind me of Jack Weller's experience in *Yesterday's People*: "The people and I seemed to be living on two different levels of thinking, and at only a few places did we meet and understand one another. We spoke the same language, but we did not communicate."[1] My daughter felt this difference. By this I mean a difference to her middle class collective experiences of the San Diego area, Upstate New York (Saratoga Springs), Corvallis (home of Oregon State University), the Puget Sound Region, and Charleston, South Carolina.

On the positive side, she noticed how everyone waved at one another when they met on the one lane roads prevalent in the area. She also noticed a general sense of courtesy toward one another. She and her sister obviously enjoyed the swim in a large pond at a relative's house. She also enjoyed the visits to my paternal grandmother's home, where my father also lives. "It is quiet and peaceful and everyone seems really nice," she told me. (Grandma Bonnie's homemade biscuits didn't hurt either.)

Some things she viewed in a less positive light. She discussed a general lack of planning for the future from many of the people her age when she spoke to them; particularly disturbing to her was one teenager who had already set his lifelong goal as working in the dangerous, decaying, and unpredictable coal mining industry.

Other observations, while more ambivalent, speak to the legacy of enduring images about the region. My daughter saw a few run-down homes, their yards overrun with weeds and filled with junked cars. The house across from her aunt's provided a constant stereotypical monolith throughout our stay; siding was missing, a broken-down and rusted-out car sat in the yard, and the steps were falling apart due to decay. In addition to the visual images, she overheard many people talk about how bad drugs were in the area. Similar discussions take place throughout the region.[2] Along with the drug problem had come a rash of car break-ins in Nicholas County. As a message to would-be thieves, a group of men used an old car for target practice, towed the car to the corner of the main intersection in Summersville and attached a sign: *This is what happens to people who break into cars.*

A trip to the nearby Braxton County Fair elicited even more questions. The Confederate battle flag was ubiquitous; it was on T-shirts, class rings, hats, and blankets, and several participants in the mud races (the draw of the fair) displayed large flags from their trucks. "West Virginia didn't fight for the South, did it?" asked my daughter. I replied that West Virginia, while it was created due to the residents' desire to remain with the Union, did have a large number of people from its southern counties, including Stonewall Jackson, choose to stay with Virginia and fight for the Confederacy. "And besides," I told her, "it's a cultural thing."

This personal story is provided to demonstrate how perceptions are generated. The previous story, taken at face value, reinforces many of the stereotypes about the region. To many people, dual visions of beauty and destruction, kindness and depravity, natural intelligence and colossal ignorance exist side by side in the region. Many outsiders perceive residents to "appear to be poor, lazy, isolated, violent, illiterate, and hard-drinking but perhaps also as having common sense, the spirit of individualism, a strong sense of loyalty, and a deep knowledge of their environment."[3] The goal of this chapter is to look beyond the outer layer of perception and stereotyping and explore what makes things such as the Confederate battle flag being flown proudly in a state that was formed out of a desire to remain with the Union "a cultural thing."

This chapter will endeavor to present how an Appalachian culture has evolved due to both internal and external forces to create an identity, or set of identities, prevalent in southern West Virginia. This meshing of culture and identity, for good and bad, impacts contemporary issues such as education, employment and welfare programs, health and dental care, crime, infrastructure development, environmental issues, political involvement, and the future for the region beyond coal.

What is culture? How is a culture developed? What role does culture play in a society? All of these questions have been answered and debated in volumes of works related to the social sciences. For the purpose of this work, rehashing these debates will not be necessary. The common knowledge understanding of culture, bounded by the area of southern West Virginia, will suffice. How a culture is developed as well as the role it plays in society, however, is vital to explaining contemporary problems in the region. By examining how this culture developed, through the eyes of both the residents and outsiders, one can establish how identities related to this culture are formed. These identities, and the perceived roles within these identities, create the foundation for discussing how the region's past still plays a significant role in contemporary problems.

Appalachian, and more specifically southern West Virginian culture, developed over generations and has been profoundly influenced by several key formative elements. These factors helped to shape residents' perceptions of their place in the family and society. The prevalence of subsistence farming from the earliest settlement of the region established the fundamental elements of mountain society, which included individualism, justice based on reciprocity, and a barter-trade system, all of which were bounded by control of small areas ruled by family patriarchs. The Industrial Revolution and growth of company towns forever altered the landscape. Wealthy, capital-rich industrialists worked through, and often usurped, the authority of local elites. At the same time, massive demographic and societal changes were underway as people flocked to the towns not only from the mountains but from the Deep South and Europe.

Out of the chaotic early days of company towns rose problems related to political corruption and disenfranchisement. These problems were only exacerbated as subsistence farming became even less profitable and the economy was weakened by dependence on mineral and resource extraction, the profits of which usually went out of state. When the Great Depression struck the nation, these weaknesses collapsed into a devastating poverty that for some have lingered down through the generations.

Subsistence farming provided much more than an economy for the region prior to the 20th century; it involved "a total system of social relationships and values."[4] Subsistence farming was a difficult task, one that involved the efforts of all family members. This reality was obvious even prior to the Civil War, when one author wrote, "The people are miserably poor among these wild hills and the small snatches of soil they cultivate ... are hardly enough to cultivate the necessities of life."[5]

This need for family support translated into strong kinship bonds. These bonds were further strengthened by patriarchal inheritance practices which helped maintain strong family relationships even as division of land increased the difficulty of agriculture. An important aspect of these close bonds was familial responsibility. The practice of inheritance, combined with kinship bonds, tied families and therefore individuals to the land in ways difficult for many middle class Americans to understand. Kinship bonds and the influence of extended family have historically played important roles in mountain society. Such groups worked to provide and enforce social control and moral codes, provide emotional support, and create a web of mutual assistance within extended families.[6] In many cases, this bond is not to Appalachia, or even West Virginia, but to the "holler" or "hill" upon which one's ancestors lived.[7] This particular bond was noted as "peculiar" as early as 1929 when Millard Peck wrote that the "people are bound by ties of sentiment and tradition to a region which for generations has been their ancestral home."[8]

Several authors have discussed the power of these kinship bonds. Sociologist Marion Pearsall wrote that for the mountaineer, "the family is the center of the individual's universe. To a remarkable degree, it is his universe."[9] Betty Crickard spoke of the mountaineers' love of home and family as well.[10] Janet Welch noted the "whole-hearted devotion and affection" the region received from its citizens, a fact which to her made "little sense in view of the Little Mountain State's economic woes."[11] A small survey completed by 11th grade students in Nicholas County elicited similar conclusions. Several students stated they would not leave the area because "that's where my family is."[12]

Weller found further fault in mountain kinship bonds, calling family "not so much a mutually supporting group, as it is a group in which each member demands support from the others."[13] Weller further blamed this form of familial dependency for several perceived short-comings of mountaineer character: "Because the mountaineer's security is dependent upon his relationships with those in his family and reference group, he must always rely on someone else. His security is not based within himself, on his own abilities and talents. Thus he can never be sure of himself as a person in his own right."[14]

Weller's analysis, while placing too much weight on the role of kinship in determining individualism and self-reliance, does illustrate that it is an important element. Many authors, while focusing on the explanation of how kinship bonds hinder southern West Virginians, have failed to mention the benefits of such a supportive structure. It has been an important factor in the survival of small farms and the family itself, especially during the Great Depression.

This support network of extended family is evident today. Sari Tudiver provided an excellent example of the positive aspects of Appalachian kinship bonds in her dissertation:

> Martha Rudd, a widow in her early 70s, did not answer the phone over a several hour period and no one could determine where she was, someone was dispatched to her house where she was found seriously ill. Her nephew drove her to the hospital ... and notified her children in Ohio. While she was away, her garden and flowers, chickens and dog were attended by her brother-in-law ... her brother, and several other neighbors and kin. When she returned home, many people brought her food until she recovered.[15]

This family support, however, if not tempered with personal motivation to improve one's condition, can lead to the creation of a family structure that supports poverty instead of creating a safety net against it. It is this pitfall that Welch alluded to when she warned that "love of place sometimes keeps us in places where there is no hope of creating decent lives."[16]

Another facet of subsistence farming was the emergence of self-sufficiency. By providing the majority of their foodstuffs themselves, with hopefully enough to sell or trade for a few other necessities, early subsistence farmers were beholden to few. Out of this self-sufficiency grew strong feelings in relation to personal freedoms and individualism (within the kinship structure). This sense of personal freedom was challenged by the coming of the company towns. Coal and lumber towns brought with them forces which worked to weaken the dominance of patriarchal control, marginalized the barter-trade system with an influx of capital and capitalistic ideas, and eroded mountaineer self-sufficiency, in some cases replacing it with dependence on the new supportive mechanisms in the region — coal, railroad, and lumber industries.

Independence and self-sufficiency have proven to be both societal virtues and vices, depending on how they evolve and are utilized within a community or society. In southern West Virginia, these traits, as well as how they are envisioned, interpreted, and acted upon, are but two of the cases in which secondary and tertiary outcomes result. According to Welch, "Appalachia is a mind-boggling paradox and its entire history up to and including present day is overwhelmingly ironical."[17] The development of mountaineer self-sufficiency and individualism is no different.

Relative isolation from the greater society and economy of Virginia (and therefore the United States) from colonial days until the end of the 19th century created a necessity of survival-driven reliance on self and family that came with subsistence farming. At least initially, the traditional independence of Scots-Irish settlers and the environment itself played a role in the development of individualism and self-sufficiency in the region.[18] The ethnic labeling of Scots-Irish of the Old Country or American Highlanders, however, provides only a small portion of the basis for a discussion of present-day southern West Virginians, other than it provided a homogenous foundation for evolving cultural norms.

Billings and Blee noted a "sense of personal independence and resentment of being bossed," while Marion Pearsall described Appalachian men as "easily angered at real and fanciful attacks on their freedom to come and go, work or not, as they please."[19] Weller provided even more damaging commentary, stating the mountaineers had rebelled against "a form of government that imposed its rule from the top" and that "these people reverted to system of private justice based on the personal relationships to the clan."[20] Weller further stated that in denouncing government, and therefore American middle class society's norms, mountaineers allowed "no hierarchy, authorities, or experts ... to form in this society; no pressure from outside was allowed to gain entrance."[21] While Weller again overstates his argument, it demonstrates what he witnessed in the southern West Virginia hills mid–20th century. His second comment also weakens his first in that, particularly by the 1950s and 1960s, pressures — and indeed people and ideas — had gained entrance to the region. Weller failed to realize was that what he was seeing was also an internal struggle between traditional culture that had developed over generations and the growing pressure of greater American culture and norms on the region.

Individualism still remains strong in the region. This can be seen in many forms. A myriad of independent churches have sprung up as denominations splintered over religious concepts, doctrine, and methodology. Welch saw this individualism act as a barrier to community bonding. As the focus was on self and kinship, this left little care for the community and therefore people "kept to their own business."[22] And they expected people to leave them to their business as well. Individualism is also supported by strong feelings of personal liberty in relation to not only the individual but the land. For many, the right to hunt, fish, and make use of the land overrides government regulations and laws. Occasionally, the combination of very intense perspectives on personal liberties and a distrust of the legal system have led some to conduct extra-legal activities when slighted.

An excellent example of both the fierce stance on personal rights and mountain justice was retold by a resident of Nicholas County interviewed for this project. The interviewee and his father (a retired miner) were visiting a friend (a farmer and retired miner himself). These visits were a Sunday tradition on this particular hill. While the women were at church on Sunday, the men would visit each other and talk about hunting, the mining downturn (it was the mid–1980s), farming, or the weather, and share a few drinks.

On this occasion the men were outside leaning on the hood of a truck discussing one of the usual topics. During the visit, a green Jeep Cherokee drove past the farmer's house on the small dirt road. In this region, a green Jeep Cherokee meant one thing — the game warden. Most people in the region believed the game warden carried more authority than local police officers and as such, the game warden passing by one's house was usually cause to call neighbors and let them know the "law was on the hill."

As the Jeep drove past, the farmer ended his conversation and walked into his house, shortly exiting again with a rifle in hand. The interviewees' father asked the farmer what he was doing and the man replied that he was planning to shoot the game warden. Luckily, the farmer was calmed and disarmed by his visitors. It turns out the game warden had previously caught the man killing a deer out of season on the farmer's own large tract of land. The farmer had killed the deer on private property but was loading the animal into his truck on a county road. The game warden confiscated the deer and the man's rifle, and assessed a fine. The farmer acquiesced but warned the game warden the confiscations and fine "wasn't right" because he had taken the deer on his own property and therefore the deer was his to do with as he pleased. Later, when the game warden drove past the man's farm, he saw it as the last act of encroachment on his 'rights' that he could tolerate.

The man was well known in the mountain community and, besides a tendency to drink a little too much homemade wine, was well liked. Virtually every male youth in the area had worked for him putting up hay. Both the man and family were polite, he paid extremely well, and his wife always brought sandwiches and homemade milkshakes to the teenagers working for him in his fields.[23] On this day something was different, however. This transition from the neighborly farmer to an armed man looking to do violence was initiated by what he felt was the game warden's (and by proxy the government's) invasion of his right to do as he pleased on his land.

Self-sufficiency had downsides as well. While families could sustain themselves through farming and help from kinship groups, few gained the necessary resources to advance beyond the subsistence level. Some argue this egalitarian nature has resulted in a condition under which there is an aversion to not only the accumulation of excess resources but also taking leadership roles within the community.[24]

Weller argued a major factor in this unwillingness to lead is a sense of apprehension about the unknown and a fatalism that "pervades his [the mountaineers'] whole life."[25] While other authors have spoken to aspects of fatalism in the culture, recent scholarship has found fatalism to be varying and rarely projected to the future of one's children.[26] What has continued to demonstrate viability is a tendency to avoid leadership roles. Welch found in a survey of 100 southern West Virginians that not one respondent envisioned themselves as leaders.[27] According to Billings and Blee, this generated a "good enough for grampa" mentality that stifled individual growth and family advancement. Under this paradigm, "life was geared to self-sufficient survival with no special emphasis on the acquisitions of material possessions as status symbols and even labor saving devices."[28] The Rural Appalachian Youth and Families Consortium also believed the "Appalachian culture of subsistence" made it difficult for the region's youth to move beyond their heritage, only perpetuating the problem.[29]

Heritage is obviously a poorly chosen word. It is entirely possible for a mountain heritage to exist and thrive in coexistence with modern ideas. The "good enough for grampa" mentality, however, when combined with the acceptance of social welfare as a way of life, can be a key determinant in the creation of the culture of poverty and resultant generational trend of poverty for some families in the region. It is this very culture of poverty theory, promoted by those who choose to take from the community rather than contribute to it, that helps to portray "the mountaineers' culture, mores, and value system as antiquated and inferior."[30]

Although subsistence farming did much to mold key elements of early regional culture and society, the coming of the Industrial Revolution both directly and indirectly challenged many of those norms. Huge demographic changes altered the mostly Scots-Irish homogeneity of the region, at least for a while. These immigrants and many local farmers moved into the rapidly growing company towns. The towns in turn posed the real challenge to the patriarchal, land-owning power base that existed.

Southern West Virginia was undoubtedly a different place after the Industrial Revolution came, not only environmentally, but socially and culturally. This does not mean, however, that the old ways were extinguished. As is often the case when two cultures come into contact, the

A tuberculosis victim and her children during the Great Depression. Images such as these not only revealed the challenges of public health in the region, but helped to generate enduring stereotypes (Library of Congress).

weaker is not completely destroyed but adapts to meet the challenges of the more dominant culture; such was the case with southern West Virginia.[31] Residents in varying degrees accepted, challenged, or adapted the new concepts into their everyday lives and indeed their culture. What remained, even with influence from mainstream, capitalist America, was a distinctly Appalachian culture in a similar manner that modern Native Americans, blacks, Latinos, and other groups still maintain a proud, vibrant, and positive cultural distinction within a greater national cultural construct. Some scholars have even spoken of an Appalachian nationalism which has grown out of a defense of mountain culture and identity.[32]

Company towns offered cash economies and capitalist ideals which challenged the subsistence living, barter-trade economy that previously existed. These towns provided opportunities previously non-existent in the region but also brought mechanisms which fostered political corruption, coercion, and intimidation. For those living in or affected by these negative influences, self-sufficiency was replaced with a dependency on cash and the company for a livelihood. By the time of the Great Depression many mountaineers found themselves not strong, independent farmers making a hard living from a difficult land but unemployed, hungry former laborers for mining companies with little or no control over their paychecks, their government, or their future.

The impact of subsistence farming and the subsequent arrival of big industry have been discussed in detail in earlier chapters. Taking this foundation of knowledge, one can begin to develop a model of the current Appalachian culture and how it exists in southern West Virginia. First, it must be stated that not everyone fits a model; residents of this region will fall well outside descriptions set forth, but most people in the region should be aware of how these cultural factors affect southern West Virginian society. Secondly, this model is drawn from the work of several scholars — Dwight Billings, Kathleen M. Blee, Janet Welch, and to a lesser degree Jack Weller.[33] Key elements of this contemporary cultural model include traditionalism, individualism, family-centered focus, lukewarm faith in political processes and government, and a collective concern for how modernity fits into the people's own Appalachian or mountain culture.

The traditionalism prevalent in the region today does not involve a strong bond to Scots-Irish or Highlander traditions. It does not even necessarily involve a strong desire to maintain generations-old family customs. Traditionalism, as it applies in this case, refers to a desire to retain lifestyles and societal aspects that many feel are being adversely impacted by greater American society. According to Weller, this regressive outlook is in contrast to middle class America's progressive outlook; for the mountaineer "does not look forward to tomorrow with pleasant anticipation ... but backward to a yesterday which was remembered, perhaps nostalgically."[34] Welch's study found this traditionalism to be less based on tomorrow than out of a disgust with and fear of the present.[35] For those subscribing to this type of traditionalism, modernity comes with a price they are not willing to pay. This price includes increased crime, an attack on fundamental religious doctrines, increased pressure to modify gender roles to meet contemporary conditions, and a subsequent breakdown of kinship and familial bonds.[36]

Just as outsiders form perspectives of Appalachia, Appalachians form perspectives of the outside world. Through the television many see images of "crime ridden urban settings" which they fear and "sophisticated lifestyles" in which they have no inclination partake.[37] Despite their wishes, some unseemly aspects of the outside world have made their way into the mountains. As residents and law enforcement officials alike realize an increase in crime, most blame the rising crime rates on increasing cases of drug abuse and addiction. In addition, the production, trafficking, and abuse of methamphetamines has become a major problem in the region. Again, geography and economic vulnerability have not been kind to the region; William Garriott III argued in his dissertation on meth abuse in rural areas that "West Virginia's rural character, its poverty and its proximity to major metropolitan areas and drug trafficking routes, made it fertile ground for methamphetamine."[38]

Between 2003 and 2005 alone meth lab discoveries tripled in West Virginia.[39] In fact, a candidate for prosecuting attorney in one county stated drug related crimes were the biggest problem facing the rural county: "Without a doubt, drugs continue to the biggest threat ... the number one contributing factor to crime in the county is drugs. Most crimes are a direct result of drug abuse, i.e. stealing to get money for drugs, forging checks to get money for drugs, or domestic assault with underlying drug/alcohol abuse."[40]

The string of car break-ins in Summersville is only one of many such examples. When addicts run out of money, they turn to theft. One man was arrested for stealing the entire contents of one home to exchange for meth. Everything was taken — the washer, the dryer, the coffee maker. The tractor was also stolen to help the thief haul his loot.[41] With drug use driving significant public health and societal problems, many traditionalists have good ammunition from which to make their arguments.

Other traditionalists fear an erosion of religious piety which they believe comes with modernization. Although fundamentalism was not as prevalent as she expected, Welch interviewed several residents which she noted as having fundamentalist ideals, and at least 10 percent believed the Biblical apocalypse was near.[42] Fundamentalists aside, religion plays at least a nominal role in many families and a primary role in some.[43] This is especially true due to strong kinship bonds where religious views of patriarchs and matriarchs can influence several nuclear families within the group.

Another aspect of traditionalism is the impact of a socio-economic makeup that has challenged long-standing gender roles. In the region, men have historically entered the work force at a younger age than women. During the early years of coal mining education mattered little and as a result it was not uncommon for women to receive a higher level of education than men. As the mines became more automated and mining jobs were replaced by service industry and retail positions, however, basic education became more important.

As a result of the changing economic climate, namely the growth of the retail and service sector, many women have found themselves better suited for employment than their brothers, fathers, and husbands. In 2006, Kristin Mallory determined that graduates from West Virginia community colleges were two times as likely to be female.[44] At the same time (2005), however, West Virginia ranked dead last (including the District of Columbia) in terms of the percentage of women with four-year degrees.[45] Likewise, increased technical education has not often resulted in promotion, as West Virginia ranks 49th in terms of white women employed in managerial or professional jobs. Black women fared slightly better, coming in 44th.[46] In addition to limitations on advancement, women continue to face disparity in pay. In 2002, an income gap of almost $10,000 a year still existed between men and women in West Virginia.[47]

While women began to take limited advantage of their education, many men came to realize "that the education [he] never got (or wanted) is the very thing that the society holds up to him as necessary."[48] For many families the role reversal of primary bread winners has been troubling, not only to men but to women, as both sexes tend to have strong feelings toward traditional gender roles. These gender roles, developed by the division of labor involved in subsistence farming, were further stratified by the influx of mining and lumber operations. As men became more physically separated from their wives, by forests and miles of earth, gender roles became even more stratified, with women belonging to the house and the children while men belonged to the "outside" world. Research by Judith Fiene found that in addition to men, women generally preferred traditional roles.[49] Several women interviewed by Welch also stated they would not vote for a woman because politics was "a man's place."[50]

Under this type of traditional perspective, people have access to the outside world but some chose to retreat from it instead.[51] Weller believed one reason for this trepidation to be that many mountaineers took issue with outside organizations, whether they be government, business, or other entities, when they could not act in the same personal, individually specific manner as people within their family/kinship group or community.[52] Subsequent concerns over outside influences have sometimes worked to stifle the influx of business and therefore jobs. One prominent member of Nicholas County believes the struggling town of Richwood turned down recent offers for a regional prison and a brewery due at least partly to concerns over their impact on personal security and traditional moral issues.[53]

Individualism, while snugly bound to personal rights, paradoxically allows for the primacy of the family as well. Weller saw a society where, for adults, the focus was "almost entirely family based, including the immediate family, cousins, and uncles, with a few close relatives."[54] Young adults who pursue education and are forced to out-migrate for employment represent a deterioration of the familial bonds. While many southern West Virginians have strong desires for their children to receive a quality education, others see "too much" education as divisive force on the family. Welch also believed that "too much" success can place one outside their reference group.[55] In fact, many first generation college students face a "cultural margin between their family and the college community."[56]

Some scholars have also discussed fatalism as an aspect of Appalachian culture. Weller found that youths had "few relative hopes or ambitions and were seldom able to articulate goals, or even [were] reluctant to talk about the future."[57] Two decades later, Welch reported that evidence of fatalism still existed.[58] Welch, however, considered mountaineer fatalism to be "ambivalent" and concluded that one could argue it was as much realism as fatalism.[59] In 1997, Robert Bickel and Meghan McDonough studied this realism as an influence on reckless activities of adolescents.

They found that in many cases, adolescent behavior, in terms such as high school graduation and teen pregnancy, are seated in realistically based self-evaluations of their positions in their homes, communities, and the greater regional economy.[60] Although not extensive enough for definitive data, a survey of Nicholas County 11th graders showed little fatalism in terms of their future. Close to half of the 30 students surveyed had definite future educational and career goals in mind, particularly in the health and medical fields.[61] A major contributor to this prevalence of medical/health careers is no doubt the fact that the Summersville Memorial Hospital is a major employer for the county and therefore generates much needed professional role models for the immediate area.

Another explanation might be a sense of frustration and concern. When concerns related to traditionalism and individual or family focused self are examined in relation to increased pressure from outside forces and the region's continuing economic woes, people may have difficulty coming to grips with living in a condition they do not desire but fearing the most likely road to advancement. In their mind, accepting the outside world brings the danger of losing the positive aspects of the same culture that creates the condition they wish to escape.

Not all southern West Virginians prescribe to this fear of the future, however. A West Virginia University study completed by John Photiadis showed that three sub-groups were developing in relation to dealing with conflicts of culture and modernization. The first group identified was those who were breaking away from traditional thinking and looking more to American mainstream ideals. Staunch traditionalists made up the second group, who worked to establish buffer mechanisms against outside intervention. Finally, Photiadis identified a culture of poverty group which had become wholly dependent on public assistance and accepted welfare as a way of life.[62] Welch likewise identified two groups or classes in her study — a welfare class and an anti-welfare class.[63]

This "culture of poverty" group has had a significant impact on the state's economy. Not only does this group subsist, at least in part, from tax dollars of others, but often refuses to take part in supporting the development of infrastructure and the production of goods and services. In 2004 the state's unemployment rate was 5.3 percent. This data indicated that of 795,000 West Virginians above the age of 16 looking for employment, 42,000 were unemployed. What this did not account for was the number of working age persons who were not pursuing any form of employment. Over 657,000 residents were listed as not in the work force. When tallied, the actual percentage of residents greater than 16 not working was 54.7 percent. This number was by far (5 percent) the highest in the nation. When the data is adjusted to account only for those between 25 and 64, 67.7 percent were not working; this was again the highest in the nation (by 6 percent).[64]

The Welch and Photiadis models demonstrate three things. A traditionalist contingent still exists that fears the assimilation into greater American society will result in a disintegration of fundamental elements of Appalachian culture such as family, religion, personal security (as an extension of personal freedom), and other positive elements. A progressive, modernizing element also exists that seeks to improve infrastructure, education, and the economy. In some cases, progressives wish to break completely from all aspects of traditional stereotypes in hopes that by obliterating traditional paradigms, modernity will fill the void. Finally, a third cadre has developed that has become dependent on public assistance and often offered support by kinship groups. This group exemplifies the culture of poverty model scholars have put forth. Characteristics include a failure to value education, a lack of interest in upward mobility, holding on to outmoded ways of living, and an exaggerated willingness to live off welfare.[65]

Future success for the region will rely on the ability of the citizens to promote positive aspects of both culture and progress to aid in modernizing efforts. If progressives are effective, some traditionalists can be won over to modernization. As for the unconvinced, they will still play a vital role in maintaining the importance and relevance of traditional mountain culture. The "welfare class," however, will be the most difficult to address. Reform from this group will first require fundamental changes in the concept of their role in society as well as the advancement of economic and social systems that can provide motivation for them to leave the welfare lists.

Just as important as how a culture develops is how that culture is perceived by others. The prism through which the rest of America has viewed the region and how southern West Virginians (and greater Appalachia) have responded to this perception has formed distinct identities for residents. These identities play a major role in the ongoing evolution of Appalachian culture and American stereotypes regarding the region. For modernizing efforts to be successful in the region, everyone (mainstream America, traditionalists, progressives, and the welfare class) must face these identities and come to grips with the realities and myths associated with each. Until this can be done, "the 'Almost Heaven' bumpers stickers cannot dispel the fact that most of the problems that West Virginia had a hundred years ago are even more pronounced today."[66]

Identity is a tricky thing. Identity can apply to a person, a culture, a nation, or a myriad of other things. One identity is likewise not exclusive of another. They can be based on careers, political affiliations, gender, sexuality, religion, or other elements of one's personal and public life. In addition to being complicated, issues of identity are extremely important, particularly in examining how people perceive, understand, and act upon information and events. This section will examine first how mainstream America came to perceive, understand, and act upon Appalachia (more specifically southern West Virginia) and then how residents responded to developing stereotypes, myths, and methodologies which worked to define, categorize, and sometimes marginalize the region.

Allen Batteau argued that "Appalachia is a creature of the urban imagination."[67] The creation of this "creature" began as early as the 1830s with Charles Hoffman's *Winter in the West*, in which Hoffman described the harshness of subsistence farming. During the 1860s, Frederick Law Olmstead's *A Journey in the Back Country* identified the region and its people as not only different from mainstream America but from the greater South as well, creating a "double otherness" associated with Appalachia.[68]

The post–Civil War rush to exploit the mineral and natural resources of the region generated even more national attention. By the 1880s the "otherness" of the region, highlighted by violent and sensationalized feuds such as the Hatfield and McCoy feud, had become solidified in greater American thought. Although recent scholarship has argued the feuds had origins in the "coming of industrial capitalism and the emergence of new class relationships in the region," instead of kinship bonds and isolationism, this turn of the century concept of Appalachia relied on the perception that "southern mountain life was not consonant with new notions about the nature of America and American civilization which gained currency during this period."[69] Between this time and the turn of the century, most literature regarding the region could be defined as classic Orientalism-style listing, naming, categorizing, and domination of discourse in regard to the region at the hands of urban middle and upper class literati and academics.[70]

Examples of this Appalachian Orientalism include Mary Noailles

Murfree's *The Star in the Valley*, in which an urbanite man, Reginald Chevis, travels to the Appalachian hills. Once there he falls in love with a mountain beauty. The two can never be together, however, and the story is resolved by the death of the hero's love interest.[71] Around 1890, many writers shifted focus from the quaintness of a backward people to their depravity and viciousness.[72] This shift was supported by the growing popularity of stories related to the constant, deadly feuds that took place between a minority of mountain families.[73] As literature created caricatures of mountaineers as deviant, anti-social vigilantes, academics were generating evidence to support their perspective based on prevailing ideas on race and ethnicity.

During this period much effort was put forth by academics to highlight the dominance of Anglo-Saxons. Using elements of Darwinism and the Teutonic theory, academics sought to demonstrate how Anglo-Saxons represented the highest level of culture and civilization. There was one problem; what to do about the mountaineers? Academics found their answer in Max Nordau's *Degeneration*, written in 1895. Nordau's work provided ammunition for the Darwinists by arguing than even with good biological stock, degeneration could occur if morbid instincts arose and were allowed to pass from one generation to the next. Due to their isolation and continued desire to partake in deviant behavior, the mountaineers had become degenerate.[74]

This argument was furthered by the writing of Henry Cabot Lodge, who promoted the dominance of Puritan New England over cavalier Virginia in America's post–Civil War perspective of history.[75] Other works, such as Horace Kephart's *Our Southern Highlanders* (1913), promoted the notion that the Scots-Irish heritage of the mountaineers was the basis for Appalachian violence and anti-social behavior.[76] William Frost, president of Berea College from 1892 to 1920, also wrote of the uniqueness of the region. If fact, it was Frost who provided the region with its name when he wrote that the area was "one of God's grand divisions, and in default of any other name we shall call it Appalachian America." Frost argued against the degenerate argument, saying the region was not degraded but "not yet graded up."[77]

The "creation" of Appalachia in the American conscious was continued through a series of cartoons by Paul Webb than ran in *Esquire* from 1935 to 1948. In Webb's drawings, mountaineer men were often lounging under a tree or on a porch in overalls and straw hats while women carried out the daily work. The only scenes in which men showed action were activities such as hunting, fishing, feuding, or moonshining. This literary and pop culture fascination with the region's otherness continued to define Appalachia through the 1950s. A *Harper's* article in 1958 focused on the growing population of Appalachian residents who left for cities such as Chicago to find employment and took their customs along with them. The article spoke of a "hillbilly" invasion of Chicago and described the group as "poor, proud, primitive, and fast with a knife."[78]

This process of characterization continued as media attention generated from the Kennedy campaign was magnified by President Lyndon Johnson's War on Poverty. Through legislation such as the Economic Opportunity Act of 1964, which created the Office of Economic Opportunity (OEO), and the Public Works and Economic Development Act (PW & EDA), dozens of anti-poverty organizations were created and millions of dollars of aid flowed into Appalachia.[79] Additionally, Johnson continued support of Kennedy's President's Appalachian Regional Commission (PARC) through the Appalachian Regional Development Act of 1965, which funded the Appalachian Regional Commission (ARC). The ARC is a confederation of thirteen (originally eleven) Appalachian states which focused on economic development, namely improving transportation routes and infrastructure such as schools and hospitals.[80]

As the War on Poverty ramped up, academics, missionaries, progressives, and politicians set their sights on the mountains of southern West Virginia as one of the focal points in Johnson's Great Society. Groups of students and other activists formed groups not unlike a "domestic Peace Corps" to bring education to isolated mountain communities. Organizations such as the Appalachian Volunteers (AV) and Volunteers in Service to America (VISTA) were organized to combat rural poverty.[81] The national media came along for the ride.[82]

The results of the War on Poverty turned out similar to the current War on Terror, however. A declaration of war on an idea or conceptualized reality, whether it is poverty, drugs, or terror, is at best difficult to quantify and at worst an ill-defined foray into the impossible. William Haddad provided the following assessment of the final objectives of the War on Poverty: "Though the War on Poverty can chalk up many victories in cities and the more industrialized areas, it is stalemated in some rural counties of the South — notably in Appalachia, where the local politicians could teach big-city bosses a trick or two."[83]

Many volunteers soon came to the frustrating realization that the "war" they had enlisted for was not as easily won as they had first envisioned. Planning was incoherent at the county and district level and little support was given from the target of their efforts. In fact, one of the biggest disappointments to the volunteers was the inability to achieve what they deemed to be "maximum feasible participation" from the poor. Many community action groups had hoped to fully involve and empower the poor, uneducated, and unemployed in the reform process. Unfortunately, just as Weller and Welch have argued, many residents had no desire to take a leadership role in the community. Additionally, even when residents from the lower economic and educational levels were placed in important roles, they were found to not have the skills necessary to aid in reform. As the volunteers became disenchanted and frustrated, animosity sometimes arose over educational, economic, and class differences between the volunteers and the residents.[84]

Local officials sometimes challenged the volunteers' methods of reform as well. In some cases it was out of class- and traditionalist-based concerns and fears. Other times, it was a straightforward struggle for control of the citizenry. Raleigh County Sheriff Okey Mills accused VISTA members of supplying the poor with alcohol and drugs and prodding them to subvert local and state authority in what he called "a communist trick to pit people against people."[85] In a nearby Kentucky town, an AV representative who helped a farmer fight against strip mining on his property was charged with sedition. Throughout Appalachia, "coal operators, county officials, and their allies moved to halt the insurgency" of the reformers.[86] In the end, most community action ventures in southern West Virginia were marginally effective at best.

Local politicians seeking to redirect funding for their own purposes, residents balking at opportunities to take leadership roles in reform, and an overall resistance to outside influence doomed the reform effort. The reforms and the government funded programs began to dwindle away. OEO funding shrank until it was shut down under the Nixon Administration; to many residents it had become yet another "intrusive government agency" anyway.

Perhaps the best epitaph for the War on Poverty can be seen in the narratives of those who fought the good fight. In John Glen's article, "The War on Poverty in Appalachia" published in the *Oral History Review*, many of those directly involved in the community action endeavors "readily agree that the War on Poverty produced no fundamental economic or political changes in Appalachia."[87]

The 1960s popular culture view of Appalachia was further solidified through the images seen on television. CBS broadcast the laughable exploits of the Clampetts in the *Beverly Hillbillies*. Although the series often used the lovable mountain bumpkins as a critical backdrop against which the more negative aspects of middle class lifestyle (greed and excess) were highlighted, the stereotypical nature of the characters provided a powerful caricature of "hillbillies."[88] Besides the fictional depiction of mountaineers out of place and time, two key documentaries added to the collection of mainstream American knowledge of the region. *Depressed Area USA* and *Christmas in Appalachia*, both broadcast by CBS, highlighted the joblessness, poverty, inept or impotent local leadership, and the general lack of education prevalent in Eastern Kentucky.[89]

Television was not the only medium by which Appalachia was presented to the American conscious. In 1963, a *New York Times* article by Homer Bigart titled "Kentucky Miners: A Grim Winter" painted a bleak picture. Speaking to the "usual disorder of coal country," Bigart then vividly detailed the destitution, decay, and poverty that he saw. Bigart presented the story as a secret that had finally been brought into the light: "Few tourists who venture into the area seldom see the pinched faces of hungry children, the filth and squalor of cabins, the unpainted shacks that still serve as schoolhouses." Describing the devastated landscape, infrastructure, and family were not enough; Bigart also had to warn America of the degeneration of character he witnessed as well: "The erosion of the character of the people is more fearsome than the despoiling of the mountains.... The welfare system has eroded the self-respect of the mountain people. Gone is the frontier bravado, the sense of adventure, the self-reliance."[90]

Bigart's presentation of Appalachia wiped away the mountaineer independence and vitality of earlier writers. Self-reliance, individualism, and hardiness were replaced with dependency, depravity, and hopelessness. Bigart was only one of a flood of filmmakers, reporters, and the like which "inundated America with photographs and moving images of dirty and barefoot children, rundown shacks, sewage-clogged streams, and desperate-eyed miners."[91]

Many residents felt ashamed of the images by which their region was being defined. Noakes calls this outcome "collateral damage" of the War on Poverty. The images of poverty, dependency, and decay were in stark contrast to mountaineer concepts of self-reliance, independence, and pride in self and home.[92] The impact on southern West Virginians (and throughout Appalachia) is significant. A survey completed by Nicholas County high school students asked the questions *How are West Virginians perceived outside of the state? Why?* Of 30 students completing the survey, 43 negative terms were used in their answer and ranged from uncivilized, uneducated, and low-class to illiterate, inbred, and ignorant. The most frequently used descriptors were hillbillies, ignorant, uneducated, stupid, and rednecks.[93]

Some academics, particularly from within or near Appalachia, fought to present a different perspective of the region than was being portrayed in popular culture. One such scholar was Bill Best, a professor at Berea College. Instead of providing a balanced approach, however, Best often "articulated the anger and suffocation felt by many within the region toward outside efforts to define them."[94] In *Stripping the Appalachian Soul*, Best provided an emotional attempt to "heal the scars left on Appalachian psyche."[95] Such is the state of "Appalachian psyche" today; the ongoing battle between tradition and modernity is still being fought in the hearts and minds of mountaineers. This struggle is complex, dynamic, and lies at the heart of southern West Virginia's current state of affairs.

Traditionalists decry the negative aspects of modernization and hold tightly to the virtues of tradition. This is the driving factor behind the symbolic nature of the Confederate battle flag in the region. To some traditionalists, and many youth, the Confederate flag does not represent slavery or even rebellion. It represents resistance to unwanted intrusion from outside, a nostalgic history of subsistence farming, and the staunch independence that early mountaineers (and Southerners in general) felt in the antebellum years. Traditionalists (including the author's grandmother) likewise see the title "hillbilly" as a badge of honor and a source of pride.[96] In fact, Welch found that only 5 out of 100 interviewees had problems with the "hillbilly" identity.[97] It is also interesting that while most adults view the term hillbilly as a positive description of their culture, the majority of high school students from the Nicholas County survey used it in a derogatory manner.

Progressives argue that modernization is necessary to improve the region's precarious economic, and subsequently social, condition. To them the loss of many aspects of mountain culture is not only acceptable but necessary to regional development. This balancing act is a difficult task, one that some progressives are well aware of. As the executive director of

Eight. Culture, Identity, and Modernization

Area Development District of Big Sandy River Region remarked, "We walk a fine line between being very proud of our heritage and trying to dispel the typical idea the rest of the world has. It remains a sensitive point. A lot of people would rather not remember the past, but it gave us a heritage to be proud of."[98]

When the importance of tradition is overlooked by progressives, however, problems arise. West Virginia Governor Joe Manchin, trying to improve the state's image, changed the state slogan from "Wild and Wonderful" to "Open for Business."[99] The move proved an abject failure in southern West Virginia. Traditionalists, among others, saw it as an attack on "hillbilly" tradition and vehemently opposed it. Now doubt many also saw the slogan "Open for Business" as being reminiscent of the mindset that opened up the region to industrialist exploitation at the turn of the century. Others opposed his modernizing program because it challenged local festivals which relied to some degree on mountaineer stereotypes to draw tourists and their money into the region.[100]

Finally there is the third class. The welfare class — those mired in the "culture of poverty"— in many cases only focus on obtaining the necessary resources to eke out a meager existence. It is this group that more often than not comes to mind when people think of the region. This group generally does not focus on the past as traditionalists or the future as progressives; they look to the now. Development, education, infrastructure, and employment must be corrected before this group can be reformed. In order for this group to have any real chance at reform, traditionalists and progressives must find a common ground upon which to improve the region's education, infrastructure, economy, and employment opportunities. Until then, the welfare class will act as an anchor to regional advancement.

NINE

Mountaintop Removal and the Battle for the Hearts and Minds

With labor laws the way they are right now in this country ... you can't do a legal organizing drive and it be successful. As soon as you start a drive, they fire 20 to 30 guys; they have hearings; they hold up the day of the election as long as they can; they bring in non-union, union buster company that pays big bucks to brainwash and scare the employees.[1]

People in communities like this are backwards. People come in from out of state, harass 'em and they'll give in.[2]

You can't find an attorney around here ... because all of them's got coal mining money in their pockets. All of them.[3]

These are not quotes from UMWA activists or frustrated miners from the late 19th or early 20th century. These comments were recorded by anthropologist Bryan McNeil during research for his 2005 dissertation "Searching for Home Where Mountains Move." While the anthropological nature of McNeil's work (he was focusing on the rise of activist groups as community stewards) is highly biased in favor of mountaintop removal (MTR) opposition groups, it demonstrates the enduring struggle between traditionalists and progressives over the future of southern West Virginia. Perhaps no other contemporary topic highlights the way in which economic instability, political corruption, and struggle for cultural identity still play prominent roles in the struggle for modernity as much as MTR.

McNeil thought that "running through the conflict over the mountaintop removal coal mining is a sense that conditions in Appalachia's coalfields violate basic expectations of how citizens should be treated in the

United States."[4] Throughout the state's post–Civil War history, similar statements have been made in regards to living conditions in company towns, treatment of striking miners, the general lawlessness during the mine wars, the desperation of the Great Depression, and the legacy of political corruption in the region. Just as with all aspects of the region's history, the current struggle over mountaintop removal is much more dynamic than either side would have one believe.

Environmentalists, activists, and others who oppose mountaintop removal draw upon the shocking photos of the mountaintop removal process and its resultant impact on the environment, public health, and cultural identity as the foundation of their argument. Organizations, through the promotion of traditional mountaineer values, have in many cases replaced the UMWA as the archenemy of King Coal.[5] Likewise, coal companies and their supporters (such as the Friends of Coal organization) highlight the need for jobs, the effectiveness of land reclamation, the importance of coal in meeting America's energy needs as well as the "radicalism" of mountaintop removal opposition groups.[6]

While the activists and coal companies square off against one another, two other groups gingerly tip-toe through the political minefield of MTR. The West Virginia Department of Environmental Protection, the organization responsible for many facets of mountaintop removal oversight, is often maligned as nothing more than a government front for the interests of coal power. Also trapped in the political dead-man's land between coal companies and mountaintop removal opposition groups is a weakened UMWA. Struggling to maintain its relevance and at least a fraction of its former influence, union leaders have thrown their lot in with mountaintop removal, much to the dismay of traditionalists and many struggling underground miners in the region.

Much is at stake in this emotional struggle. If mountaintop removal continues in earnest, some jobs will be spared and much needed money could find its way back into the communities from which the coal is extracted. In an area where jobs are scarce and subsidies from industry are minimal, the end of mountaintop removal could cause even more economic problems for families and local economies alike. From the viewpoint of those opposing MTR, however, the handful of jobs created (in comparison to traditional mining) and uncertain expectations of revenue for the local communities are outweighed by concerns over environmental (and therefore cultural) loss and dangers to public health and safety. As with other hot-button issues in the area, it is once again a case of traditionalists and progressives drawing lines in the sand.

Mountaintop removal began in 1970 at Bullpush Mountain in Fayette County.[7] The practice soon expanded throughout southern West Virginia in the following decades as the oil crisis of the '70s led to a renewed emphasis on coal. When the industry again began to struggle during the 1980s, operators sought the most economical means of recovering coal; they found their answer in mountaintop removal. The financial advantages were again reinforced in the 1990s due to an amended Federal Clean Air Act, which called for more restrictions on emissions and therefore an increased demand for low-sulfur content coal. Between 1992 and 2002, over 90,000 acres were affected by mountaintop removal operations with 12,000 new acres permitted in a single 9-month period in 2002.[8] Overall, over 26 percent of the state's 158,835,584 tons of coal (2006 figures) came from mountaintop removal operations.[9]

While traditional surface mining operations basically chip away at a particular seam of coal, mountaintop removal uses a much more aggressive approach. The practice involves large scale blasting operations and results in the removal of several hundred feet of mountain by massive excavating machines called draglines. The resultant rubble is pushed into nearby valleys. The coal is then sent to massive processing plants where it is cleaned and stored for shipment throughout the U.S. and the world. Waste from cleaning, and other processes, are stored behind massive slurry impoundments, some of which are several hundred feet tall. Once the land has been cleared of its coal, the site is then "reclaimed" for either future economic development or returned to as close to its natural state as possible.[10] Almost every aspect of the MTR process has drawn protest from residents and environmentalist organizations. From topsoil removal and blasting to slurry impoundments and the nature and effectiveness of land reclamation, opponents of MTR argue against the practice on the grounds of environmental preservation, public safety, and the defense of mountain traditions and heritage.

Well known mountaintop removal opposition groups include the Ohio Valley Environmental Coalition (OVEC), West Virginia Highlands Conservatory (WVHC), Coal River Mountain Watch (CRMW), ilove mountains.org, and Appalachian Voices. These and other organizations challenge powerful coal companies, state and federal governments, pro-coal organizations, and citizens dependent on mountaintop removal for their livelihood over how the region's resources should be extracted. Unlike previous periods of unrest in the region's past, however, those opposing mountaintop removal have rarely resorted to violence. Instead, they have directly challenged, and often won, legal cases against both coal companies and the government agencies involved with regulating mountaintop removal.

Most of these cases have involved the failure of the state to properly administer and regulate federal requirements that have been entrusted to them to enforce.[11] In fact, the majority of mountaintop removal opposition has been presented in terms of legal frameworks by opposition groups and the media alike.[12] Just below the surface of these legal arguments, however, are strong feelings of tradition and culture associated with the close bond between person and place that has developed over generations. When Bryan McNeil stated that the residents "often equate the profound violations of the social and physical landscape [of MTR] with rape,"[13] he was speaking of this bond and to the very personal sense of pervasive intrusion felt by many local residents.

There is also power in this land-self relationship if properly focused. McNeil discussed this power when he said, "The movement against mountaintop removal draws strength from the combination of political savvy, emotional fever, religious sentiment, and the ability to speak to the people's hearts and to their minds."[14] The combination of cultural awareness and environmentalism, both of which are tied strongly to a sense of self and family in southern West Virginia, is key to the continued success of mountaintop removal opposition. Furthermore, by focusing on the needs of the residents and promoting their health, welfare, and culture over that of industry, these mountaintop removal opposition groups have gradually replaced a weakened UMWA as leaders in community activism in the region.

The environmental impact of mountaintop removal has been a focal point for opposition groups. By highlighting the possible negative outcomes for streams, wildlife, and humans as a result of the altered environment, as well as fears of inadequate or ignored regulations, opponents have made a strong case against the practice. Through support from elements of the scientific community and aggressive public awareness programs, many environmentalist-driven opponents of mountaintop removal have been successful in making the public aware of the potential dangers of the practice.

Protection of the region's streams is of particular importance. According to the Environmental Protection Agency (EPA), can affect streams through deposition of minerals harmful to fish and macroinvertebrates, covering by overfill, and an increase in base flow in streams below valley fills.[15] A 2008 report published in the *Journal of North American Benthological Society* supported the negative impact, stating that mountaintop removal is "strongly related to downstream biological impairment."[16] Other scientists, such as the University of Maryland's Dr. Margaret Palmer, have been more definitive. In July of 2009, Palmer testified before the Senate Environmental and Public Works Committee that streams at the bottom of valley fills receive water that is "so polluted that entire groups of organisms can no longer live in it." She further stated that these and other impacts "are immense and irreversible."[17]

Mountaintop removal affects other forms of wildlife by the transformation of the physical environment through deforestation, mining operations, and subsequent reclamation (depending on the method of reclamation utilized). Although recent regulations call for a more scientific effort to return land to its pre-mining characteristics, there have been shortfalls. This is particularly so at older sites. Specific issues include the fragmentation of forest environments, the slow re-growth of trees and woody plants on reclaimed land due to compacted soil, and the replacement of the original environment with other types of vegetation, particularly grasslands.[18]

The alteration of the physical nature of the land in turn impacts wildlife. Aside from the initial displacement or migration of wildlife during the mountaintop removal operations such as blasting and the operation of heavy machinery, longer-lasting outcomes can also occur depending on how, and to what extent, the land is reclaimed. Some winners as a result of the environmental changes include grassland birds, small mammals such as mice, and larger animals including turkey and deer, all of which can thrive in grassland or less forested environments. There are losers, however. Woodland bird populations have decreased in some areas, particularly red-shouldered and broad-winged hawks. Salamanders and Eastern chipmunks also do not perform as well in sites which are not returned to their original environment. Perhaps the biggest loser is the black bear. Already dealing with continuing encroachment by the expansion of towns, the state animal fails to thrive in these less forested reclamation sites.[19]

If promoting the danger to streams and wildlife did not generate enough evidence for the opposition of mountaintop removal, activists also challenge mining operations from the perspective of public safety. Just as mountaintop mining operations destroy the original environment, it also creates new public health concerns. Through the construction of massive slurry impoundments, processing plant operations, and drastic increases in coal transportation, coal companies have built an environment that not only creates nuisances but poses serious threats to residents' health and safety as well.

Mountaintop removal operations are kicked off with a bang — literally. Once the site has been deforested and topsoil removed, the first layers of rock and earth are blasted away. These massive explosions can be heard for miles. Many residents near Massey Energy's site near Sylvester have complained about flying debris, damaged home foundations and wells, broken windows, and other problems caused by the blasting.[20] Once the cover has been blasted away and the coal removed, it is trucked to a processing plant to be distributed to national and international consumers. Many residents and opponents of mountaintop removal argue that the volume of coal trucks on the road, their massive size, and heavy weight also pose significant hazards to the community.

The powerful explosions used in mountaintop removal not only blast thousands of pounds of earth away from coal seams but create noise, dust, and debris problems for nearby citizens (courtesy Giles Ashford).

In many communities in southern West Virginia, the sight of a coal truck rumbling down a ragged, pot-hole spotted two-lane road has become part of daily life in the region. Many opponents of mountaintop removal, however, claim the increased activity around large operations has reached ludicrous levels. An example is the town of Sylvester, where 15 million tons of coal passed through in 2002. Increased traffic, sometimes running around the clock, has resulted in several points of contention for nearby residents. First, the non-stop parade of coal trucks has created increased noise, dust and traffic nuisances. Secondly, the combination of massive coal trucks and small winding roads can often make meetings with other vehicles dangerous and sometimes deadly. Any person who has spent significant time in the region most likely has a story of a near-miss with a coal truck in a blind turn. The increased volume of coal traffic has only increased the likelihood of accidents with other vehicles and pedestrians.[21]

Besides the problem of congestion, roads deteriorate more quickly under the constant weight of coal trucks. The poor state of many rural roads and bridges, exacerbated by overweight coal trucks, only enhances traffic dangers on the narrow, winding roads. Eager to promote the continued patronage of coal companies, local and state governments have at times not only ignored the problem but made it worse. In 2003, weight limits in several counties were doubled to support mining operations. Many roads and bridges over which these massive trucks traveled, however, were never rated for the volume and weight of traffic which now rolls over them daily.[22] In that same year, the cost to repair the state's damaged and worn out roads was estimated at $2.8 billion.[23]

Perhaps the most imposing threat to public safety is the existence of coal slurry impoundments. When coal is washed to remove ash, the resultant ash-water mixture is held in large reservoirs called slurry impoundments.[24] Often the size of lakes, there are over 100 such impoundments in West Virginia.[25] Many of these man-made lakes have been built near populated areas under questionable circumstances and pose legitimate threats to public safety. Three particular impoundments heighten residents' fears. These are the Shumate Coal and Brushy Fork impoundments, both located in Raleigh County, and the Joe Branch Coal Refuse in Wyoming County.

The Shumate Coal impoundment stands over 385 feet and holds almost 3 billion gallons of slurry.[26] Located at the bottom of the impoundment is Marsh Fork Elementary School. If the dam were to be breached, the school would have less than 3 minutes to evacuate.[27] The reaction by residents, parents, and grandparents regarding the safety and emergency response plans to potential impoundment problems resulted in the arrest of 20 protesters at Massey Energy's headquarters in Richmond, Virginia, in June of 2005.[28] North of the Shumate impoundment is the Brushy Fork impoundment. At 900 feet tall, the massive earthen dam holds back over 8 billion gallons of water and waste.[29] If this dam were to break the towns of Sylvester and Whitesville would be endangered. In fact, the threat is such that some residents of Sylvester sleep in their clothing when it rains in order to allow for a more rapid escape in case of a breach. Due to fears of flooding from the impoundment and the abundance of coal dust which required the utensils and appliances of Sylvester Elementary School to be covered in plastic when not in use, the Boone County Board of Education chose to close the school and consolidate with the older Whitesville Elementary School. Whitesville Elementary, while still prone to flooding, was farther away from the impoundment.[30]

A breach of Wyoming County's Joe Branch impoundment would also place a school in danger. The 2 billion gallons of the impoundment, if released, would cause a 21 foot wall of water and coal ash to cover Wyoming East High School as well as a nearby retirement home. The nearby towns of Pineville and Marianna could see flooding as high as 11 feet. Coal companies should not be held completely to blame for this situation, however, as the school was constructed after the impoundment was created.[31]

Even more frightening is the fact each of these structures has been classified as a Class C impoundment by WVDEP and as high hazard potential by the Mine Safety and Health Administration (MSHA). Class C dams are those located where failure may cause a loss human life or serious damage to homes, industrial and commercial buildings, important public utilities, primary highways or main haul roads. High hazard potential facilities are those whose failure could reasonably be expected to cause loss of human life, and serious damage to houses, industrial and commercial buildings, important utilities, highways, and railroads.[32]

At Brushy Fork an additional hazard is added. Directly below the impoundment lies an abandoned underground mine. Although Mayfork Coal Company has reported the old mine will provide adequate support for the 900 feet of earth pressing down on it, many people are still concerned about a collapse of a portion of the mine and subsequent failure of the impoundment.[33]

Their concerns are not unwarranted. In October of 2000, in Martin County, Kentucky, slurry from the Big Branch Coal Refuse impoundment broke through an underground mine. Although the impoundment remained intact, the rupture emptied 300 million gallons of slurry into the abandoned mine, which eventually resulted in waste water reaching the Tug Fork and Big Sandy Rivers. Over $77 million in damage and environmental cleanup cost was incurred by Massey Energy, not including MSHA fines. Eight civil lawsuits were also filed.[34]

Beyond dangers to the environment and public safety, local residents have also challenged mountaintop removal on a much more personal level—one of cultural survival. Drawing on the strong bonds of people and place, these "cultural activists" and traditionalists fear the loss of the mountain environment will result in a loss of a distinct mountain culture. Although difficult to quantify, there is obviously a close connection between people and the land in southern West Virginia. The importance of identity, culture, and heritage inherent in the region, when added to environmental and public safety concerns regarding mountaintop removal, create a powerful mixture of environmental stewardship, civic responsibility, and cultural preservation.

McNeil's reporting of a resident likening mountaintop removal to rape, although sensationalized, highlights the legitimate fears of the loss of identity and feelings of betrayal and exploitation at the hands of coal companies felt by many residents. Just as rape takes away from the victim, to traditionalists the "destroying of the landscape ... destroys an important element in making mountain culture."[35] This very personal attack on mountain culture begins as soon as the first tree is felled in preparation for MTR operations. To some residents, when they see a mountain cleared of trees and the soil removed in preparation for blasting, it is as if "the beauty of the state is being cut out ... torn away."[36] When the forest, the animals, and the vegetation is removed so are "hunting, fishing, berry picking, herbal medicine gathering, ginsenging, and other activities"[37] pertinent to mountain culture.

The memories of such places and activities held by these traditionalists are not ones of vague places and events. Residents remember specific locations where the best mushrooms or ginseng can be found. Many a southern West Virginian was taught to hunt or fish by their father or grandfather on traditional lands and at favorite fishing holes. Reminiscences of these locations, when combined with the kinship bonds associated with them,

A massive explosion at a mountaintop removal site. The destruction of mountain landscape in the name of economic survival has proven to be extremely divisive to the region's residents (courtesy Giles Ashford).

create enduring memories that are threatened every time forests are clearcut, ancestral hunting grounds are sold to private hunting companies, and the mountains themselves are leveled.

It is this powerful sense of place, created from childhood memories and kinship interactions, which make fears of their impending loss a significant motive and political tool for mountaintop removal opponents. By calling forth the defense of a way of life, traditionalist-oriented mountaintop removal groups have astutely tied fears over the loss of land associated with childhood and ancestral memories to the legacy of outside influence and industrial encroachment in southern West Virginia. Judy Bonds, leader of CRMW and recipient of the Goldman Environmental Prize for 2003, highlighted this dubious legacy when she stated that coal has been used "as a device to subjugate people, turning them into ashamed, acquiescent participants in their own oppression."[38]

Through adept manipulation of the region's historical baggage of exploitation, both real and perceived, opponents of mountaintop mining have created a significant challenge to coal companies and pro–MTR organizations. Tying this unsavory history with modern-day threats to traditional living have proven extremely effective. So powerful is this aspect of the struggle against mountaintop mining that government organizations and proponents of mountaintop removal must acknowledge its presence. Even the EPA lists as possible negative outcomes of mountaintop removal the existence of "social, economic and heritage issues."[39]

Capitalizing on the amalgamation of environmentalism, activism, and traditionalism, opposition groups have faced pro–MTR companies, groups, and politicians head-on. Unlike residents' and the UMWA's struggle against coal companies and in the 19th and early 20th centuries, modern-day activists have had their share of success in the courts. The most effective aspect of mountaintop removal opposition has involved legal actions relating to environmental protection regulations. This includes challenges regarding the level to which regulations are being following by coal companies and how organizations such as the United States Army Corps of Engineers and the West Virginia Department of Environmental Protection (WVDEP) are enforcing these restrictions. Using environmental protection legislation and the threat posed to the incredible biodiversity of the region, opposition groups have had several successes in halting, at least temporarily, mountaintop removal operations on several sites.

Perhaps the most discussed, and legally challenged, point of contention regarding mountaintop removal is the impact it has on valley streams. Excess earth is pushed into the valley creating fills. While coal companies claim that no streams are adversely affected by this practice, opponents argue otherwise. Of major concern is the complete loss of intermittent streams as well as the threat of increasing pollution and the resultant impact on plant and animal life throughout the watershed.[40] In 1994, the Department of Water Resources found that 74 percent of West Virginia streams and rivers were polluted.[41] Although it is sometimes difficult to prove exactly where the pollution is coming from, many blame surface mining, and particularly mountaintop removal.

Although regulations are, and have been, in place to protect streams, several important legal cases have focused on the interpretation of and compliance with both the Surface Mining Control and Reclamation Act of 1977 (SMCRA) and the Clean Water Act (CWA). In *Bragg v. Robertson* (1998), activists challenged both WVDEP and the Corps of Engineers over violations of both acts. Judge Charles Haden, ruling that the mandated 100 foot buffer zone between mining operations and intermittent and perennial streams applied to all portions of the stream, halted the expansion of Dal-Tex mountaintop removal site near Blair.[42] Although Haden's decision was later overturned by the conservative 4th Circuit Court of Appeals, the case emboldened activists to continue legal maneuvers against mountaintop removal operations.[43]

Another important case involving valley fills and stream pollution involved a fill in Nicholas County. In this case, the Corps of Engineers had authorized a permit to Green Valley Coal Company (a Massey Energy subsidiary) allowing 431 feet of the Blue Branch Creek to be filled. The long-term plans included the deposition of 1.5 million tons of coarse refuse and 510 tons of fine refuse into the stream, which eventually flowed into Hominy Creek. In the subsequent case of *OVEC vs. Bulen,* Judge Robert Goodwin ruled, "The Army Corps of Engineers could no longer approve mining valley fills through a streamlined permit process meant only for activities that cause minor environmental damage."[44] Goodwin also found that the Corps of Engineers had violated the Clean Water Act and required them to revoke 11 additional permits. Six more permits were later revoked under this order.[45]

Again, the 4th Circuit Court of Appeals overturned the case. The court did, however, provide an avenue to allow the plaintiffs to argue that the Corps of Engineers made an arbitrary and capricious decision based on erroneous information and ignoring relevant data.[46] The decision, heard by a panel of 4th Circuit Court of Appeals judges, was not unanimously supported by the court. Judge King requested the case be heard en banc (before the full court). Failing to gain the necessary votes for a full hearing, King, supported by Judges Michael and Motz, provided a dissenting opinion. King believed the court's decision "eviscerated the important distinction between individual and general permits" under the Clean Water Act and that permitting "without ... procedural hurdles" could create a situation in which the Corps of Engineers "allows an activity with the potential to have significant effects on the environment to be permitted."[47] King also felt that the corps "failed to make the required determination of minimal environmental impact before it issued the general permit" and "ignored numerous indications," deferring "its obligation to make nominal-effects determinations until after the general permit was in place."[48]

Using the opening allowed by the 4th Circuit Court of Appeals in their 2005 decision in *OVEC v. Bulen*, both OVEC and CRMW challenged the issuance of permits authorizing the discharge of dredged and fill material associated with mountaintop removal. In March 2009, Judge Goodwin determined that the corps' actions were indeed "arbitrary and capricious" in that it "did not include considerations of the ongoing impacts of past actions" and that the "impact determinations relied on the success of a mitigation process" which Goodwin could not be convinced would be "adequately policed."[49]

Added to Goodwin's decision was that of Judge Robert Chambers in the case of *OVEH v. USACE* in November 2009. In this case, the court determined that the U.S. Army Corps of Engineers violated both the Clean Water Act and National Environmental Protection Act (NEPA) by failing to provide adequate public notice at the Loadout and Fola sites and to adequately review environmental impacts at the Nellis site. Chambers directed the corps to reissue an amended notice for each permit, to receive and respond to resident comments, and to reconsider each permit with the new comments in mind.[50] The decision, however, did not stop operations. As the "court [was] sensitive to the substantial mining activity" at the site, operations were allowed to continue while Chambers' orders were carried out.[51] Chambers' decision came only weeks after the Environmental Protection Agency issued a press release stating that 79 sites in Appalachia required more in-depth reviews of their permit process.[52]

Other lawsuits have been successfully prosecuted as well. Lawsuits blaming mountaintop removal and deforestation operations for massive flooding in 2001 reached such a level that the West Virginia Supreme Court established a "flood litigation panel" to address all of the cases. In 2003, the Sylvester residents won $473,000 in a long battle with Massey Energy regarding coal dust which blanketed the town. The company was also ordered to reduce the number of trucks which passed through the town from 35,000 to 7,000 per year. Massey's cost did not include previous fines assessed by WVDEP or the $1.5 million price tag to completely incase the processing plant in a massive dome. Residents had little reason to sympathize with the cost incurred by Massey, however; the town saw an 80 percent drop in property values due to the volume of trucks and the constant coating of coal dust.[53] Also, in 2004 the West Virginia Supreme Court of Appeals overturned the order directing the forced sale of land owned by several members of the Caudill family in order to expand Arch Coal's Hobet 21 site.[54]

In addition to these court cases, coal companies have also been forced to adjust to both state and federal legislation that has grown more restrictive over recent years as mountaintop removal opposition groups grew more politically savvy and ultimately more effective in driving legislation. The most recent federal legislation is H.R. 585, the Environmental and Public Health Restoration Act of 2009. At the heart of this legislation is a renewed focus into researching the impact of mountaintop removal operations and developing ways to reverse negative impacts of mountaintop mining. In general the goal of the act is to "direct the president to enter into an arrangement with the National Academy of Sciences to evaluate certain federal rules and regulations for potentially harmful impacts on public health, air quality, water quality, plant and animal wildlife, global climate, or the environment; and to direct federal departments and agencies to create plans to reverse these impacts that are determined to be harmful by the National Academy of Sciences."[55]

West Virginia legislators have also recently proposed acts to further restrict operations related to surface mining in general. West Virginia H.B. 3279, a bill to amend the Surface Coal Mining and Reclamation Act, included a call to prohibit any permits authorizing the construction, enlargement or modification of any coal mine waste, prohibit any new permits for disposal of coal mine waste by injecting it into underground mines, and require a study of existing coal mine waste piles.[56]

Through emotional and traditionalist based propaganda, legal maneuvering, and political pressure, opponents of mountaintop removal have created a nightmare of public relations, legal battles, and political issues for coal companies and their supporters. These groups have been able to highlight dangers to the environment, public safety, and mountain culture posed by mountaintop removal. Despite the amount of publicity they garner, opposition groups provide only one side of a complicated and dynamic story. Bound in a mixture of historical, social, political, economic, and cultural issues, the role of mountaintop removal in southern West Virginia is not as straightforward as hardcore environmentalist-based opposition groups often present.

Proponents of mountaintop mining work diligently to counter the arguments put forth by opposition groups. While coal companies and their associated support groups obviously hold the economic and generally the political advantage in the fight over mountaintop removal, the nature of the debate automatically places pro–mountaintop removal organizations on the defensive, as they must respond to complaints from those opposing the practice. In defense of mountaintop mining, proponents have responded with a media blitz of their own. Scientific data is provided, the need for job stability (although limited due the overall reduction in mining jobs) is touted, and the increased occupational safety of surface mining is promoted. As for the more radical environmentalists, they are portrayed as uninformed anarchists, promoters of a welfare state, or as one coal manager put it, "chicken little environmentalists."[57]

Coal is the lifeblood of southern West Virginia. Without jobs from coal, the already weakened economy would collapse under current conditions. That is the cold, hard fact faced by many residents in the region. And matters are growing worse each year. As Fig. 25 demonstrates, while surface mining operations have increased and mining technology continues to improve, overall employment in the mining industry has plummeted. Hardest hit are the underground miners in the southernmost counties which have seen the number of jobs available drop to approximately 24 percent of those available in the early 1970s.[58] With little else in the way of adequate wages, mountaintop removal jobs, although few in numbers, provide much needed employment opportunities.

Under these conditions a legitimate argument is made regarding the need for jobs in contrast to possible damage to the environment or mountain culture. Under the mindset that "trees and culture won't feed a family,"

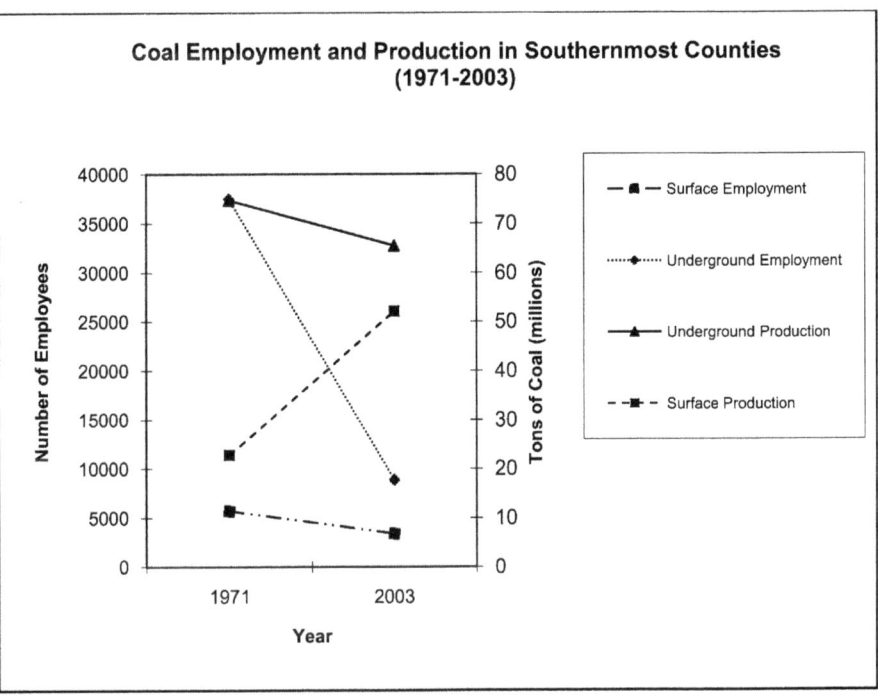

Fig. 25. Coal Employment and Production, 1971–2003, Surface and Underground Employment and Production. Source: Burns, pp. 19–39.

residents struggling to maintain work feel they have no choice but to support mountaintop mining. As one employee stated, "You don't want to bite the hand that feeds you."[59] Some opposition groups claim to understand this dilemma, or at least give it lip service. Coal River Mountain Watch provides the following summation of their stance on the economic importance of coal: "We believe public officials and agencies must fulfill their responsibility to provide a sustainable, healthy, and safe environment. Coal River Mountain Watch acknowledges that coal is the short-term economic support for our community, but we support efforts to bring together other forms of sustainable enterprise to southern West Virginia."[60]

Many pro–mountaintop removal groups focus on the importance of coal to national and worldwide energy concerns and its resultant economic dominance of the region. Organizations such as the Coal Education Development and Resource (CEDAR), Friends of Coal, and the West Virginia Coal Association (WVCA) all work to not only debunk claims by anti–

mountaintop removal groups but to promote the positive aspects of coal industry on the economy and community alike. These organizations provide a wide spectrum of policies and programs which work to get the word out on the benefits of the coal industry. Their target audience is broad, ranging from grade-schoolers to businessmen.

CEDAR works to educate K–12 children on the importance of the coal industry in the region by promoting an "understanding of the many benefits the coal industry provides in daily lives by providing financial resources and coal education materials to implement its study in the school curriculum."[61] Their programs include regional coal fairs, scholarships for post-secondary education, and approximately $34,000 in grants given to southern West Virginia schools between 2001 and 2005.[62]

The Friends of Coal picks up were CEDAR leaves off. This organization is "dedicated to inform[ing] and educate[ing] West Virginia citizens about the coal industry and its vital role in the state's future. Our goal is to provided a united voice for an industry that has been and remains a critical economic contributor to West Virginia. By working together, we can provide good jobs and benefits for future generations, which will keep our children and grandchildren closer to home."[63]

The mission statement above hits on several key points for residents. First it highlights the economic importance, especially in terms of creating jobs. Just as important, however, is the association it makes between a sustainable coal industry and the maintaining of kinship bonds. With the scarcity of jobs a driving factor for outmigration of citizens and the subsequent disruption of families, tying employment within the coal industry to family stability is an adept strategy.

The organization is extremely popular in the region. "Friends of Coal" paraphernalia, including bumper stickers, posters, billboards, and pins, is commonplace in southern West Virginia. In fact, concerns over the impartiality of Surface Mining Board, a group appointed by the governor which hears citizens' concerns over mining issues, was only intensified when members were seen driving away from one meeting in an SUV sporting "Friends of Coal" stickers.[64] The group also sponsors a series of annual football games between the state's two major college football teams, West Virginia University and Marshall University. The winner of the game receives the Governor's Cup, which is awarded by the state's head executive.[65]

Standing at the pinnacle of pro-coal organizations is the West Virginia Coal Association (WVCA). Created by coal operators themselves, the association is a trade organization representing over 90 percent of the state's mining production. Its key goals are:

- To take all necessary steps to ensure the WVCA is the leading voice for all matters related to coal in West Virginia,
- To be a strong advocate for improving safety at our members' operations through education, and legislative and administrative actions and bring positive recognitions to the safety accomplishments of members, and
- To implement an organized, focused effort to inform key demographic segments across West Virginia of the advantages of using West Virginia coal.[66]

WVCA obviously presents a much more power-based front than CEDAR or Friends of Coal. Instead of working to educate the community at large as to the importance of the coal industry to the region, WVCA specifically focuses on "key demographic segments." Also, with its members being among the wealthiest and most politically influential people in the region, it is not difficult to see how some opponents of mountaintop removal would be troubled over phrases such as "take all necessary steps." Language such as this, from an organization consisting of powerful coal operators, unfortunately provides further ammunition for opposition groups who believe that "coal companies engage in activities that will benefit their business while disregarding and denying their adverse effects on local populations."[67]

These groups, together with others, not only challenge anti–mountaintop removal groups on the grounds they are extremists and that the cessation of mining would result in "devastating consequences for the area," but on the nature of the impact on the environment as well.[68] One of the areas in which pro–mountaintop removal groups work diligently to debunk their detractors is in the area of reclamation. Led by the Appalachian Region Reforestation Initiative and supported by various area university programs, much work has been done to demonstrate that mountaintop removal sites can indeed be reclaimed to near-original conditions.

One of the major areas of concern is the poor growth record for native trees in compacted soils. Compacted soils result from the reshaping process of reclamation as earth is moved and compacted to create sloping hills over a former mountaintop removal site. New processes, such as ripping methods, which till the soil once the land is reshaped, have produced promising results.[69] In fact, due to changes in the West Virginia Surface Mining and Reclamation Rule, the use of commercial forestry (and thus the regrowth of traditional hardwoods) has seen increasing support. This trend falls in line with new regulations requiring coal companies to demonstrate a stable growth rate of trees over a 12 year bond period following the reclamation of designated sites. If insufficient growth is observed, they will incur additional cost to restore the area.[70]

Several research initiatives have shown that effective reclamation can occur. Research at Catenary Coal Company's Sample Mine in Kanawha County has shown an overall survival rate of 78 percent for trees such as oak, poplar, maple, cherry, locust, dogwood, and pine.[71] These results, and others, are the direct outcome of a new reforestation process. The process includes creating a suitable rooting mechanism for tree growth, loosely grading the topsoil to create a non-compacted growth medium, use of ground cover compatible with growing trees, planting both for wildlife stability and commercially viable trees, and using proper planting techniques.[72]

Although not all sites are designated to be reclaimed to their original condition (some have become golf courses, grasslands, wetlands, or areas for future economic development), the current research is promising. In fact, researchers are also looking at sites previously restored to pasture or grasslands with an eye on reforestation.[73] Other Appalachian states also have high hopes for reclamation. According to one University of Tennessee researcher, although it obviously takes years for a mature forest to develop, they are hoping to "shorten the time" and despite the current appearance of many sites, they are "far from useless, and it could even be beautiful again someday."[74]

Taking a page from their anti-mountaintop removal opponents, pro-mining organizations also emphasize the importance of culture. While opposition groups highlight the danger to mountain culture posed by mountaintop removal, supporters hope to demonstrate that it is the mining industry itself, including mountaintop removal, that has created the unique culture of the region. In doing so, these groups emphasize the positive aspects (and avoid the negative) of the long history of the coal industry in southern West Virginia. An excellent example of this type of strategy is the CEDAR scholarships. Part of the application process for the $1,000 scholarships is an essay on the importance of coal to West Virginia.[75]

Many of these groups are so focused on the promotion of mountaintop removal, and mining in general, that they consistently overlook, or purposely minimize, the obviously negative aspects. Coal undoubtedly will play a vital role in the region's economy and society for the foreseeable future. This fact, combined with the historical role played by the coal industry in southern West Virginia, makes arguing the importance of coal not only easy, but obvious. What is not so easy, however, and what groups such as CEDAR hope to avoid, is the fact that some of the region's culture was shaped out of a response to the negative impact coal had on local power structures, economic stability, and political corruption.

A clear-cut loser in the mountaintop removal battle is the UMWA. The once powerful labor organization has faced the difficult choice of supporting or condemning a practice that, while employing some miners, also utilizes methods which help drive overall mining employment even lower. A major contributor to this dilemma is the massive reduction in membership that has taken place over the decades. From 1941 to 2000, nationwide membership fell from 300,000 to under 21,000. Membership numbers in the region fell to a point that by the 1990s District 17 merged with District 29 due to low membership.[76]

In order to bolster their meager numbers, the UMWA has often supported mountaintop removal operations. This calculated maneuver has had its drawbacks. Highlighted by the union's position in the *Bragg v. Robinson* case, it has severely damaged the UMWA's standing amongst underground miners, activists, and community.[77] This decision, as some would argue made out of desperation, has placed the union in the crosshairs of environmentalists and the very communities they once championed. Many believe that through the political posturing of the UMWA, and the subsequent rift between the union and the community, a vacuum has been created through which Coal River Mountain Watch and other mountaintop removal opposition groups have been able to replace the depleted union as community leaders.[78]

Residents are at odds over mountaintop removal as well. A survey conducted in Nicholas County represented a population torn between jobs and the environment. In fact, of those surveyed, many demonstrated the same polarization seen in anti– and pro–mountaintop removal organizations. Residents opposed to mountaintop removal discussed how the environment was "utterly destroyed" by it, dangers to native plants, and the loss or contamination of streams. One respondent wrote that it "destroys the beauty of our mountains" in a way which "no reclamation efforts can/will ever replace." Another respondent simply stated, "I can say that I despise MTR."[79]

Anti-MTR residents also had strong feelings as to who was to blame. Although he could not identify Massey by name, one resident spoke of a need to "keep Blankenship on a tighter rein so that those who do the mining have a fair chance of making it out." Others blamed politicians for not protecting their citizens. The same residents were also equally supportive of mountaintop removal opposition groups. Respondents replied to the question *What is your opinion of MTR opposition groups?* with responses such as "Love 'em!" and "Hurray for them."[80]

There were an equal number of proponents for mountaintop removal in the survey. This group believed those opposing the practice did not understand the process and were victims of environmentalist propaganda. Supporters also touted the effectiveness of reclamation and the importance of mountaintop removal in providing jobs. In the case of these respondents, their opinions of opposition groups were also definitive. One resident felt they were driven by interests outside of the state and did not represent the "typical working man/woman in WV" while another respondent simply thought they needed to "get a life."[81]

Another group existed, however. Equal in numbers to the more polarized factions was a group which seemed to take a more measured approach. These residents, the "middle ground" residents, were able to step away from emotional and partisan perceptions to take a more balanced, analytical approach. Major concerns for this group were that only "extreme views [were] made public" and that a general lack of education on the entire process of mountaintop removal, including required reclamation initiatives, existed. This group of residents, while understanding the role mountaintop removal could play for jobs in the region, was aware of the environmental dangers as well. From this group of respondents came the most calls to hold politicians and coal operations more responsible for both day-to-day operations and long-term reclamation of sites. These "middle grounders" also viewed opposition groups in a different light. One resident felt that neither the opposition groups nor the coal operators were being truthful and that both utilized "shock value" to gain support. Another believed that although their intentions were honorable, the opposition groups "do not take into consideration what would happen to the miners and their families."[82]

Unfortunately, the "middle grounders" are often overshadowed by the more extreme factions, and many become disenchanted with the entire political process. In the end, this allows political parties and often democracy itself to be torn between ideological extremes. What results is a vicious cycle which swings from one end of the political spectrum to the other — often missing its mark regardless of whether it started from the left or right. As with other problems regarding the region's modernization, for any real headway to be made between the traditionalist-progressive battle over mountaintop removal, middle-grounders need to become more vocal and not fall prey to whims of political polarization and extremism.

As southern West Virginia continues to struggle toward modernization, mountaintop removal will not only play a part in the future of the region's economy, but will provide an iconic symbol of the struggle between progressives and traditionalists over southern West Virginia's future. The reason for the symbolic nature of mountaintop removal is the manner in which the arguments it generates address so many aspects of the region's social, economic, and cultural existence. Unfortunately, both sides have often entrenched themselves as either adamant pro or anti camps. The obstinate stances of both sides, similar to other aspects of regional modernization, often overlook valid arguments and the reality of life in southern West Virginia.

To opponents, mountaintop removal represents the continued domination of coal power over the economy, politics, culture, heritage, environment, and even the lives of local residents themselves. By taking the leading role in opposing the wealthy and politically powerful coal operators, organizations such as Coal River Mountain Watch and the Ohio Valley Environmental Coalition had usurped the role of community advocates and protectors once held by a now struggling and politically weak UMWA. In their zeal to protect the environment and traditional living of southern West Virginians, however, many anti–mountaintop removal groups have failed to address the current reality of the economic necessity and increased safety and productivity of mountain top mining as well as the growing research regarding effective reclamation techniques.

Supporters of mountaintop mining likewise call upon the vital role that this process, and mining in general, plays in providing much needed jobs. Additionally, proponents promote a one-sided history of the coal industry and highlight the importance of coal to the region while avoiding arguments related to possible environmental harm, questions of political corruption, and the fact that while coal is vital to jobs and the economy in the region, it also supports an inherently unstable mono-economy which provides little in the way of alternatives.

The explosion at Upper Big Branch Mine in Raleigh County on April 5, 2010, drew national attention not only on the accident, but shed light on the lives of coal mining families. Other aspects brought to the surface by the frenzy of media attention were the questionable safety history of Massey Energy and the company's public relations shortfalls. Slow to provide public information, contact families, and respond to questions, Massey's lackluster response was not well received in the early stages of the accident. This was perhaps highlighted no better than when the governor of West Virginia was unaware of the whereabouts of Massey's CEO, Don Blankenship, during a briefing for national news media on the second day of the accident.[83]

Blankenship, in many ways, is cut from the same cloth as the wealthy and influential capitalists that dominated the state's economy, politics, and society at the turn of the 20th century. Similar to the great industrialists of old, Blankenship was described by a childhood acquaintance as "very, very competitive" and that during his high school years, while "not overly gifted" in athletics, "he made himself what he was by working hard ... he hated losing."[84] Like his robber-baron predecessors, Blankenship also seems to believe his ideology on labor provides the best hope not only for his own enrichment but for the future of the United States as well. A legal opponent of Blankenship even conceded that while the industrialist often "comes off as cold ... he honestly believes what he is doing is materially benefiting the lives of the people who work for him." From the old-school capitalist perspective that unfettered competition, hard work, and a willingness to take chances (even in the mines) will provide the highest economic, and therefore social outcome, Blankenship's calculus equates.[85] Unfortunately, to many others it does not, and the hard-bitten, often callous approach does not help in the war of public opinion.

A review of Massey Energy's Web site on day two of the accident also indicated a disconnect between the corporation and southern West Virginia residents. Massey's Web site featured the company's safety record in a section titled "2009 Was Another Record Setting Year for Safety." The leading newsroom link on the site until approximately 1:00 P.M. Eastern time was Massey's Fourth Quarter Results; until then updates on the accident could only be found through additional links.[86] Once posted, however, the combination of an update on the deadly accident followed by newslinks related to stocks and fourth quarter profits highlight the same conflict between profit and employee safety which has troubled the mining industry for generations.

Perhaps no single event accentuates the polarization over mountaintop removal and a more widespread practice of political and ideological partisanship over the future of the region than the heated debate between Don Blankenship and Robert F. Kennedy, Jr., at the University of Charleston in January 2010. Kennedy, the liberal, Democratic champion of the environmental faction, emphasized the dangers of pollution, climate change, and occupational safety, using a myriad of factual talking points. Blankenship, the conservative, Republican defender of industry, countered with a much less fact-based argument. What Blankenship lacked in statistical data and scientific citations (not to say some do not exist on some of these issues), he made up for in emotional and nostalgic rhetoric. Calling Kennedy's argument "a bunch of rhetoric and untruths," Blankenship touted the role of coal in making "this country great" and warned that if that fact was forgotten, Americans might as well "learn to speak Chinese."[87] Blankenship continued, saying, "Coal is what made the industrial revolution possible. If windmills were the thing to do, if solar panels were, it would happen naturally."[88]

Unfortunately, this complete polarization mimics the growing divide of American politics in general, as liberals and conservatives dig in to their entrenched ideals and view each individual challenge as direct threat to their very existence. In response, many only barricade themselves deeper into ideological bunkers. This is also the case between progressives and traditionalists in the argument over the future of southern West Virginia. Whether it be economic diversity, industrial expansion, or the practice of mountaintop removal, little will be accomplished as long as both sides remain entrenched at polar opposites. What must occur in the battle over mountaintop removal (and other areas related to modernization and the economy) is the development of a more centralized focus on mountaintop mining. This centralized focus should operate under the following realities:

- Mountaintop removal operations can severely damage the environment if not properly managed, regulated, and the land effectively and scientifically reclaimed
- The removal of mountaintops carries a significant personal and traditional meaning to local residents

- With the questionable position of government organizations in relation to coal companies, government organizations at all levels must work harder to ensure their actions are taken with the best long-term interests of the community in mind, and
- Coal mining, and mountaintop removal, are currently necessary economic endeavors for not only employment but local and state revenues.

The need for a more diverse, environmentally-friendly economy in the region is undeniable. This will not occur overnight, however. Government leaders and citizens must continue to work toward a future free of the encumbering attachment to the coal industry. This does not mean an eradication of coal mining in the region but an evolution of southern West Virginia's economy and society. Until then, much as Thomas Jefferson said of the antebellum South's reliance on slavery, "we have a wolf by the ear, and we can neither hold him, nor safely let him go."[89] Such is the situation for southern West Virginia, until alternative forms of economic viability are developed, and accepted by local residents, the region's citizens must hold on.

Conclusion

Southern West Virginia's history is rich, complex, and still relevant. Born out of the Civil War, the state represents America's rural and industrial history and the sometimes violent clash between the two. One (among many) of the struggles between the Confederacy and the Union was the defense of old traditions pitted against industrialization and modernization. In this conflict over the fate of America's future, both sides offered positive and negative arguments for their legitimacy. In the end, it was the North's gritty determination, seemingly unlimited manpower, and industrial might that outlasted Southern audacity and spirit.

Immediately following the Civil War, industrialists from the victorious North and Europe swarmed over the hills and into the valleys of southern West Virginia. This wave of modernity and industrialization carried with it new and powerful ideas, social systems, and ways of thought. The changes brought on by this social and economic revolution were dramatic, including demographic upheaval, the influx of capitalism, and the growth of company towns. These transformations directly challenged the established systems of subsistence farming and patriarchal, land-owning political and social authority. Although not eradicated, both subsistence farming and local patriarchal power bases took a back seat to absentee industrialists and life in the new company towns. These company towns served as the hub of new opportunities for many, but also worked to establish a system that fostered economic dependency and political corruption.

The legacy of the Industrial Revolution in southern West Virginia involved not only the introduction of the region to modernization but created a mono-economy reliant upon the wildly unstable coal industry, a level of political corruption that now borders on tradition, and a distrust of outsiders, politicians, and law enforcement. In the midst of these problems, the devastation of the Great Depression, exacerbated by floods and drought, broke the weakened economy and to some degree the social fabric of the region. Some scholars have argued that the region has "never emerged from the effects of the Great Depression."[1]

Following the Depression, many residents found themselves even more disenchanted with government and still dependent on either surviving mining operations or public assistance. The struggle to subsist, let alone prosper, was presented to a greater American society in both popular culture and the news media as well as through scholarly endeavors, particularly in the 1930s, 1960s, and again in the 1980s. This picture of poverty, poor education, substandard public health, and widespread unemployment was overlaid with pop culture's stereotyping of "mountain folk." This popular labeling described Appalachian residents as violently feuding clansmen, moonshining anti-social degenerates, and backward-looking but lovable bumpkins.

This "created" version of Appalachia posed an alternative to the positive attributes the mountaineers themselves held as key components of their culture, such as independence and self-sufficiency. John Photiadis implied the "real culture shock" felt by Appalachian people when the two opposing constructs were compared.[2] A "crisis of identity" thus ensued, and continues, between modernity and tradition. In this crisis, people's perceptions and beliefs are influenced as much by the region's post–Civil War history as they are by modern-day constructs. In an area where kinship bonds remain strong and family groups live in the same location for generations, local history is readily passed down from one generation to the next and has therefore remained influential. What has resulted is a living history that is vibrant, relevant, dynamic, and sometimes at odds with greater American societal perspectives.

The contemporary southern West Virginian wrestles intellectually, morally, and culturally with this history. The struggle impacts almost every element of the region's society, from public health to the development of individual identities. Actions of modern-day industrialists, such as Massey Energy's CEO, Don Blankenship, only complicate the issues. Through the use of skewed traditional ideologies, patriotic rhetoric, and the dumping of hundreds of thousands of dollars into local projects such as baseball fields and swimming pools, Blankenship plays the role of the benevolent capitalist focused on the well-being of the community.[3] On the other hand,

Blankenship's hard-nosed opposition to unions, gruff demeanor, and ruthless business practices often put coal above safety. Only months before the deadly Aracoma fire in January of 2006, he warned his workers: "If any of you have been asked by your group presidents, your supervisors, engineers or anyone to do anything (ie build overcasts, do construction jobs, or whatever), you need to ignore them and run coal. This memo is necessary only because we seem not to understand that the coal pays the bills."[4]

Through such acts of duplicity, Massey and other companies have created a tenuous symbiosis between the job-hungry residents and the coal industry through which the former are chained by a powerful and historically generated paradigm conceptualized through generations of economic, cultural, and traditional conditioning. This complex, embedded, and often misleading combination of economic need, familial heritage, and personal identity and pride have helped to sustain and perpetuate the mountaineer-mining relationship for generations.

Despite the complexities of the southern West Virginia experience, three broad themes have continued to play themselves out against the misty backdrop of the rolling hills. These themes represent the experience and ideologies of traditionalists, progressives, and the welfare class. The story of how these themes have molded the politics, society, and ideologies of the region's citizenry has been vital to not only the historical but also the contemporary and future experiences of southern West Virginians.

Tradition-minded residents have historically struggled against an introduction of industry which has sought to make use of the land and its people, often offering little in return. In addition to this refusal of industrial encroachment was a resistance to the steady, growing, and pervasive influx of new ideas. To traditionalists, this combination of industrial and ideological pressures on southern West Virginia has created a widespread, and some would argue deliberate, challenge to traditional mountain society, politics, and culture. Defending a way of life, the hardcore traditionalists in turn reject modernization for the perceived (and sometimes real) evils of drug addiction, crime, industrialization, and the damage these elements would do to families, communities, and the environment.

Progressives, on the other hand, often accepted both industrialization and the new ideologies that came with modernization. In fact, most accepted modernization with open arms. From their perspective, for the region to advance, modernization is necessary. And there was merit in their argument. Diversity of ideas and cultures enriches communities and modernization would bring much needed capital and jobs to the region.

Besides, some aspects of traditional culture needed to change. The barter-trade system was ill-equipped to deal with a modern national economy, public health and medical care improvements were needed, and subsistence farming, while nice for some, could not form the basis for an entire society. The problem with progressives, however, occurred when progress and modernization were not driven by civic virtue but by greed and lust for power, or when it completely overlooked the importance of cultural norms. It was this mindset that opened the door, or at least left it untended, to wholesale exportation of land and mineral ownership from the region's citizens to absentee landowners and corporations.

The majority of struggles, both ideological and physical, have revolved around how stubborn and unyielding tradition-minded citizens have dealt with progressives bent on modernization without regard to its impact on the people and the environment alike. Again, this is not to say that all traditionalists and progressives fit this extreme model; more centered elements of each group exist. The problem is that, just as in contemporary national politics, the squeaky wheel gets oiled. As such, the most fundamental traditionalists have come to represent the region's Appalachian heritage while the most hard-nosed industrialists and radical reformers preach the complete eradication of "hillbilly" culture. Depending on the circumstances, both tout King Coal as a universal good or monolithic evil to suit their needs. In many cases both groups have (and continue to) utilize convenient and skewed concepts of the region's history and culture for their own agendas.

Hope still exists for a measured modernization, however. Sari Tudiver laid out a framework of the group of the mountaineers that have found a balance between tradition and modernization. Although not all inclusive or exclusive, Tudiver's description of successful residents in a small Appalachian community shows how people can still honor their mountain heritage while advancing their lot in life: "They work long and hard, particularly in their young and middle adult years.... Many are frugal.... They avoid very expensive farm equipment and have retained many labor intensive methods. They pride themselves on not being indebted to others and having a plain, homey lifestyle."[5]

These same people pursue higher education, including graduate degrees, save enough money to send their children to college, and occasionally vacation in various locations both within and beyond the borders of the U.S. They do this while living and maintaining the same land, kinship bonds, and footing (if only symbolic) in subsistence living as their ancestors have for generations. The difference is that they maintain this existence with personal, family, and community growth in mind. It is this small but growing subset, and others with similarly judicious approaches, that has found the balance between remaining true to their familial bonds and traditional roots while at the same time working hard to maintain their financial stability, which in turn allows them the resources to expand their view beyond the next valley and into the national and global context of human experience.

Beyond the traditionalist and progressive factions is a third, and arguably the most troublesome, group — that of the welfare class. This element includes a large portion of people who cling to a warped vision of the subsistence farming heritage while at the same time take full advantage of, and often abuse, government assistance programs. The welfare group is neither forward- nor backward-looking but lives in the moment at the whim of the fickle coal industry, the benevolence of government programs, and the support of family. Even more than fundamentally minded traditionalists, this culture of poverty mindset and its all-too-media ready images have worked to perpetuate all that is wrong with Appalachian culture. Unfortunately, these images and stereotypes often overshadow the many positive aspects of the region's rich traditional culture.

For the region to escape poverty, outmigration, and the scrutinizing eye of mainstream America, jobs need to become available and education needs to improve. For this to happen, progressives must balance the necessity of modernization and the influx of industry against occupational safety and traditionalists' uncertainties regarding the impact of modernization on the region's society and culture. Traditionalists, likewise, must look beyond their fears to understand the benefits offered by increased industry, economic diversity, and other aspects of modernization. Only after these two groups have reached common ground will the progression toward a new southern West Virginia begin. This new future must be comprised of a southern West Virginia which is proud of its history but aware of, and ready to face, its shortcomings. This new future will provide the economic, social, and cultural motivators to finally challenge the welfare class, a necessary but too powerful coal industry, and the stereotypes both generate.

Chapter Notes

Introduction

1. Crandall A. Shifflett, *Coal Towns: Life, Work, and Culture in Company Towns of Southern Appalachia, 1880–1960* (Knoxville: University of Tennessee Press, 1991), 6.
2. John Edmund Steally III, "Kanawha Prelude to Nineteenth-century Monopoly in the United States: The Virginia Salt Combinations," *Virginia Magazine of History and Biography*, 107, No. 4 (1999), 349–477, www.jstor.org/stable/4249802. Rebecca J. Bailey, "Matewan Before the Massacre: Politics, Coal, and the Roots of Conflict in Mingo County, 1793–1920" (Ph.D. dissertation, West Virginia University, 2001). John Sherwood Lewis, "Becoming Appalachia: The Emergence of an American Subculture, 1840–1860" (Ph.D. dissertation, University of Kentucky, 2000).
3. Randall Gene Lawrence, "Appalachian Metamorphosis: Industrializing Society on the Central Plateau, 1860–1913" (Ph.D. dissertation, Duke University, 1983), 48.
4. Shifflett explains this in detail in *Coal Towns*.
5. Shifflett, 11.
6. Russell Sobel, *Unleashed Capitalism: Why Prosperity Stops at the West Virginia Border and How to Fix It* (Morgantown: Public Policy Foundation of West Virginia, 2007), 57.
7. Significant portions of inhabitants of Appalachia in the late 19th century were direct descendants of the Scots-Irish who came to America in major migrations in 1610, 1690, and 1717. Shifflett, 12.
8. Jack E. Weller, *Yesterday's People: Life in Contemporary Appalachia* (Lexington: University Press of Kentucky, 1965), 24. Weller's portrayal and analysis of southern West Virginians provides some astute observations of behavior patterns and alludes to possible anthropological and historical causation, but tends to present the native residents in much the same way as 18th and 18th century writers portrayed Middle Eastern peoples. Determinations of an entire group of people as "fatalistic" and "apprehensive" limit the ability for further investigation and dialog, just as similar labels have done with Middle Eastern peoples.
9. Dwight Billings and Kathleen Blee discuss this breakdown of old social norms in *The Road to Poverty: The Making of Wealth and Hardship in Appalachia*. Although most of the work focuses on Appalachian Kentucky, the fundamental arguments and hold true for southern West Virginia as well.
10. Shifflett, 145.
11. Lawrence William Boyd, "The Economics of the Coal Company Town: Institutional Relationships, Monopsony, and Distributional Conflicts in American Coal Towns" (Ph.D. dissertation, West Virginia University, 1993), 3. Kenneth Bailey, "A Judicious Mixture: Negroes and Immigrants in the West Virginia Mines 1880–1917," 117–132, in *Blacks in Appalachia*, William H. Turner and Edward J. Cabbell, eds. (Lexington: University Press of Kentucky, 1985), 120.
12. Allen Hayes Loughry II, "'Don't Buy Another Vote. I Won't Pay for a Landslide': The Sordid and Continuing History of Political Corruption in West Virginia" (Ph.D. dissertation, American University, 2003), iv.
13. Ibid.
14. Dwight B. Billings and Kathleen M. Blee, *The Road to Poverty: The Making of Wealth and Hardship in Appalachia* (Cambridge: Cambridge University Press, 2000), 161.
15. Richard A. Brisbin, Jr., Rober Jay Dil-

ger, Allan S. Hammock, and L. Christopher Plein, *West Virginia Politics and Government*, 2d ed. (Lincoln: University of Nebraska Press, 2008), 2.

16. Loughry, iv.

17. Jennie Noakes, "From the Top of the Mountain: Traditional Music and the Politics of Place in the Central Appalachian Coal Fields" (Ph.D. dissertation, University of Pennsylvania, 2008), 124.

Chapter One

1. Billings and Blee, 16.

2. Another work, released the same year as Henry Shapiro's *Appalachia on Our Mind*, relating to the development of otherness is Edward Said's *Orientalism*. While the work focuses on the development of the Middle East as a place of "otherness," the fundamental concepts are comparable.

3. Henry D. Shapiro, *Appalachia on Our Mind: The Southern Mountains and Mountaineers in the American Consciousness, 1870–1920* (Chapel Hill: University of North Carolina Press, 1978), xiii.

4. Allen W. Batteau, *The Invention of Appalachia* (Tucson: University of Arizona Press, 1990), 3.

5. Billings and Blee, 157.

6. Lawrence, 26.

7. Billings and Blee, 170.

8. Lawrence, 15, 31. A major thesis of Lawrence's work is the capitalization of and resistance to industrialization within the communities of southern West Virginia.

9. Ronald L. Lewis, *Transforming the Appalachian Countryside: Railroads, Deforestation, and Social Change in West Virginia 1880–1920* (Chapel Hill: University of North Carolina Press, 1998), 32–33. John Lewis, 96. Rebecca Bailey, 10.

10. Steally, 353, 357.

11. Ibid., 363.

12. John Lewis, 68–69, 81–82.

13. Rebecca Bailey, 12.

14. John Lewis, 76.

15. Ronald Lewis, 106.

16. Richard Hofstadter, *The American Political Tradition and the Men Who Made It* (New York: Vintage Books, 1989), 219.

17. Roger L. Ransom, *Conflict and Compromise: The Political Economy of Slavery, Emancipation, and the American Civil War* (New York: Cambridge University Press, 1989), 51. Roger Ransom, "Economics of the Civil War," *EH.Net* Encyclopedia, Robert Whaples, ed. (August 24, 2001). http://eh.net/encyclopedia/article/ransom.civil.war.us. (accessed 8/20/2009).

18. Amy Belasco, *The Cost of Iraq, Afghanistan, and Other Global War on Terror Operations Since 9/11*, September 2, 2010, Congressional Research Service 7-5700, RL33110, www.crs.gov. (accessed 2/1/11)

19. Hofstadter, 213.

20. Ibid., 216, 213.

21. Ibid., 220.

22. Lawrence, 28.

23. Jed Hotchkiss, "The Timber Trees of West Virginia," *Science*, 19, No. 476 (March 18, 1892), 161, www.jstor.org/stable/1766424, 161.

24. Ronald Lewis, 141.

25. Ibid., 95.

26. Ibid., 98.

27. Sari Lubitsch Tudiver, "Political Economy and Culture in Central Appalachia: 1790–1977" (Ph.D. dissertation, University of Michigan, 1984), 51.

28. Shifflett, 29.

29. Lawrence, 37–40. Norfolk and Western Historical Society, www.nwhs.org (accessed 8/2/2009). Chesapeake and Ohio Historical Society, www.cohs.org/history (accessed 8/22/2009).

30. Lawrence, 38–39. The N&W was particularly interested in the development of coal and timber along its lines. The C&O, while initially working to link transport lines between the Ohio River markets and Virginia, became heavily involved in coal and timber in the 1880s.

31. Shifflett, 39.

32. Lawrence, 42.

33. Rebecca Bailey, 35–37, 40.

34. Nicholas *Chronicle*, April 22, May 20, and October 13, 1881.

35. Ronald Lewis, 67.

36. *Men of West Virginia*, Vol. 1 (Chicago: Biographical Publishing Co., 1903), 37. Ronald Lewis, 68, 69, 76.

37. *Men of West Virginia*, 40–41.

38. Charles M. Pepper, *The Life and Times of Henry Gassaway Davis 1823–1916* (New York: Century, 1920), 46, 92.

39. Ibid., 96.

40. Orlando Oscar Stealy, *Twenty Years in the Press Gallery* (New York: Publishers Printing, 1906), 270–271.

41. Ronald Lewis, 76.

42. Ibid., 77.

43. Ibid., 90–91.

44. Nicholas *Chronicle*, April 22, May 20, and October 13, 1881.

45. Amanda J. Griffith, "The Life Cycle of a Coal Town: Widen, West Virginia, 1911–

1963" (master's thesis, West Virginia University, 2003), 3.
  46. Nicholas *Chronicle*, September 29, 1881.
  47. From Rasmussen, *Absentee Landowning*, as quoted in Rebecca Bailey, 26.
  48. David H. Bennett, *The Party of Fear: The American Far Right from Nativism to the Militia Movement* (New York: Vintage, 1995), 160.
  49. Kenneth Bailey, 118.
  50. Although Native Americans lived in the region throughout the colonial and early American period, the displacement movements of the early 19th century removed most from the area.
  51. Ronald Lewis, 90, 157, 166.
  52. Charles Peter Davis, "The Impact of the Coal Industry on McDowell County, West Virginia" (master's thesis, San Jose State University, May 1997), 13.
  53. U.S. Census, Falls District, Fayette County, 1880.
  54. Lawrence, 144.
  55. Talmage A. Stanely, "The Poco Field: Politics, Culture, and Place in Contemporary Appalachia" (Ph.D. dissertation, Emory University, 1996), 136–137.
  56. Ibid., 83.
  57. Ibid., 84.
  58. Ibid., 56–57.
  59. Ibid., 77.
  60. U.S. Census, Summersville District (Township), 1870, 1900, 1910.
  61. Lawrence, 79.
  62. Billings and Blee, 170.
  63. Ibid., 175.
  64. Tudiver, 91.
  65. Ibid., 110.
  66. Billings and Blee, 175.
  67. Boyd, 5.
  68. Davis, x.

Chapter Two

  1. Griffith, 31. Boyd, 24.
  2. Boyd, 24.
  3. Sobel, 58.
  4. Nettie McGill, *The Welfare of Children in the Bituminous Coal Mining Communities of West Virginia, 1923*, Department of Labor (Washington, D.C.: U.S. Government Printing Office, 1923), 7.
  5. Shifflett, 9.
  6. Boyd, 40.
  7. Shifflett, 61.
  8. Hearings Before a Subcommittee of the Committee on Education and Labor, United States Senate, *Conditions in the Paint Creek District, West Virginia*, U.S. Senate, 63rd Congress, 1st Session, Part I, II, III, 1913, 193. The report discusses several company stores that doubled as post offices and gathering places. Shifflett, 177.
  9. Merle Travis, "Sixteen Tons," *Folk Songs of the Hills*, Capitol Records, 1947.
  10. Griffith, 33. From Elk River Coal and Lumber Company reports, 1912. The author's grandparents grew up in towns operated by this company.
  11. Shifflett, 41
  12. *Conditions in the Paint Creek District*, 381.
  13. McGill, 10.
  14. Lawrence, 148.
  15. McGill, 6.
  16. Ibid., 11.
  17. Shifflett, 61.
  18. Ibid.
  19. Kenneth Bailey, 128.
  20. Bennett, 164–165, 171.
  21. Ibid., 2–3.
  22. Shifflett, 61.
  23. Bluefield *Daily Telegraph*, April 1, 1906.
  24. *Conditions in the Paint Creek District*, 999.
  25. Shifflett, 176. Many of these items were dependent upon the availability of electricity, which varied greatly from town to town.
  26. Ibid., 177.
  27. Ibid., 176.
  28. *Conditions in the Paint Creek District*, 1000, 1411, 1436.
  29. Griffith, 40.
  30. Shifflett, 51. From interview with T.B. Pugh.
  31. Lawrence, 199, 85.
  32. Stanely, 139.
  33. *Conditions in the Paint Creek District*, 71.
  34. Shifflett, 51–52.
  35. Lawrence, 183–184, 186.
  36. Bennett, 181.
  37. Weller, 30.
  38. Ronald Lewis, 208.
  39. Shifflett, 52.
  40. Ibid., 41.
  41. Griffith, 9.
  42. Keith Dix, *What's a Coal Miner to Do? The Mechanization of Coal Mining* (Pittsburgh: University of Pittsburgh Press, 1988), 22, 25.
  43. *Conditions in the Paint Creek District*, 39, 379–182, 443–444, 1292–1298, 1400–1415, 2199.
  44. Ibid., 387, 2199.
  45. Ibid., 382, 443–444.
  46. Ibid., 1401–1405.

47. Ibid., 1400, 1414.
48. Ibid., 1296.
49. Hoyt N. Wheeler, "Mountaineer Mine Wars: An Analysis of the West Virginia Mine Wars of 1912–1913 and 1920–1921," *Business History Review*, 50, No. 1 (Spring 1976), 74, www.jstor.org/stable/3113575.
50. *Conditions in the Paint Creek District*, 382, 388.
51. Ibid., 382, 387.
52. Boyd, 17.
53. *Conditions in the Paint Creek District*, 219, 1288.
54. Shifflett, 180.
55. *Conditions in the Paint Creek District*, p. 223, 575.
56. Shifflett, 180.
57. *Conditions in the Paint Creek District*, 220, 221, 224. Shifflett, 184.
58. Boyd, 45.
59. Shifflett, 180.
60. *Conditions in the Paint Creek District*, 382.
61. Loughry, 454. Paul H. Rakes, "Acceptable Casualties: Power, Culture, and History in the West Virginia Coalfields, 1900–1945" (Ph.D. dissertation, West Virginia University, 2002), 1.
62. Shifflett, 103. Richard D. Lunt, *Law and Order vs. the Miners: West Virginia, 1906–1933* (Charleston, WV: Appalachian Editions, 1992), 14.
63. Rakes, 26. Griffith, 23.
64. Shifflett, 103. Rakes, 31.
65. Sharon A. Brown, *Historic Resource Study, Kay Moor: New River Gorge National River, West Virginia* (U.S. Department of Interior, July 1990), Appendix 10. www.nps.gov/history/history/online_books/neri/hrs1/index.htm.
66. Lunt, 13.
67. Rakes, 42–44. Shifflett, 101.
68. Shifflett, 83.
69. Brad Paisley, "You'll Never Leave Harlan Alive," *Part II*, Darrell Scott, Arista Nashville, 2001.
70. Dwight Yoakam, "Miner's Prayer," *Guitars, Cadillacs Etc., Etc.*, Capitol Records, 1986.
71. Lawrence, 118.
72. Ibid., 18. From William Graebner, *Coal Mine Safety in the Progressive Period* (Lexington: University Press of Kentucky, 1976).
73. Rakes, 24. One of the major causes of explosions was the rapid increase of methane gas production as mining operations grew larger and machinery was introduced.
74. Ibid., 47.
75. Lawrence, 120.
76. Rakes, 23. Lawrence, 117.
77. From Lawrence, 117. As reported by *1908 U.S. Immigration Commission Report*.
78. Rakes, 16. Lunt, 37. Lunt believes the true cause was the large number of non-union mines in West Virginia.
79. *Conditions in the Paint Creek District*, 1657.
80. Ibid., 387.
81. Ibid., 948, 1050, 1311.
82. Ibid., 1336.
83. Kenneth Bailey, 119–120.
84. *Conditions in the Paint Creek District*, 35.
85. Rebecca Bailey, 282.
86. McGill, 62–63.
87. Shifflett, 109.
88. Lawrence, 120.
89. Ibid., 121.
90. Ibid., 120.
91. *Conditions in the Paint Creek District*, 387.

Chapter Three

1. Rebecca Bailey, 40.
2. Ibid., 41–42.
3. Ibid., 43.
4. Lunt, 12–13.
5. Ronald Lewis, 157.
6. Ibid., 163.
7. *Conditions in the Paint Creek District*. Various interviewers discuss the important role the company store played in the residents' lives, as well as how the operators used the store and the threat of eviction as coercion against unionization.
8. Lawrence, 217.
9. Herbert R. Northrup, "The Coal Mines," in *Blacks in Appalachia*, William H. Turner and Edward J. Cabbell, eds. (Lexington: University Press of Kentucky, 1985), 165.
10. Shifflett, 117.
11. Northrup, 165.
12. Lunt, 15. Shifflett, 128–129.
13. *Hitchman Coal and Coke Co. vs. Mitchell*, U.S. Supreme Court, 245 U.S. 229 (1917), http://supreme.justia.com/us/245/229/case.html. Lunt, 21–22.
14. Lunt, 25–26.
15. *Report of the Proceedings of the 42nd Annual Convention of the American Federation of Labor*, American Federation of Labor (Washington, D.C.: Law Reporter Printing Co., 1922), 42.
16. Lunt, 21, 45.
17. Ronald Lewis, 180.
18. David A. Corbin, "Betrayal in the West Virginia Coal Fields: Eugene V. Debs and the

Socialist Party of America, 1912–1914," *The Journal of American History*, 64, No. 4 (March 1978), www.jstor.org/stable/1890733, 989.
  19. Lunt, 14. *Conditions in the Paint Creek District*, 383, 522.
  20. *Conditions in the Paint Creek District*, 522.
  21. Cribbing was the use of wood partitions to extend the size of coal cars, therefore allowing more than the standard amount to be loaded. Miners were only paid for the standard amount even if cribbing was used.
  22. Wheeler, 70. Checkweighmen verified the actual weight of a car of coal and inspected the coal for impurities and deducted pay accordingly.
  23. Northrup, 165.
  24. *Conditions in the Paint Creek District*, 1088, 1092–1093, 1096.
  25. Shifflett, 56.
  26. *Conditions in the Paint Creek District*, 1261.
  27. Wheeler, 70.
  28. Ibid., 71.
  29. *Conditions in the Paint Creek District*, 695, 697, 712, 718, 720.
  30. Dix, 12.
  31. Kenneth Bailey, 120. *Conditions in the Paint Creek District*, 697, 707.
  32. *Conditions in the Paint Creek District*, 697, 712.
  33. Ibid., 720.
  34. Ibid., 86–87.
  35. Ibid., 84–85.
  36. Kenneth Bailey, 120. Lunt discusses a superintendent and two guards indicted for peonage in Mercer County in 1913.
  37. Ronald Lewis, 178–179.
  38. Ibid., 179.
  39. Ibid., 171–173.
  40. Nicholas *Chronicle*, October 10, 1912.
  41. Loughry, 112.
  42. *Conditions in the Paint Creek District*, 987.
  43. Ibid., 987–988, 990.
  44. Ibid., 1141.
  45. Shifflett, 40.
  46. Boyd, 63–64.
  47. *Conditions in the Paint Creek District*, 193, 211, 222.
  48. Ibid., 1302.
  49. Ibid., 1101, 1303.
  50. Ibid., 1303, 1406.
  51. Ibid., 1406.
  52. Ibid., 124, 378.
  53. Ibid., 483.
  54. Ibid., 504–506. Bluefield *Daily Telegraph*, October 1, 1912.
  55. Ibid., 380.
  56. Ibid., 478, 1090.
  57. Corbin, 989.
  58. Wheeler, 71.
  59. Loughry, 112
  60. Wheeler, 71.
  61. *Conditions in the Paint Creek District*, 372.
  62. Bluefield *Daily Telegraph*, July 24, 1912, September 3, 1912.
  63. Wheeler, 71–72. Loughry, 108.
  64. Bluefield *Daily Telegraph*, September 3, 1912.
  65. Wheeler, 72. *Conditions in the Paint Creek District*, 80. Numbers of pistols and amount of ammunition varies with the source. Wheeler lists 556 pistols and 225,000 rounds of ammunition, while the Senate report lists 482 pistols and 163,300 rounds of ammunition.
  66. *Conditions in the Paint Creek District*, 26.
  67. Ibid., 343.
  68. Ibid., 245.
  69. Wheeler, 72. *Conditions in the Paint Creek District*, 447.
  70. Wheeler, 72.
  71. *Conditions in the Paint Creek District*, 2261.
  72. Wheeler, 72–73. Lunt, 28.
  73. *Conditions in the Paint Creek District*, 370.
  74. Ibid., 408–409.
  75. Ibid., 418, 426.
  76. Lunt, 32.
  77. Wheeler, 73. *Conditions in the Paint Creek District*, 264, 275–282, 399–400.
  78. Boyd, 43.
  79. Loughry, 109.
  80. *Conditions in the Paint Creek District*, 1305–1306.
  81. Corbin, 988–989.
  82. Ibid., 993.
  83. Roger Fagge, "Eugene V. Debs in West Virginia, 1913: A Reappraisal," *West Virginia History*, 52 (1993), www.wvculture.org/history/journal_wvh/wvh52-1.html. Lunt, 32. Corbin, 994.
  84. Fagge. Corbin, 998–999.
  85. Corbin, 1003–1004.

Chapter Four

  1. Lunt, 34.
  2. April D. Wolfe, "World War One and the Miners of Southern West Virginia," *West Virginia Historical Society Quarterly*, 16, No. 1 (January 2002), www.wvculture.org/history/wvhs1601.html.
  3. Wolfe.

4. Lunt, 37–38, 15–16.
5. Ibid., 44–45.
6. Boyd, 69–71.
7. Ibid., 70.
8. Ibid., 72.
9. From Loughry, 151.
10. Wheeler, 79.
11. Loughry, 129, 150–151.
12. Robert Shogan, *The Battle of Blair Mountain: The Story of America's Largest Labor Uprising* (New York: Basic Books, 2004), 15.
13. Rebecca Bailey, 407–408.
14. Shogan, 3.
15. Rebecca Bailey, 386, 413.
16. From Lunt, 78.
17. Lunt, 78. Wheeler, 76–77.
18. Lunt, 78.
19. Wheeler, 77.
20. Lunt, 79.
21. Rebecca Bailey, 411–412.
22. Ibid., 407–408.
23. Ibid., 409–410.
24. Wheeler, p. 77.
25. Ibid.
26. Shogan, 16. Rebecca Bailey, 427.
27. Shogan, 22–23. Wheeler, 77–78.
28. Wheeler, 77–78. Shogan, 24–25. Rebecca Bailey, 446.
29. Rebecca Bailey, 439, Wheeler, 77–78.
30. Wheeler, 78.
31. Ibid.
32. *New York Times*, August 2, 1921, 1–2.
33. Wheeler, 78.
34. Clayton D. Laurie, "The United States Army and the Return to Normalcy in Labor Dispute Interventions: The Case of West Virginia Coal Mine Wars, 1920–1921," *West Virginia History*, 50 (1991), www.wvculture.org/history/journal_wvh/wvh50-1.html.
35. Wheeler, 78.
36. Laurie.
37. Loughry, 115–116.
38. Ibid.
39. Wheeler, 80.
40. Laurie. Wheeler, 80.
41. Shogan, 190. Wheeler, 80.
42. Shogan, 193, Wheeler, 81. Shogan stated the U.S. Army believed the number of belligerents to be between 10,000 and 20,000 combined.
43. Wheeler, 80–81.
44. Wheeler, 81. Laurie. Shogan, 208.
45. Elliott J. Gorn, *Mother Jones: The Most Dangerous Woman in America* (New York: Hill and Wang, 2001), 273. Loughry, 116–117.
46. Wheeler, 81.
47. Ibid., 91. Taken from Winthrop Lane's *Civil War in West Virginia*.
48. Loughry, 117.
49. Wheeler, 81.
50. Ibid., 91. Taken from Lane's *Civil War in West Virginia*.

Chapter Five

1. Jerry Bruce Thomas, *An Appalachian New Deal: West Virginia in the Great Depression* (Lexington: University Press of Kentucky, 1998), 26–27.
2. Ronald Lewis, 276.
3. Paul Salstrom, *Appalachia's Path to Dependency: Rethinking a Region's Economic History: 1730–1940* (Lexington: University Press of Kentucky, 1991), 123.
4. A.R. Mangus, *Rural Regions of the United States*, Works Progress Administration (Washington, D.C.: United States Government Printing Office, 1940), 19, 37.
5. Millard Peck, "Farm or Forest in the West Virginia Appalachians?" *Journal of Farm Economics*, 11, No. 3 (July 1929), 422–435, www.jstor.org/stable/1229853, p. 435.
6. Salstrom, xxii, 43.
7. Ibid., xxiii.
8. Rebecca Bailey, 386.
9. Salstrom, 84.
10. Thomas, 9.
11. Griffith, 24. Thomas, 8.
12. Thomas, 8.
13. Tomas E. Posey, "Unemployment Compensation and the Coal Industry in West Virginia," *Southern Economic Journal*, 7, No. 3 (January 1941), www.jstor.org/stable/10530 44, 349.
14. Kevin Cahill, "Fertilizing the Weeds: The New Deal's Rural Poverty Program in West Virginia" (Ph.D. dissertation, West Virginia University, 1999), 18.
15. Ronald Lewis, 264.
16. Thomas, 15, 163, 179–181. Salstrom, 96.
17. Clyde G. Booker, "Dying for a Job: African Americans, Industrial Hegemony, and the Hawk's Nest Tunnel, 1930–1936" (Ph.D. dissertation, University of Kentucky, 2005), 4. Thomas, 27, 31.
18. Thomas, 27. Salstrom, 107. Charleston *Gazette*, January 26, 1937. Charleston *Daily Mail*, January 27, 1937.
19. Thomas, 14.
20. Ibid., 31.
21. Cahill, 30.
22. Thomas, 31.
23. Mark Myers, "Coal Mechanization and Migration from McDowell County, West Virginia, 1932–1970" (master's thesis, East Tennessee State University, August 2001), 48.

24. Thomas, 26, 60.
25. Ibid., 60.
26. Cahill, 49.
27. Ibid., 35.
28. Writer's Program, Works Progress Administration, *West Virginia: A Guide to the Mountain State* (New York: Oxford University Press, 1941), 70.
29. Cahill, 91.
30. Thomas, 60-61.
31. Cahill, 36.
32. Beckley *Post-Herald*, February 22, 1935.
33. Booker, 5. Thomas, 32.
34. Bluefield *Daily Telegraph*, February 13, 1936.
35. Thomas, 32.
36. Charleston *Gazette*, March 11, 1931.
37. Raleigh *Register*, January 17, 1932.
38. Thomas, 44.
39. Ibid., 46.
40. Beckley *Post-Herald*, March 30, 1935.
41. Thomas, 61-63, 87.
42. Ibid., 63.
43. Ibid., 70.
44. Herman Guy Kump, *Inaugural Address, March 4, 1933*, West Virginia Archives and History, www.wvculture.org/history/kumpia.html. Thomas, 70-90. Thomas discusses the impact of the Tax Limitation Act in detail throughout his book.
45. Thomas, 90.
46. Appalachian State University, *Land Ownership Patterns and Their Impacts on Appalachian Communities: A Survey of 80 Counties* (New Market, TN: Highlander Research and Education Center and Washington, D.C.: Appalachian Regional Commission, 1981), 27.
47. Ibid., 27.
48. Ibid., 145.
49. Ibid., 152.
50. Ibid., 170-171.
51. Sobel, 73-74, 78.
52. Ibid., 18-20.
53. Ibid., 16.
54. James T. Patterson, *America's Struggle Against Poverty, 1900-1985* (Cambridge: Harvard University Press, 1986), 57. Thomas, 112-113.
55. Patterson, 57.
56. Thomas, 92, 136. Robert Jay Dilger, Eleanor H. Blakely, Melissa Latimer, Barry L. Locker, F. Carson Mencken, L. Christopher Plein, Lucinda A. Potter, and David Williams, *Welfare Reform in West Virginia* (Morgantown: West Virginia University Press, 2004), 64.
57. Griffith, 26. Thomas, 92-93.
58. Thomas, 105-107.
59. Ibid., 98.
60. Ibid., 101.
61. Salstrom, 90-93. Thomas, 108.
62. Thomas, 108.
63. Booker, 13-14, 20.
64. Thomas, 41. Booker, 15, 19. Charleston *Daily Mail*, January 19, 1936.
65. Thomas, 115.
66. Ibid., 126.
67. Ibid., 115-116.
68. Ibid., 121.
69. Milton Harr, "The Civilian Conservation Corps in West Virginia: Civilian Conservation Corps (CCC) Companies and Camps in West Virginia, 1933-1942," West Virginia Archives and History, www.wvculture.org/history/ccc.html.
70. *The Panther Pioneer*, CCC camp newsletter, 1, No. 3 (August 8, 1936). Camp McDowell Company 3542. ID# DC01-0008. West Virginia Memory Project, CCC Collection, MS85-17, www.wvculture.org/history/wvmemory.
71. *The Panther Pioneer*, 1, No. 3 (August 8, 1936). CCC camp newsletter, "Memo," *Weekly Education Bulletin* (July 12, 1937). CCC Camp 3510. ID# DC01-0012. *The Beaver's Log*, CCC camp newsletter, 2, No. 6 (August 1935). Company 1522 Clifftop. ID# DC01-0079. *The Beaver's Log*, CCC camp newsletter, 4, No. 1 (January 29, 1936). Company 1522 Clifftop. ID# DC01-0083. West Virginia Memory Project, CCC Collection, MS85-17, www.wvculture.org/history/wvmemory.
72. *The Panther Pioneer*, 1, No. 3 (August 8, 1936).
73. *Skillethead*, camp newsletter, 4, No. 2 (March 30, 1939). Company 2589. ID# DC01-0029. West Virginia Memory Project, CCC Collection, MS85-17, www.wvculture.org/history/wvmemory.
74. Letters regarding Ralph Matz, ID# DC01-0061. West Virginia Memory Project, CCC Collection, MS85-17, www.wvculture.org/history/wvmemory.
75. Thomas, 197-199.
76. Patterson, 63. Thomas, 136.
77. Thomas, 137, 145-151.
78. Patterson, 46, 64-65.
79. From Cahill, 225-226.
80. Thomas, 54-56.
81. Cahill, 56-58.
82. Thomas, 168. The Eleanor Roosevelt Papers Project, George Washington University, www.gwu.edu/~erpapers.
83. Cahill, 137, 140. Thomas, 172. "Quality residents" was a term of the times. No blacks were selected to resettle.
84. Thomas, 173.

85. Thomas, 173. Cahill, 161.
86. Cahill, 161. Thomas, 172–173.
87. Cahill, 148. The Eleanor Roosevelt Papers Project.
88. Cahill, 145–146. Thomas, 173.
89. Cahill, 136, 167.
90. Thomas, 174, 188.
91. From Cahill, 167.
92. Ibid., 168,
93. Ibid., 162, 168.
94. Ibid., 19.
95. Cahill, 232. Thomas, 166.
96. Thomas, 162–163. From Benita Asch and A.R. Mangus, *Farmers on Relief and Rehabilitation*, WPA, Department of Social Research, Monograph VIII, 1937 (New York: Da Capo Press, 1971).
97. Cahill, 83.
98. Ibid., 123, 119.
99. Ibid., 119, 91.
100. Ibid., 107–108.
101. Sobel, 180.
102. Cahill, 113. Some local and regional administrators worked around the regulations and provided limited assistance to farmers in six counties.
103. Ibid., 116.
104. Thomas, 175.
105. Cahill, 175.
106. Thomas, 119.
107. Salstrom, 107–109.
108. Thomas, 176.
109. Cahill, 226–228.
110. Thomas, 177–178.
111. Cahill, 231, 225–226.
112. Dilger, et al., 2.
113. Posey, 347, 351.
114. Ibid., 350–351, 356, 359–361.
115. Glen Edward Taul, "Poverty, Development, and Government in Appalachia: Origins of the Appalachian Regional Commission" (unpublished dissertation, University of Kentucky, 2001), 13.
116. Shifflett, 199.
117. Elizabeth Carter McGaha, "WV WORKS ... Does It? An Examination of Post Welfare Hardship in West Virginia" (Ph.D. dissertation, West Virginia University, 2002), 29.
118. Dilger, et al., 2, 67, 71. Chang Fisher, "Evaluating the Impact of Mandatory Work Programs on Two Parent Welfare Caseloads" (Ph.D. dissertation, University of Maryland, 1996), 23.
119. L. Christopher Plein, "Welfare Reform in a Hard Place: The West Virginia Experience," *Rockefeller Report*, 13 (Albany: Nelson A. Rockefeller Institute of Government, November 2001), 12. Dilger, et al., 2.
120. Dilger, et al., 71. Fisher, 23. Plein, 12.
121. Ernst W. Stromsdorfer, "Determinants of Economic Success in Retraining the Unemployed: The West Virginia Experience," *The Journal of Human Resources*, 3, No. 2 (Spring 1968), www.jstor.org/stable/145128, 139–140, 145, 156.
122. Dilger, et al., 72.
123. David S. Walls and John B. Stephenson, eds., *Appalachia in the Sixties: Decade of Reawakening* (Lexington: University Press of Kentucky, 1972), 4.
124. Kavita Pandit and Suzanne Davies Withers, eds., *Migration and Restructuring in the United States: A Geographic Perspective* (New York: Rowman and Littlefield, 1999), 18.
125. McGaha, 9.
126. Weller, 103.
127. Ibid., 104.
128. Semoa C.B. Sousa, "An Economic Analysis of the Relationship of Poverty and Income Inequality in Rural West Virginia" (master's thesis, West Virginia University, 2000), 19–20.
129. Janet Gail Boggess Welch, "A Study of Appalachian Cultural Values as Evidenced in the Political and Social Attitudes of Rural West Virginians" (Ph.D. dissertation, University of Maryland, 1984), 179. Interviews: James Milam, Nicholas County prosecuting attorney, and Robert Fletcher, DDS, September 2009.
130. Dilger, et al., 79–80. McGaha, 10.
131. Plein, 12–13. Dilger, et al., 80, 82. Fisher, 25–26.
132. Fisher, Chang, 33.
133. Ibid., 122.
134. Sousa, 74.
135. Dilger, et al., 34.
136. Ibid., 42–43.
137. Walls and Stephenson, 131, 166.
138. Plein, 14. Pandit and Withers, 20.
139. Pandit and Withers, 22, 24, 26, 28.
140. McGaha, 30.
141. McGaha, 1. Dilger, et al., 2, 5.
142. McGaha, 12.
143. Dilger, et al., 111, 117. Plein, 15.
144. Dilger, et al., 158.
145. McGaha, 15–16.
146. This incentive was important because TANF does not allow higher education to substitute for employment.
147. Plein, 23. McGaha, 33.
148. McGaha, 13.
149. Dilger, et al., 80, 157–158.
150. McGaha, 16.
151. Plein, 16.
152. McGaha, 18.

153. Dilger, et al., 274.
154. McGaha, 42.
155. Dilger, et al., 278–279.
156. Plein, 33.
157. Ibid., 35.
158. Ibid., 11.
159. Hearing Before the Select Committee on Hunger, House of Representatives, *Appalachia Revisited: The Persistence of Hunger and Poverty in West Virginia*, 100th Congress, Serial No. 100-28 (Washington, D.C.: U.S. Government Printing Office, 1988), 2.
160. U.S. Census Quick Fact Database, www.quickfacts.census.gov.

Chapter Six

1. Tony Dokoupil, "Hillbilly No More," *Newsweek* (February 27, 2009). www.newsweek.com/id/186715/page/1.
2. Sandra Lee Barney, *Authorized to Heal: Gender, Class and the Transformation of Medicine in Appalachia, 1880–1930* (Chapel Hill: University of North Carolina Press, 2000), 5.
3. Ibid., 4–5, 8.
4. Ibid., 25.
5. Ibid., 3–4, 7, 21, 27, 117.
6. Ibid., 22.
7. Ibid., 35.
8. West Virginia State Medical Association, *West Virginia Medical Journal*, 10, Nos. 1–5 (July–November, 1915). Various articles.
9. Barney, 102.
10. Children's Bureau, *The Promotion of the Welfare and Hygiene of Maternity and Infancy: The Administration of the Act of Congress of November 23, 1921 (Sheppard-Towner Act), Fiscal Year Ended June 30, 1924* (Washington, D.C.: U.S. Government Printing Office, 1925), 4.
11. McGill, 55–56.
12. McGill, 55. Barney, 101.
13. No author given, "Fighting Tuberculosis in West Virginia," *The American Journal of Nursing*, 23, No. 9 (June 1923), 779. www.jstor.org/stable/3407551.
14. McGill, 10.
15. Ibid., 12, 14–15.
16. Ibid., 15.
17. Ibid., 15.
18. Ibid., 8, 16–17.
19. Ibid., 47.
20. Barney, 104.
21. C. Belmont Keeney, "Soldiers and Stereotypes: Mountaineers, Cultural Identity, and World War II" (Ph.D. dissertation, West Virginia University, 2009), 38.
22. Sheppard Act report, 1925, 42.
23. Children's Bureau, *The Promotion of the Welfare and Hygiene of Maternity and Infancy: The Administration of the Act of Congress of November 23, 1921 (Sheppard-Towner Act), Fiscal Year Ended June 30, 1926* (Washington, D.C.: U.S. Government Printing Office, 1927), 72.
24. Barney, 101.
25. Marilyn A. Jarvis, Mary Pullen, and Jane Downin, "Health Care Larnin' in Appalachia," *The American Journal of Nursing*, 67, No. 11 (November 1967), 2346–2347, www.jstor.org/stable/3453682.
26. Jarvis, et al., 2345. Studies such as these tend to find what they are looking for, meaning, as the goal of the programs were to reach the most at-risk groups, statistical data obviously omits those residents living less on the margins and therefore more likely to fall prey to poor public and personal health practices.
27. Ibid., 2345.
28. Francis X. Clines, "Rural West Virginia Winning Over Health Care Workers," *New York Times* (June 21, 2001), A14, http://www.nytimes.com/2001/06/21/us/rural-west-virginia-winning-over-health-care-workers.html (accessed 4/12/2010). Dr. Paul Conley is also a high school classmate of the author.
29. Forest Lang, Kaethe P. Ferguson, Bruce Bennard, Pamela Zahorik, and Carolyn Sliger, "Appalachian Preceptorship: Over Two Decades of an Integrated Clinical-Classroom Experience of Rural Medicine and Appalachian Culture," *Academic Medicine*, 80 (August 2005), 717, 719.
30. Clines, A14.
31. *Summersville.org*, www.summersville.org (accessed 4/12/2010). Summersville Memorial Hospital, www.summersvillememorial.org/physicians/conley.htm (accessed 4/12/2010).
32. Interview with Dr. Paul Conley conducted by Betty Louise Dotson-Lewis and posted on the University of Nebraska Medical Center's website, available at Appalachian Stories, www.unmc.edu/Community/ruralmed/RMEPost/appalachian_stories.htm (accessed 4/12/2010). Dotson-Lewis conducted the interview as part of her research for a chapter titled "Rural Health Care in the Southern Appalachian Coalfields" in her book *Appalachia: Spirit Triumphant*, self-published, 2004.
33. Stacy Dawn Whittington, "Initial Assessment/Treatment of Pediatric Overweight in Rural-Based Appalachia: A Qualitative Investigation" (master's thesis, West Virginia University, November 2005), 2–3. Roni A. Neff, "In the Wrong Place? Geographic Varia-

tion in U.S. Occupational Injury/Illness Rates" (Ph.D. dissertation, Johns Hopkins University, September 2006), 98–99.

34. West Virginia Bureau for Public Health, Health Statistics Center, www.dhhr.org (accessed 4/15/2010). Data from 1997–2001.

35. Ibid., 2006 data.

36. *State Cancer Profiles*, National Cancer Institute, http://statecancerprofiles.cancer.gov/cgi-bin/quickprofiles/profile.pl?54&047 (accessed 4/15/2010).

37. Kenneth Bridford, Joseph Costello, John Gamble, Dennis Groce, Marylin Hutchison, William Jones, James Merchant, Carl Ortmeyer, Robert Reger, and William L. Wagner, "Occupational Safety and Health Implications of Increased Coal Utilization," *Environmental Health Perspectives*, 33 (December 1979), 287, www.jstor.org/stable/3429089 (accessed 4/16/010).

38. *State Cancer Profiles*, National Cancer Institute. Cancer data 1996–2000. All others, 1999.

39. Kimberly N. Fisher, "The Effect of Parent Education on the Home Food Environment of Overweight Adolescents in West Virginia" (master's thesis, West Virginia University, 2009), 9.

40. Ibid., 9, 10,12.

41. Tracy L. LeGrow, "Access to Health Information and Health Care Decision-Making on Women in a Rural Appalachian Community" (Ph.D. dissertation, Marshall University, April 2007), 76, 85–86, 89.

42. West Virginia Bureau for Public Health, Health Statistics Center, www.dhhr.org (accessed 4/16/2010).

43. U.S. Census Quick Fact Database (accessed 4/16/2010).

44. LeGrow, 91–92.

45. Ibid., 77.

46. The author has experienced this element of intellectual intimidation himself. While helping care for my mother, I saw her on many occasions accept directions and protocols from doctors without questioning their reasoning. When I asked her if she agreed with the doctor or understood the advice, she stated that she was in no place to question him, as he had been to school for medicine and she hadn't.

47. LeGrow, 72.

48. Ibid., 79–80.

49. Shaunna L. Scott, "They Don't Have to Live by the Old Traditions: Saintly Men, Sinner Women, and an Appalachian Pentecostal Revival," *American Ethnologist*, 21, No. 2 (May 1994), 229, www.jstor.org/stable/65887.

50. John D. Photiadis and John F. Schnabel, "Religion: A Persistent Institution in a Changing Appalachia," *Review of Religious Research*, 19, No. 1 (Autumn 1977), 36, www.jstor.org/stable/3509578.

51. Ibid.

52. Tudiver, 13.

53. Scott, 229.

54. Joy A. Butcher-Winfree, "Portraits of Resiliency: A Qualitative Study of Appalachian Christian Women" (Ph.D. dissertation, Marshall University, August 2009), ii.

55. LeGrow, 82.

56. U.S. Department of Labor, Bureau of Labor Statistics, "Coal Mining: Injuries, Illnesses, and Fatalities" (April 2010), www.blg.gov/iif/oshwc/osh/os/osar0012.htm (accessed 4/17/2010).

57. U.S. Department of Labor, Mine Safety and Health Administration, *Mine Accident, Injury, Illness, Employment and Coal Production Statistics*, Tables 3 and 8, www.msha.gov/stats/statinfo.htm (accessed 5/4/2010).

58. U.S. Department of Labor, Bureau of Labor Statistics, "Coal Mining: Injuries, Illnesses, and Fatalities."

59. Ibid.

60. Julian Borger, "Hillbilly Heroin: The Painkiller Abuse Wrecking Lives in West Virginia," *The Guardian* (UK) (June 25, 2001), 3 (accessed 5/4/2010 via Proquest Database). Joseph B. Prater, "West Virginia's Painful Settlement: How the Oxycontin Phenomenon and Unconventional Theories of Tort Liability May Make Pharmaceutical Companies Liable for Black Markets," *Northwestern University Law Review*, 100, No. 3 (2006).

61. Allen G. Breed, "Oxycontin Addiction Is Plaguing Appalachia: The Prescription Painkiller Is Tearing Apart Communities and Destroying Lives," *Star Tribune* (June 24, 2001), 19A (accessed 5/4/2010 via Proquest Database).

62. Borger. Breed.

63. Breed. The case was settled in 2004 for $10 million. Circuit Court of McDowell County, West Virginia, *West Virginia v. Purdue Pharma L.P.*, Civil Action No. 01-C-137-S, 3, www.wvs.state.wv.us/wvag/PDFReader/oxycontin.pdf, n.d. (accessed 5/4/2010).

64. Bridford, 285.

65. Vincent Castranova and Val Vallyathan, "Silicosis and Coal Workers' Pneumoconiosis," *Environmental Health Perspectives*, 108, Supplement 4: Occupational and Environmental Lung Diseases (August 2000), 678, www.jstor.org/stable/3454404 (accessed 4/16/2010).

66. Castranova and Vallyathan, 679.
67. Kris Maher, "Black Lung on Rise in Mines, Reversing Trend," *The Wall Street Journal* (December 15, 2009), n.p., www.online.wsj.com/article/58126083871040391327.htm (accessed 4/20/2010).

Chapter Seven

1. Thomas Paine, *Common Sense* (Mineola: Dover Publications, 1997), 3. Originally published 14 February 1776.
2. Clinton Rossiter, *The Federalist Papers* (New York: Mentor, 1999), 209. From Madison, "Federalist No. 39."
3. Loughry, iii.
4. Charleston *Daily Mail*, May 20, 1960.
5. Lawrence R. Jacobs and Robert Y. Shapiro, "Issues, Candidate Image, and Priming: The Use of Private Polls in Kennedy's 1960 Presidential Campaign," *The American Political Science Review*, 88, No. 3 (September 1994), 527–540, www.jstor.org/stable/2944793.
6. Loughry, 344–348.
7. Ibid., 350.
8. Allen W. Batteau, *The Invention of Appalachia*, 104. Janet Gail Boggess Welch, "A Study of Appalachian Cultural Values as Evidenced in the Political and Social Attitudes of Rural West Virginians" (Ph.D. dissertation, University of Maryland, 1984), 189–190.
9. Richard Ogden Hartman, "A Constitution of Our Own: The Constitutional Convention of 1872 and the Resurrection of Ex-Confederate West Virginia" (master's thesis, Marshall University, December 2004), 63.
10. Ronald Lewis, 104, 106–107.
11. Ibid., 70–71.
12. Ibid., 108.
13. Hartman, 53.
14. Ibid., 110.
15. Lewis, 110.
16. Loughry, 143–144.
17. Charleston *Daily Mail*, November 10, 1926. Charleston *Gazette*, November 13, 1926.
18. Bluefield *Daily Telegraph*, February 2, 1933.
19. Loughry, 381–382.
20. Thomas, 36–37.
21. Raleigh *Register*, November 13, 1932.
22. Charleston *Daily Mail*, June 8, 1972.
23. Loughry, 322–323.
24. Loughry, 332. Charleston *Gazette*, February 21, 2001.
25. Charleston *Gazette*, February 21, 2001.
26. Loughry, 320–321.
27. West Virginia Advisory Committee to the U.S. Commission on Civil Rights, *Coping with Police Misconduct in West Virginia: Citizen Involvement in Officer Disciplinary Procedures; A Review of Existing Law, Legislative Initiatives, and Disciplinary Models* (January 2004), www.usccr.gov/pubs/sac/wv0104/main.htm. Loughry, 246–247.
28. Tudiver, 261–263, 284.
29. Loughry, 211–212, 215, 218. Charleston *Gazette Mail*, January 28, 1968. Charleston *Gazette*, August 31, 1968.
30. Loughry, 184, 189, 192–193.
31. Ibid., 164, 168–169.
32. Ibid., 165–166.
33. Charleston *Daily Mail*, February 28, 1972. Loughry, 167–168. Committee on Coal Waste Impoundments, "Coal Waste Impoundments: Risk, Response, and Alternatives" (National Academic Press, 2002), 25.
34. Loughry, 167–168.
35. Charleston *Daily Mail*, June 8, 1972.
36. Charleston *Gazette-Mail*, August 6, 1972.
37. Charleston *Gazette*, October 6, 1972.
38. Loughry, 289–290.
39. Ibid., 309.
40. Ibid., 255.
41. Ibid., 265–267.
42. Ibid., 271.
43. Loughry, 271–272. *New York Times*, September 18, 1989.
44. *New York Times*, September 18, 1989.
45. Charleston *Gazette*, May 2, 1975. Loughry, 243.
46. Loughry, 222–223.
47. Ibid., 224.
48. Ibid., 339–340.
49. *United States of America v. John Steven LeRose*, U.S. 4th Circuit Court of Appeals, No. 99-4886, http://laws.findlaw.com/4th/994885p.html.
50. Ibid.
51. Associated Press (AP), Martha Bryson Hodel, September 30, 1999.
52. *U.S. v. John Steven LeRose*, U.S. 4th Circuit Court of Appeals.
53. Associated Press, December 21, 1998. Charleston *Gazette*, October 6, 1998.
54. *U.S. v. John Steven LeRose*, U.S. 4th Circuit Court of Appeals. Associated Press, Martha Bryson Hodel, September 30, 1999. Associated Press, August 16, 2000.
55. Associated Press, June 9, 1999.
56. Charleston *Gazette-Mail*, October 27, 1999.
57. Tom Searls, "Larry Tucker Is Back After 20 Years," Sunday *Gazette-Mail*, http://www.wvgazette.com/News/200804190452.

58. *Topix.* Comments posted in blog format regarding Summersville mayoral election, 2007. www.topix.com/forum/city/richwood-wv (accessed 10/18/2009).
59. Bluefield *Daily Telegraph*, October 2, 1926.
60. Charleston *Gazette*, November 13, 1926.
61. Walls and Stephenson, 165.
62. Loughry, 322. Walls and Stephenson, 166.
63. Loughry, 325–326. From *Life* magazine article, Slating and Lever Brothers, May 9, 1960.
64. Charleston *Gazette*, May 20, 1960.
65. Charleston *Gazette*, May 20, 1960.
66. Slating was a process by which politicians would be grouped so that a vote for one would result in a vote for others on the slate.
67. Loughry, 344–348.
68. Ibid., 357–358.
69. Charleston *Gazette*, June 16, 1960.
70. Charleston *Daily Mail*, May 20, 1960.
71. Loughry, 360, 152.
72. Charleston *Gazette*, January 7, 1928.
73. Beckley *Post-Herald*, April 20, 1931.
74. Bluefield *Daily Telegraph*, January 27, 1933.
75. Loughry, 154.
76. *Hugh M. Caperton, et al. v. A.T. Massey Coal Company Inc., et al.*, U.S. Supreme Court, No. 8-22 (June 8, 2009), www.supremecourt.gov/opinions/08pdf/8-22.pdf (accessed 4/7/2010).
77. Hoppy Kercheval, "Arcoma Settlement Satisfied No One: Investigation of 2006 Tragedy Will Keep On Going," Charleston *Daily Mail* (November 21, 2008), 4A. *NewsBank*, www.newsbank.com (accessed 4/15/2010).
78. No author given, "Only in America," *Economist*, 390 (8620) (February 2, 2009), 34 (accessed via EBSCOhost on 4/7/2010).
79. David Klein, "Can Congress Regulate All Political Speech?" *The Wall Street Journal/WSJ.com* (March 3, 2009), n.p., http://online.wsj.com/article/SG123604532738815399.html (accessed 4/7/2010). *Caperton v. Massey*, U.S. Supreme Court.
80. *Caperton v. Massey*, U.S. Supreme Court.
81. Ibid.
82. Ibid.
83. *Hugh M. Caperton v. A.T. Massey, Inc.*, West Virginia Supreme Court of Appeals, No. 33350 (November 12, 2009), www.sate.wv.us/wvsca/Fall2009.htm (accessed 4/7/2010). *Hugh M. Caperton v. A.T. Massey, Inc.*, West Virginia Supreme Court of Appeals, No. 33350, Dissenting Opinion (November 12, 2009), www.state.wv.us/wvsca/Fall2009.htm (accessed 4/7/2010).
84. Sobel, 24.
85. Rossiter, 290. Madison from "Federalist No. 51."
86. Loughry, 359.
87. Ibid., 446.
88. Ibid., 453.
89. Sobel, *Unleashing Capitalism*, 25.

Chapter Eight

1. Weller, 1.
2. William Campbell Garriott III, "A Body on Drugs: Methamphetamine and the Making of a New Criminal Type in the Rural United States" (Ph.D. dissertation, Princeton University, November 2008), 46.
3. Richard A. Straw and H. Tyler Blethen, eds., *High Mountains Rising: Appalachia in Time and Place* (Urbana: University of Illinois Press, 2004), 101.
4. Allen Batteau, ed., *Appalachia and America: Autonomy and Regional Dependence* (Lexington: University Press of Kentucky, 1983), 93.
5. Batteau, *The Invention of Appalachia*, 31.
6. Rural and Appalachian Youth and Families Consortium, "Parenting Practices and Interventions Among Marginalized Families in Appalachia: Building on Family Strengths," *Family Relations*, 45, No. 4 (October 1996), www.jstor.org/stable/585168, 390.
7. Welch, 220.
8. Millard Peck, 432–433.
9. From Billings and Blee, 158.
10. Welch, 72–73.
11. Ibid., 219.
12. Survey of 11th grade students conducted at Nicholas County High School, Summersville, WV, October, 2009.
13. Weller, 45.
14. Ibid., 49.
15. Tudiver, 224.
16. Weller, 77.
17. Ibid.,2.
18. Several authors, particularly in the late 19th and early 20th century, relied heavily on this ethnographic history of the colonial settlers to describe such contemporary actions such as clan violence (feuding). An example of this practice is John C. Campbell's *The Southern Highlander* (1921).
19. Billings and Blee, 162. Includes Pearsall quote.
20. Weller, 11.
21. Ibid.
22. Ibid., 81, 174.
23. Interview: Richard Dorsey, August 7, 2009.
24. Batteau, *Appalachia and America*, 94.

25. Weller, 49.
26. Ibid., 189.
27. Ibid., 175.
28. Billings and Blee, 161.
29. Rural Appalachian Youth and Families Consortium, 391.
30. Thomas Kiffmeyer, *Reformers to Radicals: The Appalachian Volunteers and the War on Poverty* (Lexington: University Press of Kentucky, 2008), 46.
31. In this sense weaker does not necessarily mean less rich, significant, or valuable, but simply the less dominant in its ability to impart its norms on the other.
32. Batteau, *Appalachia and America*, 163.
33. Billings and Blee, *The Road to Poverty*. Welch, "A Study of Appalachian Cultural Values as Evidenced in the Political and Social Attitudes of Rural West Virginians." Weller, *Yesterday's People*.
34. Weller, 34.
35. Ibid., 165.
36. Ibid., 166–167.
37. Ibid., 166.
38. Garriott, 29.
39. Garriott, 29.
40. Roderick Q. Neal, "Identifying At-risk Youth for Delinquency in Southern West Virginia" (master's thesis, Marshall University, Fall 2004), 12. Interview: James Milam, September 2, 2009.
41. Garriott, 1.
42. Welch, 168.
43. Ibid., 214.
44. Kristin L. Mallory, "Employment Success of Community and Technical College Programs Graduates as an Indicator of Economic Development in West Virginia" (Ph.D. dissertation, Marshall University, 2006), 60.
45. Institute for Women's Policy Research, Women's Data Center. www.iwpr.org/femstats (accessed 5/7/2010).
46. Ibid.
47. AFL-CIO, *How Are Women in West Virginia Doing?* (June 2004), www.aflci.org/issues/jobseconomy/women/speakout/upload/wv.pdf (accessed 5/7/2010).
48. Weller, 77.
49. Jennifer Mae Burns Babbs, "Women and Men in Central Appalachia: A Qualitative Study of Marital Power" (Ph.D. dissertation, University of North Texas, August 1994), 4, 21–21.
50. Weller, 215, 170–172.
51. Ibid., 173.
52. Ibid., 56.
53. Interview: Robert Fletcher, September 2, 2009.
54. Weller, 58.
55. Ibid., 216, 197–198.
56. Kimberly S. Cowley, "Investigating West Virginia Students' Perceptions of Factors Affecting Their Education Aspirations" (Ph.D. dissertation, Marshall University, 2008), 2.
57. Weller, 36.
58. Ibid., 197.
59. Ibid., 200.
60. Robert Bickel and Meghan McDonough, "Opportunity, Community, and Reckless Lives: Social Distress Among Adolescents in West Virginia," *Journal of Social Distress and the Homeless*, 6, No. 1, 1997, 42.
61. Student survey, Nicholas County High School.
62. From Welch, 90.
63. Ibid., 184.
64. Sobel, 172–173.
65. Bickel and McDonough, 31–32.
66. Welch, 19.
67. Batteau, *The Invention of Appalachia*, 1.
68. Ibid., 31, 36–37.
69. Tudiver, 112. Shapiro, x–xi.
70. Ibid., 33, 62. Orientalism describes the "creation" of the Middle East in the mind of Westerners as presented in Edward Said's controversial classic titled *Orientalism*.
71. Ibid., 69.
72. Batteau, *The Invention of Appalachia*, 57. Shapiro, 102.
73. Shapiro, 104–106.
74. Batteau, *The Invention of Appalachia*, 60.
75. Batteau, *The Invention of Appalachia*, 61. Shapiro, 96.
76. Batteau, *The Invention of Appalachia*, 89. Shapiro, 108.
77. Batteau, *The Invention of Appalachia*, 74, 77.
78. Ibid., 127, 145.
79. Dennis Roth, "The Johnson Administration and the Great Society," U.S. Department of Agriculture, National Agricultural Library, www.nal.usda.gov/ric/ricpub/rural_development_chap5.pdf, 2. John M. Glen, "The War on Poverty in Appalachia: Oral History from the 'Top Down' and the 'Bottom Up,'" *The Oral History Review*, 22, No. 1 (Summer 1995), www.jstor.org/stable/4495357, 69.
80. Glen Edward Taul, "Poverty, Development, and Government in Appalachia: Origins of the Appalachian Regional Commission" (Ph.D. dissertation, Lexington: University Press of Kentucky, 2001), 1.
81. Glen, 72. Kiffmeyer, 1.
82. Kiffmeyer, 49, 70–72.
83. As quoted in Richard H. Leach, "The

Federal Role in the War on Poverty Program," *Law and Contemporary Problems*, 31, No. 1, Antipoverty Programs (Winter 1966), www.jstor.org/stable/1190527, 32.

84. Glen, 78.
85. Ibid., 86.
86. Ibid., 76.
87. Ibid., 76, 89, 90.
88. J.W. Williamson, *Hillbillyland: What the Movies Did to the Mountains and What the Mountains Did to the Movies* (Chapel Hill: University of North Carolina Press, 1995), 56.
89. Kiffmeyer, 100–102.
90. *New York Times*, October 20, 1963.
91. Noakes, 125.
92. Ibid., 126.
93. Student survey, Nicholas County High School.
94. Batteau, *The Invention of Appalachia*, 189.
95. Ibid., 190. Best's "Stripping the Appalachian Soul" was published in *Mountain Review*, 5, No. 2 (October 1979), 1–6.
96. Noakes, 139.
97. Welch, 194.
98. Straw and Blethen, 110.
Start here
99. Tony Dokoupil, "Hillbilly No More," *Newsweek* (February 27, 2009). http://www.newsweek.com/id/186715/page/1.
100. Straw and Blethen, 107. Dokoupil.

Chapter Nine

1. Bryan T. McNeil, "Searching for the Home Where Mountains Move: The Collision of Economy, Environment, and an American Community" (Ph.D. dissertation, University of North Carolina at Chapel Hill, 2005), 10.
2. Ibid., 11.
3. Ibid., 12.
4. Ibid., 4.
5. Shirley L. Stewart Burns, "Bringing Down the Mountains: The Impact of Mountaintop Removal Surface Coal Mining on Southern West Virginia Communities, 1970–2004" (Ph.D. dissertation, West Virginia University, 2005), 46.
6. General information about the goals and activities of the organization can be found at www.friendsofcoal.org/.
7. Burns, ii.
8. Burns, ii, 8, 14.
9. Friends of Coal, "Coal Facts 2007," *West Virginia Coal Association*. www.wvcoal.com/docs/coalfacts_07.pdf, 10 (accessed 3/14/2010).
10. Burns, 7. Requirements for the type of reclamation that must take place as well as arguments over what type of reclamation, and their effectiveness, will be discussed later.
11. Ibid., 149, 45.
12. Amanda Womac, "Frames of Mountaintop Removal in Print Journalism," 6, cci.utk.edu (accessed 3/10/2010).
13. McNeil, 2.
14. Ibid., 77.
15. Environmental Protection Agency, "Mid-Atlantic Mountaintop Mining," http://www.epa.gov/Region3/mtntop/ (9/11/2010) (accessed 3/22/2010).
16. Gregory J. Pond, Margaret E. Passmore, Frank A. Borsuk, Lou Reynolds, and Carole J. Rose, "Downstream Effects of Mountaintop Coal Mining: Comparing Biological Conditions Using Family- and Genus-level Macroinvertebrate Bioassessment Tools," *Journal of North American Benthological Society*, 27, No. 3 (July 2008), 274. Accessed via Environmental Protection Agency Web site, http://www.epa.gov/Region3/mtntop/ (accessed 3/15/2010).
17. Federal News Service, "Laboratory Director Palmer Testifies on 'Impacts of Mountaintop Removal Coal Mining on Water Quality in Appalachia' Before Senate Panel," Washington, D.C. (July 2009), n.p. (accessed via ProQuest Database 3/11/2010).
18. Environmental Protection Agency, "Mid-Atlantic Mountaintop Mining," http://www.epa.gov/Region3/mtntop/ (9/11/2010) (accessed 3/22/2010).
19. Ibid. Burns, 191–196.
20. Burns, 69–70. Penny Loeb, "Shear Madness," *U.S. News and World Report* (August 11, 1997), n.p. (accessed via Lexus Nexus on 9/27/2009).
21. Burns, 12, 72–73.
22. Ibid., 74, 126.
23. McNeil, 16.
24. Coal Impoundment Location and Information System, http://www.coalimpoundment.org (accessed 3/23/2010).
25. Burns, 76–77.
26. Coal Impoundment Location and Information System.
27. "End Mountaintop Removal," www.ilovemountains.org (accessed 3/14/2010).
28. Appalachian Voice, "Across Appalachia" (Summer 2005), 7, www.appvoices.org/images/AppVoiceJun05_AcrossApp.pdf (accessed 3/23/2010).
29. Coal Impoundment Location and Information System.
30. Burns, 77–79.
31. Coal Impoundment Location and Information System. Burns, 80.

32. Coal Impoundment Location and Information System.
33. Burns, 78.
34. Coal Impoundment Location and Information System. Burns, 77.
35. Ibid., 75.
36. Burns, 71.
37. Ibid., 91.
38. Joyce Barry, "Mountaineers Are Always Free? An Examination of Mountaintop Removal in West Virginia" (Ph.D. dissertation, Bowling Green State University, May 2004), 83, 85.
39. Environmental Protection Agency, "Mid-Atlantic Mountaintop Mining," http://www.epa.gov/Region3/mtntop/ (9/11/2010) (accessed 3/22/2010).
40. Ibid., 91, 96.
41. Loeb, n.p.
42. Burns, 151–156. Edward M. Green, "The Mountaintop Mining Litigation: How Far-reaching Will Its Impacts Be?" *Crowell and Moring Mining Law Monitor* (November 2000), n.p. http://www.crowell.com/NewsEvents/Article.aspx?id=309 (accessed 3/15/2010).
43. Burns, 156.
44. Burns, 157–161.
45. Ibid., 160.
46. U.S. 4th Circuit Court of Appeals, *OVEC v. William Bulen*, No. 04-2129, November 23, 2005.
47. U.S. 4th Circuit Court of Appeals, *OVEC v. William Bulen*, dissenting opinion, No. 04-2129(L) CA-03-2281-3.
48. Ibid.
49. U.S. District Court for the Southern District of West Virginia, *OVEC v. Dana R. Hurst*, Civil Action No. 3:03-2281, March 31, 2009.
50. U.S. District Court for the Southern District of West Virginia, *OVEC v. USACE*, Civil Action No. 3:08-0979, November 24, 2009.
51. Ibid.
52. Environmental Protection Agency, "EPA Releases Preliminary Results for Surface Coal Mining Permit Reviews," www.epa.gov/Region3/mtntop/ (9/11/2010) (accessed 3/15/2010).
53. Burns, 170, 162–168.
54. Ken Ward, Jr., "Court Blocks Forced Sale of Lincoln Family's Land," www.wvgazette.com/News/MiningtheMountains/200405080003 (May 8, 2004) (accessed 3/24/2010). Burns, 168.
55. Environmental and Public Health Restoration Act of 2009, U.S. House, 111th Congress, 2nd Session, 2010.
56. *Amendment and Reenactment of Surface Coal Mining and Reclamation Act*, State of West Virginia, H.B. 3279, March 2009.
57. Burns, 83.
58. Ibid., 19–39.
59. Ibid., 73.
60. Barry, 82.
61. Burns, 73.
62. *Coal Leader*. www.coalleader.com/2005/CEDAR_west_va_05.htm (accessed 3/24/2010). Burns, 73.
63. Friends of Coal, www.friendsofcoal.org (accessed 3/8/2010).
64. McNeil, 148, 159–159.
65. Friends of Coal.
66. West Virginia Coal Association. www.wvcoal.com (accessed 3/24/2010).
67. McNeil, 71.
68. Burns, 83.
69. Appalachian Regional Reforestation Initiative, "Students Enjoy Earth Day at Nicholas Energy." ARRI News, 1 (4): 4, http://arri.osmore.gov/PDFs/Pubs/ARRI_newsletter_V01.1.1ss.4.pdf (accessed 3/23/2010). Story provided by the Nicholas *Chronicle*.
70. Jeff Skousen and Jim King, "Tree Survival on Mountaintop Mines in Southern West Virginia," West Virginia University Extension Service, n.p., 2004.
71. P. Emerson, J. Skousen, and P. Ziemkiewicz, "Survival and Growth of Hardwoods in Brown versus Grey Sandstone on a Surface Mine in West Virginia," *Journal of Environmental Quality*, 38 (2009), 1824–1825. Also available as a posted paper from the Division of Plant and Soil Science and Water Research Institute, West Virginia University, 2009, at ARRI, http://arri.osmre.gov.
72. Jeff Skousen, Jim Gorman, Eugenia Pena-Yewtukhiw, Jim King, Jason Stewart, Paul Emerson, and Curtis Delong, "Hardwood Tree Survival in Heavy Ground Cover on Reclaimed Land in West Virginia: Mowing and Ripping Effects," *Journal of Environmental Quality*, 38 (2009), 1401. Also available as a posted paper from the Division of Plant and Soil Sciences, West Virginia University, 2009, at ARRI, http://arri.osmre.gov.
73. Ibid., 1402.
74. *Mine Reclamation Video: Zeb Mt. Reclamation Site*, University of Tennessee Institute of Agriculture, AgResearch. http://agresearch.tennessee.edu/video/research.asp?t=mine%20Reclamation&=40 (accessed 3/11/2010).
75. 2009 CEDAR of Southern West Virginia, Inc., scholarship application for Southern West Virginia Community and Technical College, 2009, http://southernwv.edu/files/CEDAR%20Scholarship%20Application09.pdf.

76. Burns, 59.
77. Ibid., 65–66.
78. McNeil, 129.
79. Resident survey conducted May 2010 in Nicholas County. While not scientific in nature, the purpose of survey was to obtain general resident attitudes toward mountaintop removal. Survey sheets were distributed to patients at a dentist's office. While respondents ranged in age, sex, education, and employment, there were no unemployed respondents. This fact does exclude one of the three major groups of discussion for this work. Additionally, while Nicholas County does have mountaintop removal operations in progress and several residents work in the mining industry in and outside of the county, it has not seen widespread operations similar to other counties. It was the author's goal to obtain data from a region that was aware of, but not fully engrossed with, mountaintop removal operations to obtain a wider range of opinions. This point, as well as the author's familiarity with the area, were factors in using Nicholas County. Robert Fletcher, DDS, of Fletcher and Fletcher Dentistry supported this survey.
80. Ibid.
81. Ibid.
82. Ibid.
83. Governor Joe Manchin, Upper Big Branch Mine accident briefing, CNN (4/6/ 2010).
84. Ian Urbina and John Leland, "A Mine Boss Inspires Fear, but Pride, Too," *New York Times* (April 8, 2010), A1(L), *Custom Newspapers* database (accessed 4/9/ 2010).
85. Ibid.
86. Massey Energy Company, www.massey energyco.com/ (accessed 4/6/2010).
87. "Mountain Duel: Kennedy Takes on the Coal Baron," *Guardian* (London, England) (January 23, 2010), 28, *Custom Newspapers* database (accessed 4/9/2010).
88. Ibid.
89. Thomas Jefferson to John Holmes, Monticello, Library of Congress (April 22, 1820), http://memory.loc.gov/master/mss/ mtj/mtj1 (accessed 4/6/2010).

Conclusion

1. Taul, 11.
2. Welch, 83–84.
3. J.D. Charles, "Massey Gives County 300K," Logan *Banner* (May 12, 2008), n.p. *NewsBank* database (accessed 4/15/2010). Jeffrey Reynolds, "Finally: Racetrack Funding Secure," Williamson *Daily News* (September 5, 2008), n.p. *NewsBank* database (accessed 4/15/2010).
4. Amy Goodman, "Massey Disaster Not Just Tragic, But Criminal," Altus *Times* (OK) (April 14, 2010), 9. *NewsBank* database (accessed 4/15/2010).
5. Tolliver, 225.

Bibliography

Government Documents

Children's Bureau. *The Promotion of the Welfare and Hygiene of Maternity and Infancy: The Administration of the Act of Congress of November 23, 1921 (Sheppard-Towner Act), Fiscal Year Ended June 30, 1924*, Washington, D.C.: U.S. Government Printing Office, 1925.

Children's Bureau. *The Promotion of the Welfare and Hygiene of Maternity and Infancy: The Administration of the Act of Congress of November 23, 1921 (Sheppard-Towner Act), Fiscal Year Ended June 30, 1926*, Washington, D.C.: U.S. Government Printing Office, 1927.

Circuit Court of McDowell County, West Virginia. *West Virginia v. Purdue Pharma L.P.*, Civil Action No. 01-C-137-S, www.wvs.state.wv.us/wvag/PDFReader/oxycontin.pdf, n.d. (accessed 5/4/2010).

Environmental Protection Agency. "EPA Releases Preliminary Results for Surface Coal Mining Permit Reviews," www.epa.gov/Region3/mtntop/ (9/11/2010) (accessed 3/15/2010).

Environmental Protection Agency. "Mid-Atlantic Mountaintop Mining," www.epa.gov/Region3/mtntop/ (9/11/2010) (accessed 3/22/2010).

State Cancer Profiles. National Cancer Institute. http://statecancerprofiles.cancer.gov/cgi-bin/quickprofiles/profile.pl?54&047 (accessed 4/15/2010).

State of West Virginia, West Virginia Advisory Committee to the U.S. Commission on Civil Rights. *Coping with Police Misconduct in West Virginia: Citizen Involvement in Officer Disciplinary Procedures: A Review of Existing Law, Legislative Initiatives, and Disciplinary Models*, January 2004, www.usccr.gov/pubs/sac/wv0104/main.htm (accessed 10/16/2009).

State of West Virginia. H.B. 3279 *Amendment and Reenactment of Surface Coal Mining and Reclamation Act*, March 2009.

U.S. 4th Circuit Court of Appeals. *OVEC v. William Bulen*, No. 04-2129. November 23, 2005.

U.S. 4th Circuit Court of Appeals. *OVEC v. William Bulen*, Dissenting Opinion. No. 04-2129(L) CA-03-2281-3.

U.S. 4th Circuit Court of Appeals. *United States of America v. John Steven LeRose*, No. 99-4886, http://laws.findlaw.com/4th/994886p.html (accessed 10/16/2009).

U.S. Census, various years and counties. Data retrieved from Census Data Microfilm via Summersville Public Library, Summersville, WV.

U.S. Census Quick Fact Database. www.quickfacts.census.gov.

U.S. Department of Labor, Bureau of Labor Statistics. "Coal Mining: Injuries, Illnesses, and Fatalities" (April 2010) www.blg.gov/iif/oshwc/osh/os/osar0012.htm (accessed 4/17/2010).
U.S. Department of Labor, Mine Safety and Health Administration. *Mine Accident, Injury, Illness, Employment and Coal Production Statistics.* Tables 3 and 8, www.msha.gov/stats/statinfo.htm (accessed 5/4/2010).
U.S. District Court for the Southern District of West Virginia. *OVEC v. Dana R. Hurst*, Civil Action No. 3:03-2281, March 31, 2009.
U.S. District Court for the Southern District of West Virginia. *OVEC v. USACE*, Civil Action No. 3:08-0979, November 24, 2009.
U.S. Federal News Service, "Laboratory Director Palmer Testifies on 'Impacts of Mountaintop Removal Coal Mining on Water Quality in Appalachia' Before Senate Panel," Washington, D.C. (July 2009), n.p. (accessed via ProQuest Database, 3/11/2010).
U.S. House, Hearing Before the Select Committee on Hunger. *Appalachia Revisited: The Persistence of Hunger and Poverty in West Virginia*, 100th Congress, Serial No. 100-28, Washington, D.C.: U.S. Government Printing Office, 1988.
U.S. House. H.R. 585, *Environmental and Public Health Restoration Act of 2009*, 111th Congress, 2nd Session, Washington, D.C.: U.S. Government Printing Office, 2010.
U.S. Senate. Hearings Before a Subcommittee of the Committee on Education and Labor. *Conditions in the Paint Creek District, West Virginia*, 63rd Congress, 1st Session, Parts I, II, and III, 1913.
U.S. Supreme Court. *Hitchman Coal and Coke Co. v. Mitchell*, 245 U.S. 229, 1917, http://supreme.justia.com/us/245/229/case.html (accessed 9/17/2009).
U.S. Supreme Court. *Hugh M. Caperton, et al., v. A.T. Massey Coal Company Inc., et al.* No. 8-22, June 8, 2009, www.supremecourt.gov/opinions/08pdf/8-22.pdf (accessed 4/7/2010).
West Virginia Bureau for Public Health. Health Statistics Center, www.dhhr.org (accessed 4/15/2010).
West Virginia Supreme Court of Appeals. *Hugh M. Caperton v. A.T. Massey, Inc.* No. 33350, November 12, 2009, www.state.wv.us/wvsca/Fal12009.htm (accessed 4/7/2010).
West Virginia Supreme Court of Appeals . *Hugh M. Caperton v. A.T. Massey, Inc.* No. 33350. Dissenting Opinion. November 12, 2009, www.state.wv.us/wvsca/Fall 2009.htm (accessed 4/7/2010).

Papers/Speeches/Collections

American Federation of Labor. *Report of the Proceedings of the 42nd Annual Convention of the American Federation of Labor*, Washington, D.C.: Law Reporter Printing, 1922.
American Federation of Labor and Congress of Industrial Organizations (AFL-CIO). *How Are Women in West Virginia Doing?* (June 2004), www.aflci.org/issues/job seconomy/women/speakout/upload/wv.pdf (accessed 5/7/2010).
Appalachian Regional Reforestation Initiative. "Students Enjoy Earth Day at Nicholas Energy," ARRI News, 1 (4): 4, 6. http://arri.osmre.gov/PDFs/Pubs/ARRI_news letter_V01.1.Iss.4.pdf (accessed 3/23/2010).
Appalachian Voices. "Across Appalachia" (Summer 2005), www.appvoices.org/images/ AppVoiceJun05_AcrossApp.pdf (accessed 3/23/2010).
CEDAR of Southern West Virginia, Inc. scholarship application for Southern West

Virginia Community and Technical College, 2009. http://southernwv.edu/files/CEDAR%20Scholarship%20Application09.pdf.
Committee on Coal Waste Impoundments. "Coal Waste Impoundments: Risk, Response, and Alternatives." National Academic Press, 2002.
Eleanor Roosevelt Papers Project, George Washington University, www.gwu.edu/~erpapers (accessed 9/27/2009).
Harr, Milton. "The Civilian Conservation Corps in West Virginia: Civilian Conservation Corps (CCC) Companies and Camps in West Virginia, 1933–1942," West Virginia Archives and History, www.wvculture.org/history/ccc.html (accessed 9/26/2009).
Institute for Women's Policy Research. Women's Data Center. www.iwpr.org/femstats (accessed 5/7/2010).
Jefferson, Thomas, to John Holmes. Monticello, Library of Congress (April 22, 1820), http://memory.loc.gov/master/mss/mtj/mtj1 (accessed 4/6/2010).
Kump, Herman Guy, Inaugural Address, March 4, 1933, West Virginia Archives and History, www.wvculture.org/history/kumpia.html. Accessed on 9/23/2009.
Plein, L. Christopher. "Welfare Reform in a Hard Place: The West Virginia Experience," Rockefeller Report, No. 13. Albany, N.Y.: Nelson A. Rockefeller Institute of Government, November, 2001.
Roth, Dennis. "The Johnson Administration and the Great Society," National Agricultural Library, U.S. Department of Agriculture, www.nal.usda.gov/ric/ricpubs/rural_development_chap5.pdf (accessed 1/3/2020).
Skousen, Jeff, and Jim King. "Tree Survival on Mountaintop Mines in Southern West Virginia." West Virginia Memory Project, CCC Collection, MS85-17, www.wvculture.org/history/wvmemory (accessed 9/26/2009).
CCC camp newsletter, *The Beaver's Log*, 2, No. 6, August 1935. Company 1522 Clifftop. ID# DC01-0079.
CCC camp newsletter, *The Beaver's Log*, 4, No. 1, January 29, 1936. Company 1522 Clifftop. ID# DC01-0083.
CCC camp newsletter, *Memo*, Weekly Education Bulletin, July 12, 1937. CCC Company 3510. ID# DC01-0012.
CCC camp newsletter, *The Panther Pioneer*, 1, No. 3, August 8, 1936. Camp McDowell Company 3542. ID# DC01-0008.
CCC camp newsletter, *Skillethead*, 4, No. 2, March 30, 1939. Company 2589. ID# DC01-0029.
Letters regarding Ralph Matz, ID# DC01-0061.
West Virginia University Extension Service.
Womac, Amanda. "Frames of Mountaintop Removal in Print Journalism," ccc.utk.edu (accessed 3/10/2010).

Newspapers/News Magazines

Altus *Times*, Altus, Oklahoma. NewsBank database (accessed 4/15/2010).
Associated Press (AP). Various. Lexus Nexus (accessed 10/18/2009).
Beckley *Post-Herald*. Beckley, WV.
Bluefield *Daily Telegraph*. Bluefield, WV.
Borger, Julian. "Hillbilly Heroin: The Painkiller Abuse Wrecking Lives in West Virginia," *The Guardian* (UK) (June 25, 2001), 3 (accessed 5/4/2010 via Proquest Database).
Breed, Allen G. "Oxycontin Addiction Is Plaguing Appalachia: The Prescription Painkiller Is Tearing Apart Communities and Destroying Lives," *Star Tribune* (June 24, 2001), 19A (accessed 5/4/2010 via Proquest Database).

Charleston *Daily Mail*. Charleston, WV.
Charleston *Gazette*. Charleston, WV.
Charleston *Gazette-Mail*. Charleston, WV.
Dokoupil, Tony. "Hillbilly No More." *Newsweek* (February 27, 2009). www.newsweek.com/id/186715/page/1.
Loeb, Penny. "Shear Madness." *U.S. News and World Report* (August 11, 1997), n.p. (accessed via Lexus Nexus on 9/27/2009).
Logan *Banner*. NewsBank database (accessed 4/15/2010).
New York Times. New York, NY.
Nicholas *Chronicle*. Summersville, WV.
Raleigh *Register*. Beckley, WV.
Williamson *Daily News*. NewsBank database (accessed 4/15/2010).

Books

Appalachian State University. *Land Ownership Patterns and Their Impacts on Appalachian Communities: A Survey of 80 Counties*. New Market, TN: Highlander Research and Education Center and Washington, D.C.: Appalachian Regional Commission, 1981.
Bailey, Kenneth. "A Judicious Mixture: Negroes and Immigrants in the West Virginia Mines 1880–1917." In *Blacks in Appalachia*, edited by William H. Turner and Edward J. Cabbell, 117–132. Lexington: University Press of Kentucky, 1985.
Barney, Sandra Lee. *Authorized to Heal: Gender, Class and the Transformation of Medicine in Appalachia, 1880–1930*. Chapel Hill: University of North Carolina Press, 2000.
Batteau, Allen, W., ed., *Appalachia and America: Autonomy and Regional Dependence*, Lexington: University Press of Kentucky, 1983.
Batteau, Allen W. *The Invention of Appalachia*. Tucson: University of Arizona Press, 1990.
Bennett, David H. *The Party of Fear: The American Far Right from Nativism to the Militia Movement*. New York: Vintage Books, 1995.
Billings, Dwight B., and Kathleen M. Blee. *The Road to Poverty: The Making of Wealth and Hardship in Appalachia*. Cambridge: Cambridge University Press, 2000.
Brisbin, Richard A., Jr., Rober Jay Dilger, Allan S. Hammock, and L. Christopher Plein. *West Virginia Politics and Government*. 2d ed. Lincoln: University of Nebraska Press, 2008.
Brown, Sharon A. *Historic Resource Study, Kaymoor: New River Gorge National River, West Virginia*. U.S. Department of Interior, July 1990. www.nps.gov/history/history/online_books/neri/hrsl/index.htm (accessed 4/8/2010)
Dilger, Robert Jay, Eleanor H. Blakely, Melissa Latimer, Barry L. Locker, F. Carson Mencken, L. Christopher Plein, Lucinda A. Potter and David Williams. *Welfare Reform in West Virginia*. Morgantown: West Virginia University Press, 2004.
Dix, Keith. *What's a Coal Miner to Do? The Mechanization of Coal Mining*. Pittsburgh, PA: University of Pittsburgh Press, 1988.
Dubofsky, Melvyn, and Foster Rhea Dulles. *Labor in America: A History*, 7th ed. Wheeling, IL: Harland Davidson, 2004.
Gorn, Elliot J. *Mother Jones: The Most Dangerous Woman in America*. New York: Hill and Wang, 2001.
Hofstadter, Richard. *The American Political Tradition and the Men Who Made It*. New York: Vintage Books, 1989.
Kiffmeyer, Thomas. *Reformers to Radicals: The Appalachian Volunteers and the War on Poverty*. Lexington: University Press of Kentucky, 2008.

Lewis, Ronald L. *Transforming the Appalachian Countryside: Railroads, Deforestation, and Social Change in West Virginia 1880–1920*. Chapel Hill: University of North Carolina Press, 1998.
Lunt, Richard D. *Law and Order vs. the Miners, West Virginia, 1906–1933*. Charleston, WV: Appalachian Editions, 1992.
Mangus, A.R. *Rural Regions of the United States*. Works Progress Administration, Washington, D.C: U.S. Government Printing Office, 1940.
McGill, Nettie. *The Welfare of Children in the Bituminous Coal Mining Communities of West Virginia, 1923*. Department of Labor, Washington, D.C.: U.S. Government Printing Office, 1923.
Men of West Virginia, Vol. I. Chicago: Biographical Publishing, 1903.
Northrup, Herbert R., "The Coal Mines." In *Blacks in Appalachia*, edited by William H. Turner and Edward J. Cabbell, 159–171. Lexington: University Press of Kentucky, 1985.
Paine, Thomas. *Common Sense*. Mineola, NY: Dover, 1997.
Pandit, Kavita, and Suzanne Davies Withers, eds. *Migration and Restructuring in the United States: A Geographic Perspective*, New York: Rowman and Littlefield, 1999.
Patterson, James T. *America's Struggle Against Poverty, 1900–1985*. Cambridge: Harvard University Press, 1986.
Pepper, Charles M. *The Life and Times of Henry Gassaway Davis, 1823–1916*. New York: Century, 1920.
Ransom, Roger L. *Conflict and Compromise: The Political Economy of Slavery, Emancipation, and the American Civil War*, New York: Cambridge University Press, 1989.
Rossiter, Clinton, ed. *The Federalist Papers*. New York: Mentor, 1999.
Salstrom, Paul. *Appalachia's Path to Dependency: Rethinking a Region's Economic History: 1730–1940*. Lexington: University Press of Kentucky, 1991.
Shapiro, Robert D. *Appalachia on Our Mind: The Southern Mountains and Mountaineers in the American Consciousness, 1870–1920*. Chapel Hill: University of North Carolina Press, 1978.
Shifflett, Crandall A. *Coal Towns: Life, Work, and Culture in Company Towns of Southern Appalachia, 1880–1960*. Knoxville: University of Tennessee Press, 1991.
Shogan, Robert. *The Battle of Blair Mountain: The Story of America's Largest Labor Uprising*. New York: Basic Books, 2004.
Sobel, Russell S., ed. *Unleashed Capitalism: Why Prosperity Stops at the West Virginia Border and How to Fix It*. Morgantown: Public Policy Foundation of West Virginia, 2007.
Stealy, Orlando Oscar. *Twenty Years in the Press Gallery*. New York: Publishers Printing, 1906.
Straw, Richard A., and H. Tyler Blethen, eds. *High Mountains Rising: Appalachia in Time and Place*. Urbana: University of Illinois Press, 2004.
Thomas, Jerry Bruce. *An Appalachian New Deal: West Virginia in the Great Depression*. Lexington: University Press of Kentucky, 1998.
Walls, David S., and John B. Stephenson, eds. *Appalachia in the Sixties: Decade of Reawakening*, Lexington: University Press of Kentucky, 1972.
Weller, Jack E. *Yesterday's People: Life in Contemporary Appalachia*. Lexington: University Press of Kentucky, 1965.
Williamson, J.W. *Hillbillyland: What the Movies Did to the Mountains and What the Mountains Did to the Movies*. Chapel Hill: University of North Carolina Press, 1995.
Writer's Program, Works Progress Administration. *West Virginia: A Guide to the Mountain State*. New York: Oxford University Press, 1941.

Dissertations and Theses

Babbs, Jennifer Mae Burns. "Women and Men in Central Appalachia: A Qualitative Study of Marital Power." Ph.D. dissertation, University of North Texas, August 1994.
Bailey, Rebecca J. "Matewan Before the Massacre: Politics, Coal, and the Roots of Conflict in Mingo County, 1793–1920." Ph.D. dissertation, West Virginia University, 2001.
Barry, Joyce. "Mountaineers Are Always Free? An Examination of Mountaintop Removal in West Virginia." Ph.D. dissertation, Bowling Green State University, May 2004.
Booker, Clyde G. "Dying for a Job: African Americans, Industrial Hegemony, and the Hawk's Nest Tunnel, 1930–1936." Ph.D. dissertation, University of Kentucky, 2005.
Boyd, Lawrence William. "The Economics of the Coal Company Town: Institutional Relationships, Monopsony, and Distributional Conflicts in American Coal Towns." Ph.D. dissertation, West Virginia University, 1993.
Burns, Shirley L. Stewart. "Bringing Down the Mountains: The Impact of Mountaintop Removal Surface Coal Mining on Southern West Virginia Communities, 1970–2004." Ph.D. dissertation, West Virginia University, 2005.
Butcher-Winfree, Joy A. "Portraits of Resiliency: A Qualitative Study of Appalachian Christian Women." Ph.D. dissertation, Marshall University, August 2009.
Cahill, Kevin. "Fertilizing the Weeds: The New Deal's Rural Poverty Program in West Virginia." Ph.D. dissertation, West Virginia University, 1999.
Cowley, Kimberly S. "Investigating West Virginia Students' Perceptions of Factors Affecting Their Education Aspirations." Ph.D. dissertation, Marshall University, 2008.
Davis, Charles Peter. "The Impact of the Coal Industry on McDowell County, West Virginia." Master's thesis, San Jose State University, May 1997.
Fisher, Chang. "Evaluating the Impact of Mandatory Work Programs on Two Parent Welfare Caseloads." Ph.D. dissertation, University of Maryland, 1996.
Fisher, Kimberly N. "The Effect of Parent Education on the Home Food Environment of Overweight Adolescents in West Virginia." Master's thesis, West Virginia University, 2009.
Garriott, William Campbell III. "A Body on Drugs: Methamphetamine and the Making of a New Criminal Type in the Rural United States." Ph.D. dissertation, Princeton University, November 2008.
Griffith, Amanda J. "The Life Cycle of a Coal Town: Widen, West Virginia, 1911–1963." Master's thesis, West Virginia University, 2003.
Hartman, Richard Ogden. "A Constitution of Our Own: The Constitutional Convention of 1872 and the Resurrection of Ex-Confederate West Virginia." Master's thesis, Marshall University, December 2004.
Keeney, C. Belmont. "Soldiers and Stereotypes: Mountaineers, Cultural Identity, and World War II." Ph.D. dissertation, West Virginia University, 2009.
Lawrence, Randall Gene. "Appalachian Metamorphosis: Industrializing Society on the Central Plateau, 1860–1913." Ph.D. dissertation, Duke University, 1983.
LeGrow, Tracy L. "Access to Health Information and Health Care Decision-making on Women in a Rural Appalachian Community." Ph.D. dissertation, Marshall University, April 2007.
Lewis, John Sherwood. "Becoming Appalachia: The Emergence of an American Subculture, 1840–1860." Ph.D. dissertation, University of Kentucky, 2000.

Loughry, Allen Hayes II. "'Don't Buy Another Vote. I Won't Pay for a Landslide': The Sordid and Continuing History of Political Corruption in West Virginia." Ph.D. dissertation, American University, 2003.
Mallory, Kristin L. "Employment Success of Community and Technical College Programs Graduates as an Indicator of Economic Development in West Virginia." Ph.D. dissertation, Marshall University, 2006.
McGaha, Elizabeth Carter. "wv works ... Does It? An Examination of Post Welfare Hardship in West Virginia." Master's thesis, West Virginia University, 2002.
McNeil, Bryan T. "Searching for the Home Where Mountains Move: The Collision of Economy, Environment, and an American Community." Ph.D. dissertation, University of North Carolina at Chapel Hill, 2005.
Myers, Mark. "Coal Mechanization and Migration from McDowell County, West Virginia, 1932–1970." Master's thesis, East Tennessee State University, August 2001.
Neal, Roderick Q. "Identifying At-risk Youth for Delinquency in Southern West Virginia." Master's thesis, Marshall University, Fall 2004.
Neff, Roni, A. "In the Wrong Place? Geographic Variation in U.S. Occupational Injury/Illness Rates." Ph.D. dissertation, Baltimore: Johns Hopkins University, September 2006.
Noakes, Jennie. "From the Top of the Mountain: Traditional Music and the Politics of Place in the Central Appalachian Coal Fields." Ph.D. dissertation, University of Pennsylvania, 2008.
Rakes, Paul H. "Acceptable Casualties: Power, Culture, and History in the West Virginia Coalfields, 1900–1945." Ph.D. dissertation, West Virginia University, 2002.
Sousa, Semoa C.B. "An Economic Analysis of the Relationship of Poverty and Income Inequality in Rural West Virginia." Master's thesis, West Virginia University, 2000.
Stanely, Talmage A. "The Poco Field: Politics, Culture, and Place in Contemporary Appalachia." Ph.D. dissertation, Emory University, 1996.
Taul, Glen Edward. "Poverty, Development, and Government in Appalachia: Origins of the Appalachian Regional Commission." Ph.D. dissertation, University of Kentucky, 2001.
Tudiver, Sari Lubitsch. "Political Economy and Culture in Central Appalachia: 1790–1977." Ph.D. dissertation, University of Michigan, 1984.
Welch, Janet Gail Boggess. "A Study of Appalachian Cultural Values as Evidenced in the Political and Social Attitudes of Rural West Virginians." Ph.D. dissertation, University of Maryland, 1984.
Whittington, Stacy Dawn. "Initial Assessment/Treatment of Pediatric Overweight in Rural-based Appalachia: A Qualitative Investigation." Master's thesis, West Virginia University, November, 2005.

Journal/Periodical Articles

Bickel, Robert, and Meghan McDonough. "Opportunity, Community, and Reckless Lives: Social Distress Among Adolescents in West Virginia," *Journal of Social Distress and the Homeless*, 6, No. 1 (1997), 29–44.
Bridford, Kenneth, Joseph Costello, John Gamble, Dennis Groce, Marylin Hutchison, William Jones, James Merchant, Carl Ortmeyer, Robert Reger, and William L. Wagner. "Occupational Safety and Health Implications of Increased Coal Utilization," *Environmental Health Perspectives*, 33 (December 1979), 285–302, www.jstor.org/stable/3429089 (accessed 4/16/010).
Castranova, Vincent, and Val Vallyathan. "Silicosis and Coal Worker's Pneumoconiosis,"

Environmental Health Perspectives, 108, Supplement 4: Occupational and Environmental Lung Diseases (August 2000), 675–684, www.jstor.org/stable/3454404 (accessed 4/16/2010).

Corbin, David A. "Betrayal in the West Virginia Coal Fields: Eugene V. Debs and the Socialist Party of America, 1912–1914," *The Journal of American History*, 64, No. 4 (March 1978), 987–1009. www.jstor.org/stable/1890733.

Emerson, P., J. Skousen and P. Ziemkiewicz. "Survival and Growth of Hardwoods in Brown versus Grey Sandstone on a Surface Mine in West Virginia," *Journal of Environmental Quality*, 38 (2009), 1821–1829.

Fagge, Roger. "Eugene V. Debs in West Virginia, 1913: A Reappraisal," *West Virginia History*, 52 (1993), 1–18. www.wvculture.org/history/journal_wvh/wvh52-1.html.

"Fighting Tuberculosis in West Virginia," *The American Journal of Nursing*, 23, No. 9 (June 1923), 778–779. www.jstor.org/stable/3407551.

Glen, John M. "The War on Poverty in Appalachia: Oral History from the 'Top Down' and the 'Bottom Up,'" *The Oral History Review*, 22, No. 1 (Summer 1995), 67–93. www.jstor.org/stable/4495357.

Hotchkiss, Jed. "The Timber Trees of West Virginia," *Science*, 19, No. 476 (March 18, 1892), 161. www.jstor.org/stable/1766424.

Jacobs, Lawrence R., and Robert Y. Shapiro. "Issues, Candidate Image, and Priming: The Use of Private Polls in Kennedy's 1960 Presidential Campaign," *The American Political Science Review*, 88, No. 3 (September 1994), 527–540. www.jstor.org/stable/2944793.

Jarvis, Marilyn A., Mary Pullen, and Jane Downin. "Health Care Larnin' in Appalachia," *The American Journal of Nursing*, 67, No. 11 (November 1967), 2345–2347. www.jstor.org/stable/3453682.

Klein, David. "Can Congress Regulate All Political Speech?" *The Wall Street Journal/WSJ.com* (March 3, 2009), n.p. http://online.wsj.com/article/SG123604532738815399.html (accessed 4/7/2010).

Lang, Forest, Kaethe P. Ferguson, Bruce Bennard, Pamela Zahorik, and Carolyn Sliger. "Appalachian Preceptorship: Over Two Decades of an Integrated Clinical-classroom Experience of Rural Medicine and Appalachian Culture," *Academic Medicine*, 80 (August 2005), 717–723.

Laurie, Clayton D. "The United States Army and the Return to Normalcy in Labor Dispute Interventions: The Case of West Virginia Coal Mine Wars, 1920–1921," *West Virginia History*, 50 (1991), 1–24. www.wvculture.org/history/journal_wvh/wvh50-1.html.

Leach, Richard H. "The Federal Role in the War on Poverty Program," *Law and Contemporary Problems*, 31, No. 1, Antipoverty Programs (Winter 1966), 18–38. www.jstor.org/stable/1190527.

Maher, Kris. "Black Lung on Rise in Mines, Reversing Trend," *The Wall Street Journal* (December 15, 2009), n.p., www.online.wsj.com/article/58126083871040391327.htm (accessed 4/20/2010).

"Only in America, *Economist*, 390 (8620) (February 2, 2009), 34 (accessed via EBSCOhost on 4/7/2010).

Peck, Millard. "Farm or Forest in the West Virginia Appalachians?" *Journal of Farm Economics*, 11, No. 3 (July 1929), 422–435. www.jstor.org/stable/1229853.

Photiadis, John D., and John F. Schnabel. "Religion: A Persistent Institution in a Changing Appalachia," *Review of Religious Research*, 19, No. 1 (Autumn 1977), 32–42, www.jstor.org/stable/3509578.

Pond, Gregory J., Margaret E. Passmore, Frank A. Borsuk, Lou Reynolds, and Carole J. Rose. "Downstream Effects of Mountaintop Coal Mining: Comparing Biological Conditions Using Family- and Genus-level Macroinvertebrate Bioassessment Tools," *Journal of North American Benthological Society*, 27, No. 3 (July 2008), 274. Accessed via Environmental Protection Agency Web site, www.epa.gov/Region3/mtntop/ (accessed 3/15/2010).

Posey, Thomas E. "Unemployment Compensation and the Coal Industry in West Virginia," *Southern Economic Journal*, 7, No. 3 (January 1941): 347–361. www.jstor.org/stable/1053044.

Prater, Joseph B. "West Virginia's Painful Settlement: How the Oxycontin Phenomenon and Unconventional Theories of Tort Liability May Make Pharmaceutical Companies Liable for Black Markets," *Northwestern University Law Review*, 100, No. 3 (2006).

Rural and Appalachian Youth and Families Consortium. "Parenting Practices and Interventions Among Marginalized Families in Appalachia: Building on Family Strengths," *Family Relations*, 45, No. 4 (October 1996), 387–396. www.jstor.org/stable/585168.

Scott, Shaunna L. "They Don't Have to Live by the Old Traditions: Saintly Men, Sinner Women, and an Appalachian Pentecostal Revival," *American Ethnologist*, 21, No. 2 (May 1994), 227–244. www.jstor.org/stable/65887.

Skousen, Jeff, Jim Gorman, Eugenia Pena-Yewtukhiw, Jim King, Jason Stewart, Paul Emerson, and Curtis Delong. "Hardwood Tree Survival in Heavy Ground Cover on Reclaimed Land in West Virginia: Mowing and Ripping Effects," *Journal of Environmental Quality*, 38 (2009), 1400–1409.

Steally, John Edmund III. "Kanawha Prelude to Nineteenth-century Monopoly in the United States: The Virginia Salt Combinations," *The Virginia Magazine of History and Biography*, 107, No. 4 (1999), 349–477. www.jstor.org/stable/4249802.

Stromsdorfer, Ernst W. "Determinants of Economic Success in Retraining the Unemployed: The West Virginia Experience," *The Journal of Human Resources*, 3, No. 2 (Spring 1968), 139–158. www.jstor.org/stable/145128.

West State Medical Association, *West Virginia Medical Journal*, 10, No. 1 (July 1915); 10, No. 2 (August 1915); 10, No. 3 (September, 1915); 10, No. 4 (October 1915); 10, No. 5 (November 1915).

Wheeler, Hoyt N. "Mountaineer Mine Wars: An Analysis of the West Virginia Mine Wars of 1912–1913 and 1920–1921," *The Business History Review*, 50, No. 1 (Spring 1976), 69–91. www.jstor.org/stable/3113575.

Wolfe, April D. "World War One and the Miners of Southern West Virginia," *West Virginia Historical Society Quarterly*, 16, No. 1 (January 2002), Electronic version, n.p. www.wvculture.org/history/wvhs1601.html.

Internet

Appalachian Regional Reforestation Initiative. http://arri.osmre.gov (accessed 3/22/2010).

Appalachian Stories. www.unmc.edu/Community/ruralmeded/RMEPost/appalachian_stories.htm (accessed 4/12/2010).

Appalachian Voices. www.appvoices.org (accessed 3/14/2010).

Belesco, Amy. "The Cost of Iraq, Afghanistan, and Other Global War on Terror Operations Since 9/11" (May 15, 2009), 1. http://fas.org/sgp/crs/natsec/RL33110.pdf (accessed 8/19/2009).

Chesapeake and Ohio Historical Society, www.cohs.org/history (accessed 8/22/2009).

Clines, Francis X. "Rural West Virginia Winning Over Health Care Workers." *New York Times* (June 21, 2001), A14, www.nytimes.com/2001/06/21/us/rural-west-virginia-winning-over-health-care-workers.html (accessed 4/12/2010).

Coal Impoundment Location and Information System, www.coalimpoundment.org (accessed 3/23/2010).
Coal Leader. www.coalleader.com/2005/CEDAR_west_va_05.htm (accessed 3/24/2010).
Coal River Mountain Watch. www.crmw.net (accessed 3/23/2010).
End Mountaintop Removal. www.ilovemountains.org (accessed 3/14/2010).
Friends of Coal, www.friendsofcoal.org. (accessed 3/8/2010)
Green, Edward M. "The Mountaintop Mining Litigation: How Far-reaching Will Its Impacts Be?" *Crowell and Moring Mining Law Monitor* (November, 2000), n.p. www.crowell.com/NewsEvents/Article.aspx?id=309. (accessed 3/15/2010).
"Mountain Duel: Kennedy Takes on the Coal Baron," *Guardian* (London, England) (January 23, 2010), Custom Newspapers database (accessed 4/9/2010).
Massey Energy Company. www.masseyenergyco.com/ (accessed 4/6/2010).
Norfolk and Western Historical Society. www.nwhs.org (accessed 8/2/2009).
Ransom, Roger. "Economics of the Civil War," *EH.Net Encyclopedia*, edited by Robert Whaples (August 24, 2001). http://eh.net/encyclopedia/article/ransom.civil.war.us (accessed 8/20/2009).
Searls, Tom. "Larry Tucker Is Back After 20 Years," *Sunday Gazette-Mail*, wvgazette.com. www.wvgazette.com/News/200804190452 (accessed 10/18/2009).
Summersville.org. www.summersville.org (accessed 4/12/2010).
Summersville Memorial Hospital. www.summersvillememorial.org/physicians/conley.htm, (accessed 4/12/2010).
Topix. Comments posted in blog format regarding Summersville mayoral election 2007. www.topix.com/forum/city/richwood-wv (accessed 10/18/2009).
Urbina, Ian, and John Leland. "A Mine Boss Inspires Fear, but Pride, Too," *New York Times* (April 8, 2010), A1(L), Custom Newspapers database (accessed 4/9/2010).
Ward, Ken, Jr. "Court Blocks Forced Sale of Lincoln Family's Land," *Charleston Gazette*, wvgazette.com. www.wvgazette.com/News/MiningtheMountains/2004050800003 (May 8, 2004) (accessed 3/24/2010).
West Virginia Coal Association. www.wvcoal.com (accessed 3/24/2010).
West Virginia Coal Facts 2007. West Virginia Coal Association. www.wvcoal.com/docs/coalfacts_07.pdf (accessed 3/14/2010).

Interviews

Richard Dorsey. Interview by author. Sugar Grove, WV, August 7, 2009.
Robert Fletcher, DDS. Phone interview by author. Summersville, WV, September 2, 2009.
James "P.K." Milam, Nicholas County prosecuting attorney. Summersville, WV, May 13, 2008 (e-mail) and September 2, 2009 (phone).

Video Transcripts

Mine Reclamation Video: Zeb Mt. Reclamation Site. University of Tennessee Institute of Agriculture, AgResearch. http://agresearch.tennessee.edu/video/research.asp?t=Mine%20Reclamation&=40 (accessed 3/11/2010).
Upper Big Branch Mine Accident Briefing, Governor Joe Manchin, CNN (4/6/2010).

Index

absentee landowners 22, 28, 32, 47–48, 71, 79, 124, 183, 186
African Americans 23–24, 29, 34, 41, 43, 45, 48, 52–53, 63, 70, 83, 147; conditions in 34, 36, 54
Agricultural Adjustment Administration (AAA) 89, 91
Aid to Dependent Children (ADC) 82, 92
Aid to Families with Dependent Children (AFDC) 93, 100
American Friends Service Committee (AFSC) 86–88
Appalachian Regional Commission (ARC) 100, 110, 153
Appalachian Voices 160
Appalachian Volunteers (AV) 153–154
Arthurdale Homestead 87–88
A.T. Massey (Massey Energy) 133; legal battles 131–133, 166, 171; mountaintop mining involvement 163, 169; political power 9, 185; protests 165; public opinion 10, 178, 184–185; Upper Big Branch accident 180

Bailey, Rebecca 3
Baldwin-Felts Detectives 52, 58, 66–67
Bankhead-Jones Farm Tenancy Act of 1937 90
Barron, W.W. 124
Batteau, Allen 151
Beckley 44, 78
Beckley *Post-Herald* 77
Benjamin, Brent 132
Best, Bill 156
Bigart, Homer 155
Billings, Dwight B. 13–14, 141, 143, 145
Black Lung 40, 82, 118–119, 125
Blair Mountain 50, 67–69
Blankenship, Don 9, 132, 178, 180–181, 184–185
Blankenship, George 64, 66

Blee, Kathleen 13–14, 141, 143, 145
Blizzard, Bill 68
Bluefield *Daily Telegraph* 35, 122, 130
Boone County 58, 131–132, 165
Bradley, Joseph 22
Bragg v Robinson 169, 177
Braxton County 137
Brown, Charlie 126
Buffalo Creek Disaster 125–126
Bull Moose Special 60
Butcher-Winfree, Joy A. 115

Cabin Creek 8, 33, 38, 50–52, 55, 58, 60–62, 65
Camden, Johnson N. 20–21
Caperton v Massey 132
Chafin, Don 63–65, 67–68, 122
Chafin, Raymond 131
Chambers, Robert 170
Charleston 36, 63, 78, 123, 130–131, 136, 181
Charleston *Gazette* 130
Civil War 15, 22, 18–19, 124, 134, 139, 183
Civilian Conservation Corps (CCC) 81, 84–85, 90
Clay County 19, 22
Clean Water Act 169–170
Coal Education Development and Resource (CEDAR) 173–177
Coal River Mountain Watch (CRMW) 160, 168, 170
community college 147
Community Work Experience Program (CWEP) 94–96, 101
company houses 32–34, 49, 53, 82; evictions 52, 54–57, 61, 65–66
company store 32, 35, 37–39, 49, 55; as coercive tool 49, 52, 55; pricing 37–39, 47; social impact 33, 35, 45, 55
company towns 4, 7, 8, 27, 46–47, 51, 55; diversity 70; family dependence on 29–

215

30, 32, 49, 55; social life 24, 32, 35–36; violence 30, 37
Conley, Paul 111
Conley, William G. 78
Cornwell, John 65
corruption 2, 4, 6, 8–9, 47, 71, 120, 158–159, 177, 179; causes 30, 121–122, 133–134, 138, 145, 182; impact on political process 59, 80, 121, 133–134; judicial 132–133, 126; local 32, 65, 122–123, 127–130, 131; law enforcement 122–123; state 65, 122, 124–127
Crickard, Betty 139

Dawson, Daniel 79
Dayton, Alston 50–51, 63, 69
Debs, Eugene V. 61
disease 9, 78, 107, 109, 111; *see also* black lung, causes; common diseases; heart disease
doctors 55, 106–107, 111, 113–114
Donahue Committee 38
drought 74, 76, 184
drugs 105, 117–118, 137, 146, 185

East Tennessee State University 111
economy 73, 76–77, 80, 182, 184; coal influence 11, 30–31, 75, 145, 172, 177, 179–180; conflict with Industrial Revolution 22, 74–75, 138, 145; early economy 14–15, 27, 75, 139, 141; impact of corruption 133, 138; limitations 10–11, 27, 31, 149, 179–180, 183; role of farming *see* farming
education 100, 117, 124, 134, 138, 148–150, 153–154, 184, 186; barriers 78–79, 134, 148; company towns 36; education programs 84–85, 92, 93, 101, 107, 153; social impact of 114, 147–148, 154; women 147
Elkins, Stephen B. 20–21, 122

Farm Security Administration (FSA) 88, 91, 90
farming: effect on environment 76; government programs 89–91; Great Depression 76–77, 88–90, 134, 139, 145; impact of industrialization 5, 7, 22–23, 27–28, 32, 35, 45, 48, 70–71, 134, 144, 148, 183; impact on culture 13–14, 28, 70, 94, 134, 138–143, 145, 151, 156, 187; rehabilitation and recovery 89–90; relationship with economy 13, 23, 38, 74–75, 77, 89–90, 134, 139; subsistence 1, 4, 5, 8, 11, 13, 14, 74–75, 86, 89, 91–92, 106, 138, 144
Fayette County 160
Federal Emergency Relief Act of 1933 (FERA) 81, 83–85, 87, 89
First Community Bank 128
flooding 35, 171; impoundments 125, 165; mine hazard 40; natural floods 74, 76, 184

Friends of Coal 159, 173–175
Frost, William 153

Gassaway, Henry 20–21, 112
Glen, John 154–155
Goodwin, Robert 169
Great Depression 8, 73, 184; impact on economy 75–77; impact on farming 76–77; impact on mining 76–77, 82; impact on society 78
Grubb, James 126
Guffey-Snyder Act 82
Guffey-Vinson Act 82

Haden, Charles 169
Harding, Warren G. 68
Hatfield, Henry 60
Hatfield, Sid 64, 66–67
Hawk's Nest Tunnel 83
Hitchman Coal and Coke v Mitchell 50–51, 63, 69
Hoover, Herbert 78, 86
Hotchkiss, Jed 17
Huntington *Socialist* 61

immigrants 4, 23, 29, 32, 34–35, 41, 48, 52, 54, 70, 144; mortality in mines 34, 36, 54; pay 43–44
impoundments *see* mountaintop mining

Jackson, Naama 123
Jim Crow 4, 23, 63
Job Opportunities and Basic Skills Training Program (JOBS) 94
Johnson, Lyndon B. 6, 9, 92, 110, 153
Jones, Mary 47, 49, 54

Kanawha County 58–60, 65, 77–78, 84, 127, 176
Kanawha Salt Works 3, 13, 15
Kelly, John H. 126
Kennedy, John F. 92, 121, 131, 153
Kennedy, Robert F., Jr. 181
Kenney, C. Frank 65
Kephart, Horace 152
kinship bonds 1, 2, 11, 14, 147, 151; creation 14, 139; enduring nature 72, 105, 114, 117, 166, 184, 187; negative aspects 114, 139–140, 142, 148, 150; positive aspects 114, 139–140
Koontz, Wells 65
Kump, Herman 78, 82–83

Labor Argus 61
Labor Star 61
Lawrence, Randall 14, 24, 29, 45, 53
LeRose family 126–130
Lever Act 65
Lewis, Sherwood 3

Lick Creek 68
Lincoln County 17, 131
Lodge, Henry Cabot 152
Logan (township) 112, 131
Logan County 8, 17, 63–69, 107, 109, 112, 122–123, 126, 130
logging *see* lumber industry
Loughry, Allen 120, 126–127, 129, 131, 134
lumber Industry 4, 5, 7, 16–19, 21–23, 53–54, 91, 148; impact on economy 74, 134, 140; impact on environment 6, 76; impact on society 29, 140; unionization efforts 49, 51

Mallory, Kristin 147
Manchin, A.J. 126–127, 134
Manchin, Joe 157
martial law 8, 36, 49, 58–61, 67–68, 71
Matewan 3, 50, 64, 66
McDowell County 19, 23–24, 27, 36–37, 53, 65–67, 77, 82, 84, 104, 122, 131
McGaha, Elizabeth 101, 103
McNeil, Bryan 158, 161, 166
Mercer County 19
military courts 59–60
Mills, Okey 154
mine guards 17, 49, 52–61, 65–68, 82, 123; *see also* Baldwin-Felts Detectives
Mine Safety and Health Administration (MSHA) 165–166
miners 31, 59–60, 62–63, 82–83, 159; African American 53; demographics 23, 31, 41, 76; finances 33, 38–39, 77; health 41, 117–118; injuries 40–42, 107, 109, 113, 116–117; lifestyle 36, 41, 49; pay 42–43, 64, 75, 82, 92, 96, 117; socialism 61; unions 47–58, 65, 67–69, 71, 158–159, 177; uprisings 55, 65–66, 71
Mingo County 65–68, 86, 122–123, 130–131
mining 4, 23, 29, 31, 42, 82–83, 93, 112, 142, 154, 164, 169, 172, 175–178, 181–182; accidents 40, 42, 109, 116, 119, 180–181; methods 118, 160 (*see also* mountaintop mining); role in economy 5, 27, 30, 75–76, 79, 82, 96, 104, 145, 172–173, 179; role in society 22, 28, 30, 36, 41, 89, 96, 104, 137, 145, 147, 148, 172–173, 184–185; safety 40–41, 115–116, 118, 181
Moore, Arch 125–126
mountaintop mining: environmental impact 161–162, 165, 169; impact on culture 168; impoundments 165–166; legal cases 161, 169–171; methods 160, 163; opposition 158–160, 166, 168, 171–172, 179; public opinion 177–178; reclamation 176; regulations 171, 176; support for 159, 172–175, 177, 179
Murfree, Mary 151–152

National Coal Worker's Autopsy Study 118
National Industrial Recovery Act of 1933 (NIRA) 69, 80, 82
National Recovery Administration (NRA) 80, 82
nativism 54
New Deal 6, 8, 73, 78–79, 86, 108, 110–111, 119
Nicholas Chronicle 22, 33, 54
Nicholas County 1, 18–22, 27–28, 54, 75, 90, 126–127, 129, 137, 139, 142, 148–149, 156, 169, 177
Nordau, Max 152
nurses 89, 106–107, 109–111

Ohio Valley Environmental Coalition (OVEC) 160, 169–170
Olmstead, Frederick (Law) 151
Omnibus Budget Reconciliation Act of 1981 94
operators (coal) 9–10, 36–39, 41, 45, 47–53, 55–60, 61–69, 71, 75, 77, 82–83, 86, 121–122, 125, 154, 160, 174–175, 178–179
outmigration 148, 153

Paint Creek 8, 33, 36, 38, 43, 50–52, 54–55, 58, 60–62, 65, 67, 69
Pearsall, Marion 139
Peck, Millard 139
peonage 13, 51, 53
Photiadis, John 114, 149–150, 184
physicians *see* doctors
Plein, Christopher L. 104
progressives 10–11, 150, 156–158, 160, 179, 185–187

racism 37, 48, 54, 63; *see also* segregation
Ragland, Henry 48
railroads 26, 77, 86, 121, 165; expansion 19, 20; impact on salt industry 15; impact on society 4, 22; ties with other industries 60
Raleigh County 31, 63, 77, 107–108, 113, 154, 164, 180
Red House homestead 87–88
Red Jacket Injunction 63, 69
religion 147, 150–151, 114–115
Richwood 18, 20, 130, 148
Robertson, Donald 126
Roosevelt, Eleanor 87
Roosevelt, Franklin D. 82–83
Rural Electrification Administration (REA) 91

schools 34, 36, 79, 136, 153, 174
Schoonover, Randy 126
segregation 24, 34, 48, 63
Shifflett, Crandall 3–4, 18, 32, 35–36, 41, 50
silicosis 83, 118
Smith, Russell J. 91

Socialist Party of America (SPA) 61
stereotypes 6, 10, 13, 105, 137, 150–151, 184, 187; development 9, 144, 151, 155, 157
Summersville 27–28, 111, 126–129, 137, 146, 149
Summersville Regional Medical Center 111, 149
Surface Mining Board 174
Surface Mining Control and Reclamation Act 169, 171, 176
Swandale 22
Sylvester 163–165, 171
Sylvester Elementary School 165

taxes 80, 122, 75; burden 79–80; revenues 79; Tax Limitation Act 79, 83
Temporary Assistance to Need Families (TANF) 100–102
Testerman, Cabell 64, 66
Thomas, Jerry 82–83
Tomblin, Earl Ray 126
Tonkovich, Dan 126
traditionalists 10–11, 115, 147, 149, 150, 156–160, 166, 179, 181, 185–187
transportation men 52–54
Tucker, Larry 126, 129–130

Underwood, Cecil 125
unemployment 54, 77, 93–94, 104, 149–150, 172, 184; causes 75–77, 80, 82, 90, 96, 100, 104, 117, 177; social impact 92, 94, 104, 147, 174
United Mine Workers of America 8, 38, 48–51, 54, 58–59, 61–65, 67–69, 71, 82, 158–159, 161, 168
U.S. Commission on Civil Rights 123
U.S. Supreme Court 82, 132

Volunteers in Service to America (VISTA) 153–154

Wagner Act 82
War on Poverty 6, 9, 92, 110–111, 153–155
Washington Agreement 65
Wayne County 17
Webster County 19–20, 75, 77, 90
Welch, Janet 139–143, 145–150, 154, 156
welfare class 10, 73, 92–94, 96, 100, 102, 104, 115, 143–144, 149–150, 155, 157, 185, 187
Weller, Jack 5, 93–94, 136, 139, 141, 143, 145–146, 148, 154
Wells, Danny 126
West Virginia Coal Association (WVCA) 173–175
West Virginia Department of Environmental Protection (WVDEP) 165, 168–169, 171
West Virginia National Guard 58–59, 65, 67–68
West Virginia Supreme Court 59–60, 122, 132–133, 171
women 93, 142; in company towns 24, 27, 35–36, 45, 70; education 147; employment 85, 147; health 107, 113; roles 115, 147–148
Work Incentive Program (WIN) 93
Works Progress Administration 73, 75, 81, 84–86, 89–90
WV WORKS 100–104
Wyoming County 53, 164–165

yellow dog contracts 50, 63, 69
Yesterday's People 136

www.ingramcontent.com/pod-product-compliance
Ingram Content Group UK Ltd.
Pitfield, Milton Keynes, MK11 3LW, UK
UKHW041953140426
5217IPUK00015B/779